Climate Change Policy
in the United States

ALSO BY DIANNE RAHM
AND FROM McFARLAND

*Toxic Waste and Environmental Policy in
the 21st Century United States* (2002)

*Sustainable Energy and the States: Essays on
Politics, Markets and Leadership* (2006)

Climate Change Policy in the United States

The Science, the Politics, and the Prospects for Change

DIANNE RAHM

McFarland & Company, Inc., Publishers
Jefferson, North Carolina, and London

Maps created by Anastasia Valdes.

LIBRARY OF CONGRESS CATALOGUING-IN-PUBLICATION DATA

Rahm, Dianne.
   Climate change policy in the United States : the science, the
politics and the prospects for change / Dianne Rahm.
      p.   cm.
   Includes bibliographical references and index.

   ISBN 978-0-7864-4299-7
   softcover : 50# alkaline paper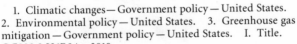

   1. Climatic changes— Government policy— United States.
2. Environmental policy— United States.   3. Greenhouse gas
mitigation — Government policy— United States.   I. Title.
QC903.2.U6R34   2010
363.738'74560973 — dc22   2009037848

British Library cataloguing data are available

Cover images ©2009 Shutterstock

Manufactured in the United States of America

McFarland & Company, Inc., Publishers
   Box 611, Jefferson, North Carolina 28640
      www.mcfarlandpub.com

Table of Contents

Preface

Thoughtful consideration of public policy must start with an understanding of the facts and the reality that confront policy makers. In the case of climate change, the facts are many and the reality is daunting. Climate change as a phenomenon is complex and not yet fully understood. As scientists continue to gather facts about our changing planet, they refine their models and sharpen their predictions. Policy makers must start with an assessment of the facts, models, and predictions coming from scientists. Accordingly, this book begins with an overview of global warming and lays out the most likely impacts of a warmer planet. Using a historical lens, the chapter begins by detailing the discoveries of the greenhouse effect and global warming. This is followed by a discussion of the contemporary understanding of the climate system and greenhouse gases and a description of the countries that are the main contributors to human-caused greenhouse gases. The current scientific understanding of the projected consequences of global warming are explored as are areas of continuing uncertainty about likely outcomes. Potential mitigation and adaptation strategies are suggested.

Chapter 2 begins with a brief look at the international treaties and agreements that form the legal basis for greenhouse gas reductions and the U.S. position, over time, vis-à-vis these negotiations and agreements. Public policy toward climate change shifted enormously from George H.W. Bush, to William J. Clinton, to George W. Bush, and finally to Barack H. Obama. George H.W. Bush committed the U.S. to the Framework Convention on Climate Change, thus beginning U.S. policy on climate change. Bill Clinton attempted to continue and expand U.S. climate change policy when he signed the Kyoto Protocol but due to opposition in the Senate the treaty was never ratified. When George W. Bush took office, he announced that the U.S. under his administration would not be a party to the agreement and would not agree to mandatory cuts in greenhouse gas emissions. For the eight years of the Bush administration, no progress toward emissions reductions was made.

1

Indeed, U.S. emissions increased throughout the Bush administration. Failure of federal leadership resulted in a series of state and state-based regional alliances that enacted policies to reduce greenhouse gas emissions. On assuming office, Barack Obama reversed federal policy and committed the United States to a leadership role in climate policy. Chapter 2 discusses the policy changes during these administrations.

The Kyoto Protocol is set to end in 2012. Negotiations to frame a successor treaty began late in 2007 in Bali, Indonesia. The meeting exposed the division between the Bush administration and the other nations—a division that nearly ended the conference. The split between the U.S. delegation and those of other nations attending the Bali conference was commitment on the part of most countries to the principles of differentiated responsibility and precautionary action-taking. These two principles conflicted with the Bush administration's call for fairness and emphasis on economic costs when uncertainties exist. Chapter 3 explores these differences. The Kyoto Protocol put in place a specific set of policy mechanisms for the implementation of the agreement. Chapter 3 also explores how well these mechanisms are working and suggests changes that should be made to the Kyoto Protocol's successor treaty.

Science is central to climate change policy yet science came under attack by opponents of policy action. A group of influential actors rooted their objection to climate change policy in the argument that the scientific understanding was too weak and uncertain to take any policy action—especially expensive policy action. This view was strongly supported and widely spread by economic interests that feared they would be on the losing side should carbon regulation take form. The opposition of oil, coal, and fossil fuel intensive industries produced well-funded lobbyist groups and anti-science skeptics. Organizations such as the Global Climate Coalition heavily lobbied Congress and the Bush administration against mandatory greenhouse gas emissions restrictions. Others concentrated on discrediting the scientific evidence pointing to climate change. Many leading political figures accepted this misinformation and used it as an excuse for inaction. Chapter 4 explores the role that these actors played in the U.S. policy debate.

The debate over climate change was framed around morality, ethics, social justice, and religious duty. Both secular and religious individuals advocated or opposed climate change policy on the basis of moral and ethical ideals. Among secular activists, Al Gore's efforts were key in moving the frame from consideration of economic losses to questions of what was right and social responsibility. Many religious organizations joined the debate on the basis of their religious obligation to care for creation. Chapter 5 discusses the framing of the debate in all of these terms and the many individuals and groups, including religious denominations, who believe that taking action on climate change is a moral and religious imperative. The chapter closes with a discussion of those actors who, for religious reasons, argue against taking any action to avert climate change.

Chapter 6 provides detailed information about the sources of U.S. emissions by sector. Separate discussions describe the production of greenhouse gases by transportation, power production, the built environment, industry, commerce, and agriculture. The impacts of land use, changes in land use, and forestry are explored. Tracking greenhouse gas emissions is the first step to controlling them. Chapter 6 explores the variety of tracking mechanisms as well as the emergence of carbon markets as a regulatory mechanism to govern emissions reduction agreements. Carbon market operations in Europe, functioning under the Kyoto Protocol, are discussed. The creation of U.S.–based emission registries and domestic carbon trading options are explored. The question of how successful these markets are and to what extent they may be utilized to regulate U.S. greenhouse gas emissions is considered. Alternatives to cap-and-trade schema are investigated.

The final two chapters look at solutions. Chapter 7 focuses on technological solutions while Chapter 8 spotlights demand side management, energy efficiency, and conservation. Potential solutions include the increased use of renewable energy, hydrogen-based energy and nuclear energy; geoengineering; new vehicles; the smart grid; landfill gas; recycling; carbon capture and storage; improved batteries; and lifestyle changes, all of which are discussed. No one solution is a magic bullet. Solving the climate crisis will involve adopting many new technologies and changing many old behaviors.

I want to thank several people for their help with *Climate Change Policy in the United States*. Alexandra Voigt and Aaron Stein provided wonderful research assistance. Anastasia Valdes produced the maps that appear in chapters 1, 2, and 3 and provided encouragement and many thoughtful comments that were of great assistance in the preparation of this volume.

Abbreviations

AAU   Assigned Amounts Units
AFOLU   Agriculture, Forestry, and Other Land Use
AMI   Advanced Metering Infrastructure
AR4   Fourth Assessment Report
BTU   British Thermal Unit
C&C   Contraction and Convergence
CAFE   Corporate Average Fuel Economy
CARB   California Air Resources Board
CCAR   California Climate Action Registry
CCS   Carbon Capture and Storage
CCX   Chicago Climate Exchange
CDC   Centers for Disease Control and Prevention
CDM   Clean Development Mechanism
CER   Certified Emissions Reduction
CH_4 Methane
CIA   Central Intelligence Agency
CITL   Community Independent Transaction Log
CO_2 Carbon Dioxide
COP   Conference of Parties
CSP   Concentrating Solar Power
DOD   Department of Defense
DOE   Department of Energy
ECI   Evangelical Climate Initiative
ECX   European Climate Exchange
EEA   European Environmental Agency
EEN   Evangelical Environmental Network
EPA   Environmental Protection Agency
ERU   Emissions Reduction Units
EU ETS   European Union Emissions Trading Scheme

EU   European Union
FAR   First Assessment Report
FERC   Federal Energy Regulatory Commission
FIT   Feed-In Tariff
FWS   Fish and Wildlife Service
GAO   Government Accountability Office
GCST   Global Science Climate Team
GHG   Greenhouse Gas
GM   Genetically Modified
GPS   Global Positioning System
GWP   Global Warming Potential
IGCC   Integrated Gasification Combined Cycle
IPCC   Intergovernmental Panel on Climate Change
ISO   Independent System Operator
ITL   International Transaction Log
JI   Joint Implementation
kWh   Kilowatt hour
LED   Light-emitting diode
LFGTE   Landfill Gas to Energy
LULUCF   Land Use, Land Use Change and Forestry
MEA   Multilateral Environmental Agreement
MGGRA   Midwest Greenhouse Gas Reduction Accord
MOU   Memorandum of Understanding
MSW   Municipal Solid Waste
MW   Megawatts
NAE   National Association of Evangelicals
NAS   National Academy of Sciences
NASA   National Aeronautics and Space Administration
NECX   Northeast Climate Exchange
NGO   Nongovernmental Organization
NiMH   Nickel-metal-hydride
NO_2 Nitrous Oxide
NOAA   National Oceanic and Atmospheric Administration
NSF   National Science Foundation
NYCX   New York Climate Exchange
OMB   Office of Management and Budget
OPEC   Organization of Petroleum Exporting Countries
PFC   perfluorocompounds
PMU   Phasor Measurement Units
ppb   parts per billion
ppm   parts per million

PTP Powering the Plains
PURPA Public Utilities Regulatory Policies Act
PV Photovoltaic
R&D Research and Development
RD&D Research, Development and Demonstration
REC Renewable Energy Certificate
REDD Reducing Emissions from Deforestation and Forest Degradation
RGGI Regional Greenhouse Gas Initiative
RMU Removal Units
RPS Renewable Portfolio Standard
RTO Regional Transmission Organizations
SAR Second Assessment Report
SF_6 Sulfur Hexafluoride
TAR Third Assessment Report
TCR The Climate Registry
Tg CO_2 Eq. Teragrams Carbon Dioxide Equivalent
UK ETS United Kingdom Emission Trading Scheme
UN United Nations
UNDP United Nations Development Program
UNEP United Nations Environment Program
UNFCCC United Nations Framework Convention on Climate Change
USCAP U.S. Climate Action Partnership
USDA U.S. Department of Agriculture
V2G Vehicle-to-Grid
WGA Western Governors Association
WHO World Health Organization
WMO World Meteorological Organization
WREGIS Western Region Electricity Generation Information System
WTO World Trade Organization

1

Climate Change
An Overview of the Problem

Climate change is a complex environmental issue that currently has and will continue to have enormous economic, security, ecological, and social impacts. This chapter provides an overview of the problem. Using a historical lens, the chapter begins by providing details about the discovery of the greenhouse effect and the phenomenon of global warming. The greenhouse effect, first detected in 1896, is responsible for making the planet Earth habitable by preventing all the solar radiation that enters the atmosphere from radiating back into space. The link between the excessive buildup of greenhouse gases in the atmosphere and human activities was first described in the 1930s. It is this extreme buildup of greenhouse gases that is causing the warming of our planet. In the succeeding decades after its discovery, with observed warming under investigation, the theory that human actions cause global warming received more attention. Increasing awareness of human impacts on the Earth resulted in the rise of the environmental movement in the 1970s and with it further investigation of climate impacts. The data were somewhat confusing, as aerosols in the atmosphere were actually lowering atmospheric temperatures and raising predictions of a new Ice Age. This misinterpretation soon passed when scientists realized that these aerosols would remain in the atmosphere only for a short time and thus their masking of global warming would cease. By the 1980s, the scientific community began to warn of the serious consequences which would result if global warming was not addressed. These concerns led governments to establish the Intergovernmental Panel on Climate Change (IPCC) to make recommendations to the world's governments.

The chapter draws on the several reports of the IPCC to discuss the contemporary understanding of the climate system and greenhouse gases. Climate is a complex and interactive system that involves the world's water, land, atmosphere, and all its living creatures. The dynamic interplay between the water, land and atmosphere influences and is influenced by plant and animal life. Together they create the patterns of average temperature, average precipitation, and average wind that we call climate. When we consider the phenomenon of global warming, each of these factors need to be part of the analysis but human actions that result in the emission of greenhouse gases into the atmosphere must be at the center of the investigation. The chapter discusses the primary gas of concern, carbon dioxide, as well as other gases with great potential for warming our planet.

The chapter also assesses emissions by the countries that are the main contributors to human-caused greenhouse gases. The United States and China are two of the largest contributors to greenhouse gases. The chapter reviews the international reporting of greenhouse gases and the current scientific understanding of the projected consequences of these emissions. The IPCC has provided a great deal of detail regarding likely outcomes associated with global warming including regional analysis of expected impacts from glaciers melting, flooding, sea level rise, intensified storms, fire, drought, and the shifting of patterns of diseases. Because of the complexity of global ecosystems and the yet not well understood impact of climate feedback loops, global warming projections continue to contain areas of uncertainty. The chapter discusses some of the greatest areas of uncertainty.

Nations are beginning to address the issue of global warming through a variety of mitigation and adaption efforts. Mitigation involves the reduction of emissions to achieve stabilization of levels of greenhouse gases in the atmosphere that will avert the more drastic likely outcomes of the climate crisis. But global warming is underway, and some impacts will not be deterred. How we adapt to those changes and find ways to live on a changed planet are discussed. The chapter provides a brief introduction to some mitigation and adaptation strategies that could be adopted.

The chapter closes with a discussion of global warming's economic considerations. An assessment of the costs associated with acting to curb global warming versus the consequences of not acting is provided. The Stern report and other path breaking economic analyses, call attention to the fact that failing to act may be very expensive indeed in terms of global Gross Domestic Product (GDP). Economic analysis suggests that action to mitigate and adapt to climate change may also contain the positive aspects of new job creation and new industries developed to live in a carbon-constrained world. The chapter discusses these.

Recognition of the Global Warming Problem

In 1896 Svante Arrhenius, a Swedish scientist, published a paper that linked the burning of fossil fuels to increases in average carbon dioxide (CO_2) levels in the atmosphere. Arrhenius' calculations also showed that heat would pass back into outer space differently in air with higher levels of CO_2 than it would in an atmosphere with lower levels of CO_2. He found that atmospheres with higher levels of CO_2 would retain more heat. These calculations led him to hypothesize the greenhouse effect — greater levels of CO_2 in the atmosphere would result in less transfer of heat back into space and the Earth would warm. Arrhenius' measurements were unreliable in part because he used very complicated calculations and also because he computed them by hand. Scientists did not consider the projections to be accurate until computers were used to model the process. That would not happen for many years after Arrhenius' initial discovery. Nevertheless, other scientists followed the path of research begun by Arrhenius and continued to investigate the relationship between global warming and carbon dioxide buildup in the atmosphere. By the 1930s, there was a general realization that the U.S. and the North Atlantic had warmed considerably since the late 1800s. Scientists generally believed this warming was the result of natural climate cycles. An amateur scientist, G.S. Callendar, however, argued that the warming being observed was due to the greenhouse effect. In the 1950s, a few scientists looked deeper into Callendar's claims. These studies were often funded by the U.S. Navy to study weather and its impact on the oceans. They supported Callendar's assertion that CO_2 could build up in the atmosphere and cause global warming.[1]

In 1947, the *New York Times* published an article with the headline "Warming Arctic Climate Melting Glaciers Faster, Raising Ocean Level, Scientist Says." This article described the work of Dr. Hans Ahlmann, a Swedish geophysicist and one of the early scientists to warn of the negative impacts of global warming.[2] At this time, though, global warming was not generally seen as a problem by most scientists. Rather, researchers pointed to potential beneficial effects such as the increased growing season for crops as well as extended fishing and shipping opportunities.[3] More importantly, there was still considerable scientific skepticism regarding the precision of global warming projections linked to CO_2 emissions. These concerns would soon be put to rest.

The highly accurate measures of CO_2 taken by Charles Keeling in Mauna Loa, Hawaii, beginning in 1958 provided excellent time series data showing changing CO_2 levels in the atmosphere. Keeling's methods also provided the evidence by which scientists could differentiate increases of CO_2 coming from fossil fuel burning versus those from the natural carbon cycle.[4] Being able to differentiate emissions in this way was vital for understanding how humans were contributing to increasing concentrations of carbon dioxide by their actions as opposed to emissions that were part of a natural rhythm of the carbon cycle.

By the 1960s, scientists verified that atmospheric CO_2 levels were increasing annually. During the decade of the sixties the scientific community made progress in better understanding the climate. Knowledge increased as advances were made by constructing increasingly better computer models that predicted greenhouse gas (GHG) concentrations. Another essential advance came from developing methods to identify historic temperatures through the use of very old pollens and fossil shells. By the late 1960s, application of these computer models and prediction techniques led scientists to forecast with some confidence that temperature might rise by several degrees within the next hundred years.[5] Anticipation of such rapid temperature increases were troubling as it was unclear how various plant and animal species, including humans, would respond to these changes.

Within the United States the decade of the 1960s was tumultuous for several reasons. There was rising domestic unhappiness with the War in Viet Nam. The large youth population was every more vocally expressing its opinion on the direction of the country was taking. Questioning the state of the nation was not just an activity of the youth. The public began to openly debate the continued expansion of industrialization and the pollution caused by ceaseless growth. Several influential books appeared that drew attention to the state of the environment. One of these was Rachel Carson's *Silent Spring* which looked at the effect of pesticide use. Another was Paul Ehrlich's *Population Bomb* which questioned how long the Earth could withstand ever increasing human populations. Both books and two highly publicized oil spills off the coast of California focused the attention of the country on the environment.[6]

The rise of the U.S. environmental movement, beginning in the late 1960s, changed the way many viewed the consequences of human behavior on the world. It had become all too clear that human actions were having vast environmental impacts. When Ohio's Cuyahoga River caught on fire because of the vast amounts of combustible substances dumped into it, the American public began to demand action to clean the nation's water. The poor air quality, especially in urban areas like Los Angeles, spurred a cry for action to clean the air. With the new awareness of environmental threats, public concern about human impacts on the climate also emerged. A 1971 report to the United Nations by thirty ecologists stated: "There can be little doubt that man, in the process of reshaping his environment in many ways has changed the climate of large regions of the Earth, and he has probably had some influences on global climate as well — exactly how much, we do not know."[7]

A great deal of uncertainty entered the debate over global warming in the 1970s because of another climate impact that was being felt. Concern began to focus on human activities that put small particles, called aerosols, into the air. These aerosols could have the effect of blocking sunlight and cooling the planet.[8] An analysis of weather statistics showed that the planet had begun cooling in the 1940s. Reports in the popular media lent doubt to concerns about global warming. The media variously reported predictions of global warming resulting in coastal flooding and sea level rise along with predictions of a new Ice Age.[9] It took some time to sort this controversy out and to demonstrate that the cooling effects of aerosols would be short-lived. Aerosols drop out of the atmosphere relatively rapidly whereas the effects of warming agents like CO_2 are long-lived because the GHG emissions persist in the atmosphere for long periods of time.

The ambiguity over what was actually happening to the world's climate continued into the 1970s. Historical events of the decade, however, did focus public attention on energy. The Organization of Petroleum Exporting Countries (OPEC) oil embargos of the 1970s resulted in a shift to the expanded use of coal to decrease U.S. vulnerability to imported sources of oil. Increased coal use was potentially troublesome because burning coal releases vast amounts of CO_2. While President Carter called for increasing coal use, concerned with the potential impact of CO_2 emissions, he also asked Congress for $5 million to study the problem.[10] Late in the Carter administration, William Nordhaus, a member of the President's Council of Economic Advisors, began to tentatively discuss potential policies for restricting the burning of coal and other fossil fuels.[11] A 1978 survey of climate specialists, sponsored by the Departments of Defense (DOD) and Agriculture (USDA) along with the National Oceanic and Atmospheric Administration (NOAA), sought to get scientific opinion on the likelihood and consequences of climate change. The survey results were mixed, revealing that the 24 climatologists surveyed were equally split on whether the planet was undergoing a warming or a cooling trend. They all agreed, though, that there would be no catastrophic weather changes for at least a century.[12]

The lack of consensus in the scientific community resulted in a call for more climate research. Using data collected by satellites and ships, new databases of global climate indicators were created. The new data allowed scientists to recognize that climate was a complex system with numerous feedback loops and that climate responded to scores of inputs. Volcanic eruptions, solar flares, shifts in ocean currents, the extent of cloud cover, the role of other atmospheric gases besides CO_2, and even small changes in the Earth's orbit were added to rising levels of greenhouse gases. Perhaps more troubling, examination of ice cores drilled from Greenland and Antarctica revealed that the climate was in a sensitive equilibrium. Analyses of these ice cores showed that even small changes in greenhouse gas concentrations in the past had set off large and sudden climate shifts. While knowledge from the new research efforts filtered through the scientific community, public opinion regarding the direction and cause of climate change remained uncertain. When global temperatures started to rise again in the late 1970s some of the public confusion began to disappear.[13] Not all did, however.

Even into the 21st century, many popular accounts of global warming discounted, and even ridiculed, the scientific evidence. Powerful actors with a self interest in denying the fact that the globe was warming seized on the notion of scientific uncertainty as a way to convince the public and elected officials that taking action to reduce GHG emissions was unnecessary. While the scientific dispute over the potential of global cooling was resolved fairly quickly when it was shown that the observed cooling could be explained by the presence of aerosols, which remain in the atmosphere only a short time, compared to steadily rising levels of CO_2.[14] Nevertheless, influential actors that thought they might be losers should the government act to reduce GHG emissions continued to spread the myth that the science of climate change was too uncertain to take any action to prevent global warming. This opposition began in the 1970s and persisted well into the first decade of the 21st century.

By the late 1970s and early 1980s, a growing number of scientists began to warn that the world should take action to reduce GHG emissions. The press was increasingly reporting on the consequences of global warming including the spread of deserts and the melting of Arctic ice which would radically alter precipitation patterns and raise sea levels.[15] In 1981, an ominous forecast from the Institute for Space Studies of the National Aeronautics and Space Administration (NASA) predicted global warming trends that might even be sufficient to melt the West Antarctic ice sheet. NASA warned that should the West Antarctic ice sheet melt, the world's oceans would rise from 15 to 20 feet within the century.[16] In the same year, scientists from Columbia University funded by the National Science Foundation (NSF), using a different technique than that used in the NASA study, reported evidence that supported the greenhouse theory of global warming.[17]

As more studies were conducted regarding global warming and its likely consequences, the issue became politically controversial. The release of several influential reports in 1983 fueled the debate. The U.S. Environmental Protection Agency (EPA) released a report with a very urgent tone that cautioned the climate would warm over the next few decades and that even drastic measures to curb the use of fossil fuels would not reverse the warming.

The EPA projected a 2 degree Celsius increase in temperature by 2050. Such an extreme rise in temperature would require significant efforts to deal with expected undesirable and frightening outcomes.[18] Three days later, the National Academy of Sciences issued a separate report, which essentially agreed with the EPA report but took a more relaxed tone. President Reagan's science advisor, George Keyworth, criticized the EPA report calling it alarmist and agreed with the finding of the National Academy that there was time to prepare for the impacts of global warming.[19]

Later in the 1980s other factors related to global warming were investigated including the role of deforestation in the rise of atmospheric CO_2 and the fact that other gases, such as methane, had also increased in the atmosphere and that these gases were potent greenhouse gases.[20] As more and more scientists looked at the phenomenon, many previously unconsidered factors were brought into the analysis. Scientists began to consider the role of cloud cover, increased plant growth in a CO_2 rich environment, whether climate shifts would be slow or abrupt, and increasing frequency or intensity of storms. It also became clear in the 1980s just how contentious the issue would become as elected officials, the business community, and environmental advocates became increasingly aware of the costs of regulating or failing to regulate greenhouse gases. The summer of 1988, the hottest ever on record till that date, focused public attention on the scientific claims of global warming. On June 23 of that year, in dramatic testimony, Dr. James E. Hansen of NASA told a Congressional committee that the evidence was clear that global warming had begun and that action should be taken to reduce greenhouse gas emissions.[21] Dr. Hansen's testimony served as a catalyst to motivate action. For the first time, a forceful and credible scientist brought immediacy to the issue and urged political action. While many who feared the cost of action chose to rely on repudiation of science as a tool to delay response, Dr. Hansen's testimony gave the issue salience and propelled it forward.

In response to the threat of global warming, the Intergovernmental Panel on Climate Change was created. The IPCC, organized by the World Meteorological Organization (WMO) and the United Nations Environment Program (UNEP), has the mission of presenting objective scientific evidence of climate change and its causes as well as the environmental and socioeconomic impact of climate change to the world's governments. The IPCC represents almost all the world's governments and their climate experts. The IPCC reports not only provide scientific assessment of the phenomenon of climate change but also recommend adaptation and mitigation strategies to deal with climate change. The IPCC produces reports on a regular basis, drawing conclusions from investigations undertaken by the world's scientists.[22] Climate change science grew almost exponentially between the years of 1951 and 1997, with a doubling of efforts each 11 years. This growth in the knowledge-base gave the IPCC a substantial foundation on which to base its conclusions.[23]

The First Assessment Report (FAR) of the IPCC was released in 1990 and had influence in the development of the United Nations Framework Convention on Climate Change (UNFCCC) which went into force in 1994. UNFCCC provides the basic policy framework for dealing with climate change issues. The IPCC's Second Assessment Report (SAR), released in 1995, provided important information for the negotiation of the Kyoto Protocol in 1997.[24] The Third Assessment Report (TAR), released in 2001, revealed that the IPCC had reached consensus and reported that it was much more likely than not that the Earth was undergoing global warming caused by human actions rather than natural climate cycles and that the consequences would be severe.[25]

Since 2001 the scientific community has solidified its consensus regarding the anthropogenic, or human-caused, sources of global warming. The complexity and sophistication of the models used from the mid–1970s to the IPCC's Fourth Assessment Report (AR4) of 2007 increased markedly. In the mid–1970s, climate models were restricted to rain, sun and CO_2. By the mid–1980s land surface, ice and clouds were added. The FAR included ocean influences. The SAR incorporated the role of volcanic activity and sulphates. The TAR included the carbon cycle, rivers, ocean circulation, and aerosols. The AR4 included atmospheric chemistry and interactive vegetation.[26]

The growing superiority of the models led to a vastly improved knowledge-base and far greater certainty. The AR4 of 2007 reported with "very high confidence that the global average net effect of human activities since 1750 has been one of warming..."[27] and that "warming of the climate systems is unequivocal, as is now evident from observations of increases of in global average air and ocean temperatures, widespread melting of snow and ice, and rising global average sea level."[28]

Contemporary Understanding of the Climate System and Greenhouse Gases

Climate is best thought of as the average weather in a geographic region. Climate is a complex and interactive system consisting of the atmosphere, land, oceans, other bodies of water, snow, ice, and living things.[29] Climate is most often described in terms of average temperature, average precipitation, and average wind over time. The most important factor that controls climate is solar radiation. Climate shifts can occur when incoming solar radiation changes through changes in the sun or the orbit of the Earth, when cloud cover and atmospheric particles or vegetation change the reflection back toward space of incoming solar radiation, or by altering the radiation from Earth back to space by changing the greenhouse gas concentration in the atmosphere. When we think of the climate system we most often think of the atmosphere because that is where the weather occurs[30] but the complex relationships between air, land, and water are also central to climate.

The Earth's atmosphere consists mainly of oxygen and nitrogen but neither of these gases plays a role in the greenhouse effect because they do not absorb the terrestrial radiation heading back toward space. Water vapor, carbon dioxide, and other trace gases in the atmosphere (such as methane and nitrous oxide), however, do absorb the terrestrial radiation that leaves the surface of the Earth. As the concentrations of these gases increase, the energy balance between land, oceans, water bodies, atmosphere, and space is altered.[31]

A measure called "radiative forcing" indicates the strength an agent has to alter the Earth-atmosphere energy balance. Radiative forcing can be caused by natural phenomena such as volcanic eruptions and variation in solar radiation as well as by human-induced changes to the composition of the atmosphere.[32] Holding all else constant, increases in greenhouse gases will produce positive radiative forcing, or warming of the Earth. Likewise, other factors, such as the presence of aerosols, tend to produce negative radiative forcing or a cooling effect.[33]

There are several important greenhouse gases to consider. These include carbon dioxide, methane, nitrous oxide, and ozone. Carbon dioxide is the chief anthropogenic greenhouse gas. At the beginning of the industrial revolution, most commonly dated as the year 1750, CO_2 concentrations were 280 parts per million (ppm). By 2005, concentrations had risen to 379 ppm. Ice cores show that for a range of time of over 650,000 years, concentrations of CO_2 have been between 180 ppm to 300 ppm. The main source of these recent increased levels of CO_2 is the use of fossil fuels. Land use changes, such as deforestation, also contribute to CO_2 levels as they remove natural sinks. Sinks, such as forests and oceans, absorb CO_2 thus not allowing it to build up in the atmosphere.[34] Methane (CH_4) is another important GHG. Concentrations of methane have increased from the pre-industrial level of 715 parts per billion (ppb) to 1774 ppb in 2005. Ice cores show these levels far exceed the historic range over the last 650,000 years of between 320 ppb to 790 ppb. The IPCC's Fourth Assessment Report stated that it is very likely that these increased levels of methane come from anthropogenic sources such as agriculture and fossil fuel use. Methane is produced through decomposition of organic matter. Methane is emitted from solid waste landfills as well as when animal waste decomposes. Methane is also formed from agricultural processes such as rice cultivation and enteric fermentation in ruminant stock animals such as cows, sheep and water buffalo. These animals have a digestive tract that includes an extra stomach or rumen that allows the animal to digest tough vegetation but in the process they produce methane. Natural gas and petroleum production, coal mining, and incomplete fossil fuel combustion each contribute to the amount of methane in the atmosphere. Nitrous oxide (N_2O) has increased from its pre-industrial concentration of 270 ppb to 319 ppb in 2005. Approximately one-third of N_2O emissions are anthropogenic and come mainly from agriculture. Nitrous oxide is generated by the production of nitrogen-fixing crops, fertilizer use, fossil fuel use, the production of nylon and nitric acid, and wastewater treatment. Ozone is present in the stratosphere as the ozone layer and in the troposphere as smog. In the stratosphere ozone works to shield the Earth from harmful ultra violet radiation. Over the past several decades, however, the release of halocarbons containing chlorine and bromine has depleted the stratospheric ozone layer. Halocarbons are used as solvents, pesticides, refrigerants, adhesives, electrical component insulating coatings, and in plastics. Examples include methyl chloride, dioxin, perchloroethylene, trichloroethane, Freon, PCBs, CFCs and DDT. The depletion of the ozone layer has resulted in a small negative radiative impact or cooling. On the other hand, changes in tropospheric ozone levels due to emission of ozone-forming chemicals such as nitrogen oxides, carbon monoxide, and hydrocarbons act to increase warming. Hydrocarbons occur in many forms and are both naturally occurring and the result of human activity including petroleum use, trash incineration, and evaporation of industrial solvents. The largest hydrocarbon contributor to urban smog comes from automobile emissions.[35] Increases in tropospheric ozone are estimated to be the third largest contributor to warming, falling directly behind CO_2 and CH_4.[36]

Other factors play a role in greenhouse gas production. Changes in the earth's reflectivity due to transformations in land cover may either decrease or increase warming. Reflection of solar radiation back into space by clouds, snow and ice provide a negative forcing effect while the presence of black carbon on snow or melting snow and ice cover which reveals dark land produces a positive radiative forcing.[37]

The presence of these greenhouse gases in the atmosphere has resulted in observed climate changes. The IPCC's 4AR outlined some of these, as follows. The years between 1995 and 2006 rank among the twelve warmest years since temperatures have been recorded (beginning in 1850). Global average temperature is increasing, global average sea levels are rising, and Northern hemisphere snow cover is decreasing. As the IPCC 4AR states, "Numerous long-term changes in climate have been observed. These include changes in artic temperatures and ice, changes in precipitation amounts, ocean salinity, wind patterns and aspects of extreme weather including droughts, heavy precipitation, heat waves and the intensity of tropical cyclones."[38] Arctic sea ice has decreased by 2.7 percent per decade since the late 1970s. Temperatures at the top level of artic permafrost have increased by 3 degrees Celsius since the 1980s. Precipitation has increased in eastern parts of North and South America, northern Europe, and northern and central Asia while drought has plagued the Sahel region of Africa south of the Sahara desert, the Mediterranean, southern Africa, and sections of southern Asia. More severe and longer droughts have occurred since the 1970s. Heavy precipitation events have increased. Heat waves have become more common in the last 50 years. Hurricanes have increased in intensity.[39]

Further warming of the Earth is projected for the next several decades, even if GHG emissions are stabilized. The IPCC warns that "continued greenhouse gas emissions at or above current rates would cause further warming and induce many changes in the global climate system during the 21st century that would *very likely* be larger than those observed during the 20th century."[40]

Main Anthropogenic Contributors

Statistics on worldwide emissions of greenhouse gases can be confusing as they have been made available by different organizations in different ways. The United Nations (UN) Statistics Division provides data on CO_2 emissions and CO_2 emissions per capita by country. These are estimated using the UN Millennium Development Goals Indicators database and the UN Population Division's world population database. They do not factor in land use or land use changes, which affect the levels of CO_2 because land use and land use changes often change the ability of sinks to absorb CO_2. The advantage of using these data, however, is that they show emissions for every country. For instance, in 2004 the U.S. was the world's largest emitter, releasing 5987.98 million metric tons or 20.4 tons per person. Emissions have grown nearly 20 percent since 1990. In comparison, China in that same year emitted 5010.17 million metric tons or 3.84 tons per person. Its emissions had grown a staggering 108.7 percent since 1990. Table 1 provides a summary of nations with emissions above 300 million metric tons in 2004.

Three important issues arise when investigating CO_2 emissions by nation. These issues are important for determining policy that affects GHG emissions. The first of these is the emissions per person by country. Figure 1 graphically illustrates these for countries emitting 300 million metric tons or more in the year 2004. As Figure 1 shows, the nations responsible for the highest per capita emissions are the United States, Canada, and Australia. Countries in the next tier of per capita emissions, those emitting between 9 and 14 metric tons per person, are the Russian Federation, Japan, Germany, the United Kingdom,

TABLE 1

CO$_2$ Emissions Per Capita in 2004

Selected Countries

Country	CO$_2$ emissions Millions of metric tons	% change since 1990	CO$_2$ emissions Metric tons per capita
United States	5987.98	19.6	20.40
China	5010.17	108.7	3.84
Russian Federation	1617.94	-32.4	11.20
India	1342.96	96.9	1.20
Japan	1285.81	12.4	10.10
Germany	885.85	-14.0	10.70
Canada	593.09	28.8	18.50
United Kingdom	562.36	-4.7	9.40
Italy	489.59	12.7	8.50
South Korea	465.64	93.0	9.77
Iran	433.57	98.5	6.31
France	417.35	5.6	6.90
Australia	381.80	36.7	19.00
Indonesia	378.25	76.8	1.69
Mexico	438.02	5.9	4.24
South Africa	437.03	31.6	9.19
Spain	354.56	55.1	8.30
Brazil	331.79	58.2	1.80
Ukraine	316.94	-55.9	6.70
Poland	316.70	-16.8	8.30
Saudi Arabia	308.39	21.0	13.38

Source: UN Statistics Division, Millennium Development Goals Indicators Database.

Table 1: CO$_2$ Emissions Per Capita in 2004 Selected Countries.

South Korea, South Africa, and Saudi Arabia. The developing countries—
China, India, Iran, Indonesia, Mexico, Brazil — are in the final tier along with
some developed nations including France, Spain, Ukraine, and Poland. If policy recommendations are based on per capita emissions, then the burden will
most heavily fall to the first tier nations.

The second consideration is how nations are changing their emissions
over time. Figure 2 shows percentage change in emissions between 1990 and
2004 for countries emitting 300 million metric tons or more. As Figure 2
shows, the largest increases in emission in that time frame have come from
China, India, South Korea, Iran, Indonesia, Spain, and Brazil while the United
States, Japan, Italy, France, Australia, Mexico, South Africa, and Saudi Ara-

CO_2 Emissions Per Capita in 2004
Countries Emitting 300 Million Metric Tons or More

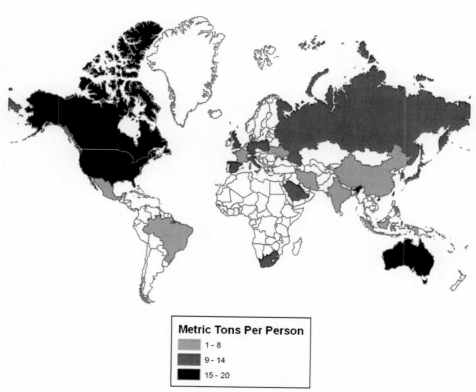

Source: UN Statistics Division, Millennium Development Goals Indicators Database.

Figure 1

bia have increased their emissions far more modestly. Finally, some countries have been successful, for a variety of reasons, in reducing their emissions. These include the Russian Federation, Germany, the United Kingdom, Ukraine, and Poland. Policy approaches that seek to reward decreased emissions over time should look carefully at Figure 2.

Finally, if policy efforts are geared toward addressing only the total amount of emissions, then Figure 3 should be the most illuminating. Figure 3 shows the world's greatest emitters in 2004 — the United States and China — each emitting more than 5,000 million metric tons. The figure also shows the countries in the mid-range of emissions, those putting off between 500 and 2,000 million metric tons. These include the Russian Federation, India, Japan,

CO_2 Emissions Percent Change 1990-2004
Countries Emitting 300 Million Metric Tons or More

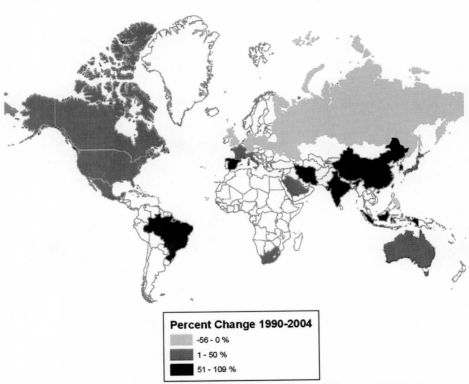

Source: UN Statistics Division, Millennium Development Goals Indicators Database.

Figure 2

Germany, Canada, and the United Kingdom. Those countries emitting between 300 and 500 million metric tons include Italy, South Korea, Iran, France, Australia, Indonesia, Mexico, South Africa, Spain, Brazil, Ukraine, Poland, and Saudi Arabia. Policy based only on quantity of CO_2 emitted should focus on Figure 3.

Greenhouse gases can also be measured as CO_2 equivalents. This measurement includes all greenhouse gases, not just carbon dioxide. The UNFCCC reporting nations provide emissions data in this format. These data also include the effects of land use and land use changes. The UNFCCC data is an excellent time series, going back to 1990, with annual reporting. All nations, however, do not report their emissions. Important omissions include China

CO_2 Emissions in 2004
Countries Emitting 300 Million Metric Tons or More

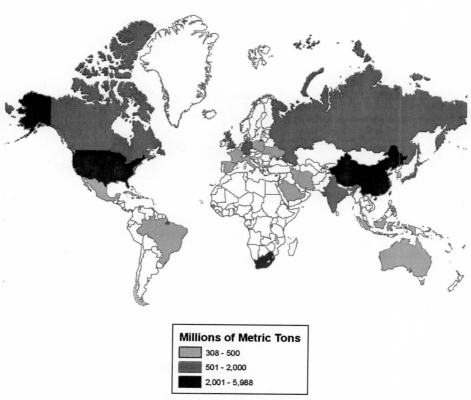

Millions of Metric Tons
308 - 500
501 - 2,000
2,001 - 5,988

Source: UN Statistics Division, Millennium Development Goals Indicators Database.

Figure 3

and India. Table 2 shows CO_2 equivalents with land use and land use change for those countries reporting that emitted more than 500 million metric tons in 2005.

Figure 4 depicts three tiers of GHG emitters. Alone in the first tier is the United States with total GHG emission in 2005 in excess of 6,000 million metric tons. A large drop occurs with the second tier countries of the Russian Federation and Japan, each emitting 2,289 and 1,263 million metric tons respectively. Those countries in tier 3, emitting under 1,000 million metric tons include Germany, Canada, the United Kingdom and Australia.

Figure 5 shows the percentage change in GHG emissions for countries emitting more than 500 million metric tons between 1990 and 2005. The country with the largest increases was Canada with a 54 percent increase. The mid-range countries, with percentage increases from 1 to 25 percent, include the United States, Australia, and Japan. Several countries show decreases in emissions over the time period including the Russian Federation, German, and the United Kingdom. Once again, it is important to point out that reporting of total GHG emissions, as opposed to CO_2, suffers from the

TABLE 2

GHG Emissions with Land Use and Land Use Changes in 2005

Selected Countries

Country	GHG emissions Millions of metric tons	% change since 1990
United States	6431.93	16.3
Russian Federation	2289.16	-27.7
Japan	1263.87	7.1
Germany	965.40	-19.5
Canada	729.71	54.2
United Kingdom	555.36	-15.4
Australia	522.18	4.5

Source: UN Framework Convention on Climate Change
(http://unfccc.int/ghg_emissions_data/ghg_data_from_unfccc/time_series_annex_i/items/38
14.php)

Table 2: GHG Emissions with Land Use and Land Use Changes in 2005 Selected Countries.

Greenhouse Gas (GHG) Emissions 2005
Countries Emitting 500 Million Metric Tons or More

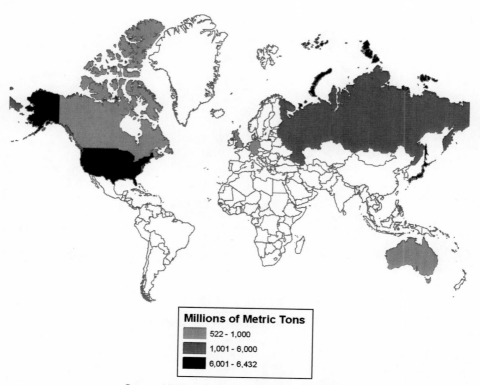

Millions of Metric Tons
- 522 - 1,000
- 1,001 - 6,000
- 6,001 - 6,432

Source: UN Framework Convention on Climate Change

Figure 4

lack of reporting by developing nations. The greatest omissions include no reports from China, India, or Brazil.

These tables and figures clearly show that the developed and rapidly developing countries are the key contributors of anthropogenic GHG emissions. Although historically the developed world by far contributed more greenhouse gases to the atmosphere through their industrialization and modernization efforts, today, the developing world is overtaking the developed world in GHG emissions. This dynamic is very important to understand because existing international agreements designed to lower levels of greenhouse gases in the atmosphere exempt developing countries from mandatory reductions. These exemptions fit with the long history of UN agreements

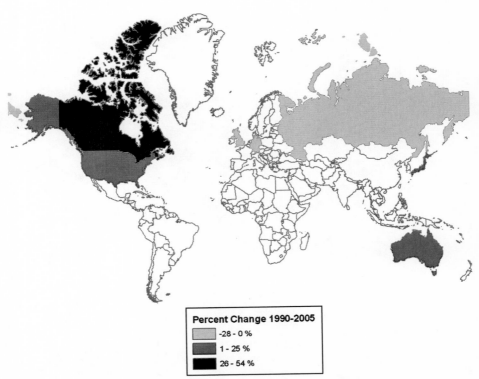

Greenhouse Gas (GHG) Percent Change 1990-2005
Countries Emitting 500 Million Metric Tons or More

Percent Change 1990-2005
-28 - 0 %
1 - 25 %
26 - 54 %

Source: UN Framework Convention on Climate Change

Figure 5

(discussed more thoroughly in chapters 2 and 3) which generally accept the notion that developed nations have a special responsibility to reduce emissions while developing nations should focus primarily on development efforts to reduce poverty. While this may seem initially somewhat odd, it has two basic justifications. First, the developed world is responsible for having generated most of the greenhouse gases currently in the atmosphere — gases generated through fossil fuel burning as they grew rich during their industrial revolutions and after. Second, many actions taken by people in developing countries who struggle on the edge of abject poverty actually result in major contributions to greenhouse gas production. These actions might include clearing forests to create farm lands for crop production. Such acts reduce sinks and thereby contribute to increasing levels of emissions. International agreements, therefore, have long held that developing countries should focus first on their efforts to develop.

Current Scientific Understanding of the Projected Consequences of Global Warming

The most authoritative source of information for current scientific understanding of the projected consequences of global warming is the Intergovernmental Panel on Climate Change. The IPCC has documented that global warming is clearly being observed. The IPCC's 4AR, released in 2007, included a separate statement regarding impacts from the warming as well as adaptive capacity and vulnerability of natural systems and humans to climate change. The IPCC assessed data sets largely collected in the period after 1970, data sets that lack full details on countries in the developing world. Nevertheless, they concluded that "[o]bservational evidence from all continents and most oceans shows that many natural systems are being affected by regional climate changes, particularly temperature increases."[41] These changes include the enlargement and increasing number of glacial lakes formed as glaciers melt, melting ice in the Arctic and Antarctic which is having an impact on predators such as the polar bear, the overall warming of lakes and rivers worldwide, the onset of earlier Springs as demonstrated by premature leaf-unfolding and untimely greening of vegetation, shifts in the ranges of plants and animals as they adapt their ranged due to warmer climates, and changes in animal migration patterns.[42]

Worldwide ecosystems are projected to endure serious impacts due to climate change. In terms of freshwater resources, it is expected that by 2050 drought-affected areas will increase while heavy precipitation events are likely to increase and pose an increased flood risk. Glaciers and snow cover will decline, so areas and populations supplied by melt water coming from these sources will have less water. Many species will face extinction over the century due to climate change and the disruptions that will stem from it such as fire, flooding, drought, insects, and ocean acidification. Making the situation more somber, by 2050 the uptake of carbon by ecosystems is projected to peak so the warming of the Earth will accelerate. Coastal areas will face increased risk of erosion due to sea level rise. Coral reefs are projected to be subject to more frequent events of bleaching and will be more likely to die off completely.[43]

People will be heavily affected by climate change worldwide. It is expected that many millions of people will be flooded every year because of sea level rise and extreme rain events. The large cities in Asia and Africa that are densely populated and located in low-lying areas will face high risks. Islands are projected to be particularly vulnerable to sea level rise. The health status of millions of people will also be impacted by climate change. It is probable that there will be increases in malnutrition due to crop loss and increases in deaths due to heat waves, floods, storms, fires and droughts. There will be vast shifts in the patterns and number of people exposed to various infectious diseases and malaria as mosquitoes and other disease-carrying agents extent their range.[44] Increased levels of pollen and mold spores in the atmosphere will add to the incidences of asthma and allergic diseases, which have already shown sharp rates of increase over recent years.[45] Perhaps more frightening, climate change is likely to result in wars that will result from demand for food and water supplies. Large numbers of environmental refugees, in search of a new place to live, are apt be created. These refugees, in turn, may pose a large burden on countries to which they migrate. By mid century, there is the potential that droughts, food shortages, and flooding will result in the creation of up to 200 million environmental refugees.[46]

While global warming is overwhelmingly a bad story for the Earth, some of the impacts of climate change will have positive regional affects. Crop productivity will increase slightly in some regions as they experience average warmer temperatures and longer growing seasons. This will likely result in an overall global increase in food if temperature increases remain within 1–3 degrees Celsius, however, if temperatures climb higher the IPCC projects that global food production will decrease. Some other regional positive trend will include increased commercial timber production for the short to medium term. Additionally, fewer people will be sickened by or die from cold-related illnesses.[47]

Despite the fact that some regions and localities will benefit from global warming, generally speaking most of the regions of the world will suffer harm. Moreover, the harm will increase if temperatures rise higher than 1–3 degrees Celsius. Overall, the IPCC 4AR states that "costs and benefits of climate change for industry, settlement and society will vary widely by location and scale. In the aggregate, however, net effects will tend to be more negative the larger the change in climate."[48] According to the IPCC, the continent of Africa is most vulnerable to the impacts of climate change. By 2020, in Africa, it is estimated that between 75 and 250 million people will be subject to water shortages. Agricultural production is expected to drop. In some African countries the drop could be as much as 50 percent by 2020. Large lake fisheries are expected to decline. By the end of the century sea level rise will affect low-lying coastal areas, where large numbers of people live.[49] In general, the World Health Organization (WHO) projects that the largest risk to life and health associated with climate change will occur in Africa, and predominantly among the youth of Africa.[50] Part of the reason for this is not only that warming will have such major impacts but also that Africa is poverty stricken and therefore has far fewer resources to help its people adapt to the ravages that climate change will bring.

Asia, too, will experience many ill effects. Himalayan glacier melt will increase flooding and rock avalanches from destabilized slopes. This melt will also affect water resources within the next 30 years with decreased flow to rivers as glaciers recede. Water scarcity will impact more than a billion people by mid-century. Coastal areas will be at risk from ocean flooding as seas rise and storms intensify. There will be regional winners and losers. Crop yields could increase by nearly 20 percent in eastern and southeastern Asia while they could decrease by up to 30 percent in central and south Asia by 2050. Deaths due to diarrhoeal disease will increase as will the toxicity and abundance of cholera in South Asia.[51] Asia is also likely to see health impacts from the spread of malaria as the climate warms and the mosquito increases its range.[52] China, however, may experience some beneficial effects. The northwest region of China, in particular, may already be seeing early signs of a shift in climate from warm and dry to warm and wet, resulting in more vegetation and fewer occurrences of sand-storms.[53]

The prediction for Australia and New Zealand is that they will experience reduced precipitation likely resulting in extended drought. Indeed, drought conditions currently persist in Australia and have greatly impacted wheat production, which in turn has negatively impacted food availability and prices worldwide. The problem of reduced precipitation in southern and eastern Australia and New Zealand is expected to intensify by 2030. One of the most important ecological features of the world, the Great Barrier Reef, will be massively impacted. The Great Barrier Reef is the largest coral reef system in the world, stretching over 1,600 miles in the Coral Sea off the coast of Queensland in northeast Australia. The Great Barrier Reef currently is a vast area containing a widely diverse collection of life but the area is expected to sustain significant loss of biodiversity by 2030 due to the impacts of climate change. Finally, Australia and New Zealand will have to deal with sea level rise that will likely threaten coastal communities. These coastal communities will also be threatened by storm of increasing severity and frequency.[54]

Almost all of Europe's regions will experience negative consequences associated with climate change. Europe is projected to experience a greater risk of inland flash floods resulting from heavy precipitation events as well as coastal flooding from rising sea levels and severe coastal storms. Mountainous area will experience retreating glaciers, reduced snow cover, and species loss. In northern Europe climate change may initially bring beneficial effects including increased crop yield and forest growth, however, as climate change progresses the region will experience negative impacts. Southern Europe will find itself with scarce water supplies, decreased precipitation, and lower crop productivity. Central and Eastern Europe will likely experience reduced summer rainfall and will experience health risks associated with heat waves.[55] Tropical viruses like chikungunya and dengue fever, will be seen in southern Europe as the insects that carry the virus will be able to live in a warmed Europe.[56]

Drastic changes are predicted for Latin and South America. Because of reduced precipitation, Latin and South America is likely to see the east Amazon shift from tropical forest to savanna. This massive change will result in an extreme loss of biodiversity in the region. The east Amazon currently is a major refuge of the Earth's plant and animal species but this safe haven will be lost. As the globe warms, the areas of Latin America that are currently already dry will experience desertification and loss of agricultural productivity due to salinization of fresh water supplies. Sea level rise will impact coastal areas, especially islands, and produce an increase in flooding in many areas. Changes in precipitation patterns and decline of glaciers will drastically reduce water available for energy generation, agriculture, and human use.[57]

North America will experience decreased snow pack in the western mountains, more winter flooding, and less summer water flow. The Southwest will grow increasingly dryer and will get less winter rainfall.[58] Some projections are for Dust Bowl–like conditions to return to the Southwest by mid-century. Projections suggest that the 10-year drought the West has been enduring may just be the beginning of a much longer, if not permanent, dry period.[59] Forests are expected to be stressed by fire, pests, and diseases. Indeed, the fire season in the West has increased its length and the West now currently is experiencing and unprecedented number of wild fires. Agricultural patterns will also change as warming increases and precipitation rates shift. Cities will become urban hot spots and will experience deadly heat waves as temperatures rise. Coastal communities will be most vulnerable to danger from increased tropical storm activity and flooding.[60] Tropical diseases, like dengue fever, are expected to spread into the United States due to a warmer climate and expanded range of mosquitoes unless there is effective mosquito control.[61] Dengue fever was largely overcome in the Americas in general due to the spraying of DDT. The disease has made a comeback already in South and Central America, the Caribbean, and Mexico. According to the Pan American Health Organization, 2007 was the second worst year on record with over 918,000 cases reported. Several cases have been reported in Hawaii and along the Texas-Mexico border region.[62]

The earliest and most dramatic effects are already widely being seen at the poles. Polar regions will continue to see the reduction in thickness and size of glaciers and ice sheets. Ice sheets will thaw and fall into the ocean. Permafrost will thaw, increasing the amounts of methane released and hastening more warming. Many animals will be endangered by these shifts.[63] The Polar Bear was listed by EPA as a threatened species in 2007. Indeed, widespread warming changes have been underway in northern Alaska and the Arctic for the last 30 years. These changes include a later freeze and earlier melt of Arctic rivers and lakes, increased intensity of storm activity, and overall rise in temperature. For the Arctic, these changes have initiated wide scale biological, climatological, and hydrologic system changes that, in turn, impact human social systems where they exist in the far north.[64]

Areas of Continuing Uncertainty

Part of the problem with climate science is that it is not an experimental science. An experimental science provides findings by conducting controlled experiments which unambiguously determine causation. Experimentation involves randomly selecting subjects into groups and controlling conditions so that only one group receives the treatment that is in question. If the treatment group reacts differently than the control group, the treatment is determined to have caused the effect. Experimental methods thus employed eliminate bias and assure that the treatment variable under scrutiny is the agent causing observed differences between the experimental and control groups.

Lacking controlled experimentation, climate science must proceed using a three step process. First, climate scientists must show that the climate has changed with some level of statistical certainty. Second, they must argue that this change is consistent with computer models that simulate human-induced changes in climate. Finally, they must demonstrate that no rival hypothesis (such as natural cycles) could account for the observed change.[65] This is difficult to do. It has taken decades for climate scientists to develop accurate models with sufficient detail and sophistication to allow a scientific consensus to emerge. That said, there are still areas of uncertainty that persist and need continuing study.

Scientific understanding of the role of stratospheric water vapor is not well understood. Water vapor is known to act as a potent greenhouse gas but just how water vapor impacts climate systems needs further investigation. The role that surface reflectivity plays perhaps is known a bit better but greater understanding is needed. How much surface reflection increases the amount of heat that is radiated back into space is unclear as are the impacts of reduced levels of surface reflectivity as ice and snow melt. The same can be said of the role of aerosols, including cloud cover. How much they provide a cooling impact needs to be explored more. The role that contrails, the vapor trails produced by aircraft exhaust, play are poorly understood.[66] Another problem is that some models in use remain inadequate or incomplete. Missing, inaccurate and non-representative data introduce a level of uncertainty into understanding climate change processes. Finally, many uncertainties regarding the socioeconomic impacts of climate change stem from attempts to forecast human behavior that is not easily predicted. In this category are factors such as political response to climate issues, movement of populations away from vulnerable areas, and the resilience of communities.[67] These factors are poorly understood.

The dramatic and unpredicted increase in the speed of glacier melt has caused scientists to wonder about what else they might have missed in their projections. Melt rates of the 3-kilometer-thick ice sheet on Greenland doubled in speed between 2000 and 2005. This was not expected. The rapidity of the melt far exceeded model projections and because of this, scientists wonder what else their models might have understated.[68] The biological and ecological complexity of the Arctic demands an integrated scientific approach to its study, which is still lacking. This combined with lack of sustained time series data provides challenges for forecasting.[69]

Finally, it needs to be said that the predictions of the IPCC depend on several assumptions that may be too optimistic. For instance, the 4AR rests on the assumption that a large amount of reduction in emissions will happen spontaneously as improved technology brings gains to energy efficiency thus reducing the amounts of greenhouse gases released into the atmosphere. However, the 4AR does not factor in the rapid increase in energy use and emissions releases coming from increased economic activity in the developing world, especially China and India. As a result of this development, it is likely that the world will continue on the path of expanded energy use. If this is the case, policy makers should begin to concentrate more closely on making sure technological advances in energy efficiency are made and that they are rapidly diffused to developing nations.[70]

Mitigation and Adaptation

Communities, regions, and nations are moving rapidly into the arena of both mitigation and adaptation. Mitigation involves the reduction of greenhouse gas emissions while adaptation involves finding ways to live with an altered climate and its consequences. As later chapters will show, multilateral environmental agreements (MEA) like the Kyoto Protocol are addressing the issues of both mitigation and adaptation.

IPCC models show that there is significant potential for reducing GHG emissions over the next several decades. Some of these mitigation strategies rest upon certain technologies and practices currently commercially available. Others require additional research and development (R&D) before they will be ready for commercial use. For instance, the IPCC suggests the energy supply sector could use off-the-shelf strategies that include switching from coal to gas, nuclear power, renewable energy, and combined heat and power. With additional R&D, carbon capture and storage may become viable and additional sources of renewable energy may become cost effective. The transportation sector could improve by using more fuel efficient vehicles, hybrid vehicles, clean diesel vehicles, biofuels, increased reliance on public transportation, non-motorized transport including walking and cycling, as well as better land use and transportation planning. Buildings could be improved by using energy efficient lighting, appliances and heating and cooling systems. Improved insulation, active and passive solar designs to aid with heating and cooling could be employed. Alternative refrigeration fluids could be used. The industrial sector could make better use of more efficient electrical equipment, heat and power recovery, recycling, and better control over non–CO_2 GHG emissions. The agricultural sector could put in place better crop and grazing management to increase soil carbon storage, improvements in rice cultivation techniques, livestock and manure management to cut down on CH_4 emissions; improved nitrogen fertilizer application techniques could reduce N_2O emissions; and energy crops could replace fossil fuel use. Forests could be planted or replanted. Deforestation could be halted. The waste management sector could make better use of methane recovery from landfills.[71] Changes in eating patterns affect mitigation. As the developing world improves its living standard, the trend is for increased meat consumption. Increases in meat consumption, especially beef, will dangerously increase methane releases. Maintenance or adoption of vegetarian eating patterns can greatly reduce greenhouse gas emissions.

In terms of adaptation, some progress is being made. The World Health Organization is setting up systems for warning vulnerable populations about heat waves, the spread of vector-borne diseases to areas previously not subject to such diseases, the increasing risk of hurricanes in the Caribbean, the potential for glacial lake outburst floods, and the safe use of wastewater in arid areas. Nevertheless, WHO thinks much more needs to be done. The concerns for health effects associated with climate change must expand to include the wider issues of health security that will address more substantive issues. One such concern is for the effects on humans and human settlements in cattle-based societies when the cattle are prevented from grazing by sustained drought. Another area of health security concerns changes that may affect the overall production of food, especially in marginally productive areas of the world.[72]

The sad truth is that it is easier for developed nations to both mitigate and adapt to climate change simply because they have the resources to initiate programs. Use of the Clean Development Mechanism (CDM) under the Kyoto Protocol does, however, provide some prospect of introducing both mitigation and adaption strategies into developing countries. Using CDM, developed countries can meet some of their greenhouse gas reduction targets by partnering with developing nations to put in place projects that produce greenhouse gas reductions in the developing country. Developed countries can also transfer clean energy technologies to developing nations to further assist with mitigation. They can also provide direct monetary assistance for adaptation projects.

Economic Impacts of Global Warming

Climate change will have enormous impacts on the Earth's people, animal species, and plant life. A key question is: What will it cost to take action to prevent the most dire consequences? An alternative question that must be asked is what will be the costs if global warming is left to proceed without interruption? The British government undertook an in-depth study to answer these questions under the direction of Sir Nicholas Stern, Head of the Government Economics Service and Advisor to the Government on the Economics of Climate Change and Development. The Stern Report, the most comprehensive economic analysis of the impacts of climate change, came to several important conclusions.

The most significant of these is that "the benefits of strong and early action far outweigh the costs of not acting."[73] Prominent in the Stern analysis is the conclusion that global warming will affect the life of humans worldwide and that hundreds of millions could suffer as the world warms. The Stern Report asserts that if no action is taken, the costs will be the equivalent to losing at least 5 percent of global GDP per year, extending far into the future. The loss in GDP could be even higher if other assumptions are included in the economic model. The costs of action, however, are estimated by the Stern Report to be about 1 percent of global GDP per year. If that investment takes place over the next 20 years, the impact of avoiding major disruptions to the world's economy can be vastly reduced. This conclusion has been supported by leading economists, including Nobel Prize winning Kenneth J. Arrow.[74]

For the United States, the cost of inaction will also be greater than the costs of action, according to a study done by the University of Maryland's Center for Integrative Environmental Research. Echoing the Stern Report, the study concluded that climate change would affect every American in significant and dramatic ways with costs rising if action is delayed. The costs are anticipated to vary regionally but will be associated with storm damage, the cost of fire suppression, flooding, and drought — each of which will damage property and crops. Losses from reduced shipping due to low water levels will drive up costs for the manufacturing sector, particularly in the Midwest. Sea level rise and storms will destroy property along the coasts. Drought will impact the South and Southwest, hurting agriculture, industry and households.[75] The U.S. Government Accountability Office (GAO) estimates that private and federal insurers are exposed to the effects of climate change, especially property and crop damage due to weather-related events, and over the course of the coming decades will experience substantially increased risks from damage settlements.[76]

The Stern Report asserts that if no action is taken to cut GHG emissions, the concentration of those gases in the atmosphere will reach twice the pre-industrial level by 2035. Such a buildup of greenhouse gases will certainly result in temperature increases over 2 degrees Celsius and in the long term perhaps as much as 5 degrees Celsius. Such a massive change in temperature will result in major changes in where people live and how they live their lives. The report concludes that

> All countries will be affected. The most vulnerable — the poorest countries and populations — will suffer earliest and most, even though they have contributed least to the causes of climate change. The costs of extreme weather, including floods, droughts and storms, are already rising, including for rich countries. Adaptation to climate change — that is, taking steps to build resilience and minimize costs — is essential. It is no longer possible to prevent the climate change that will take place over the next two to three decades, but it is still possible to protect our societies and economies from its impacts to some extent — for example, by providing better information, improved planning and more climate-resilient crops and infrastructure. Adaptation will cost tens of billions of dollar a year in developing countries alone, and will put still further pressure on already scarce resources. Adaptation efforts, particularly in developing countries should be accelerated.[77]

The scientific evidence suggests that the Earth will undergo extreme impacts from global warming if we continue to engage in business-as-usual. The Stern Report concludes that the risk of the worst impacts will be reduced if GHG levels are stabilized at between 450 and 550 ppm of CO_2 equivalent. To achieve this, emissions will have to be reduced by 80 percent of 2006 levels. While this is challenging, the Stern Report also suggests that climate change will create significant business opportunities especially for low-carbon technologies that could be worth hundreds of billions of dollars a year. The reassuring message of the Stern Report is that

> The World does not need to choose between averting climate change and promoting growth and development. Changes in energy technologies and in the structure of economies have created opportunities to decouple growth from greenhouse gas emissions. Indeed, ignoring climate change will eventually damage economic growth. Tackling climate change is the pro-growth strategy for the longer term, and it can be done in a way that does not cap the aspirations for growth of rich or poor countries.[78]

While many jobs may be created by developing a low-carbon economy, millions of jobs worldwide could also be lost. Global warming threatens the world's fisheries sector, the tourism industry, and will cause massive job loss among those displaced by its impacts. At the same time, the UN Development Program (UNDP) expects many new jobs to be created in the environment and energy technology sector as nations work to mitigate and adapt to climate change. Job loss and creation, even if they happen in the same overall number, will still be disruptive because the likelihood that they will be created in the same places and at the same time is low. The stress created by such huge shifts will be substantial.[79]

Signs of a burgeoning low-carbon industry are emerging. Google, the Internet search engine giant, created a research group focused on the development of cheaper sources of renewable energy focusing largely on solar and wind power. The project, called Renewable Energy Cheaper than Coal, is aimed at first helping Google to cut its own energy costs and then to sell its new cheaper power. The project follows an earlier initiative to lower energy costs through making its data centers more energy efficient. Its philanthropic arm, Google.org, will join these efforts by making grants to universities, firms, and laboratories working on related projects.[80] The Google phenomenon is just part of the movement towards creation of a new industry. Venture capital from Silicon Valley began moving heavily into the energy arena in 2006. Billions have been poured into energy-related start-up companies with the expressed hope of solving the energy problem within 30 years.[81]

While new companies may be created, existing companies will have to consider their risk of potential additional costs associated with climate change. These threats are more extensive than the direct physical risk associated with climate change such as droughts, floods, sea level rise, fire, and storms. The most obvious of these new costs is an increased regulatory burden in a carbon-constrained economy. This cost can be estimated based on the likely purchase price of carbon allowances traded under a cap-and-trade system or the burden of a carbon tax. Companies may also have to deal with vulnerabilities associated with supply chain disruption which might result from climate change-related issues. For instance, suppliers will likely pass along their carbon-related costs their customers. Companies that use steel, aluminum, glass, rubber, and plastics are likely to feel the impact of higher costs. On the other hand, companies that are capable of producing products that will be profitable in a carbon-constrained economy will do well.[82]

The insurance sector has a particular interest in climate change as they will underwrite much of the cost of disasters and extreme weather events. Global costs of weather related disasters increased from an average annual cost of $8.9 billion between 1977 and 1986, to an average annual cost of $45.1 billion between 1997 and 2006. These trends are expected to increase.[83] Some estimates are that weather losses could reach over $1 trillion by 2040.[84] The only way to avoid these losses is to work toward better mitigation and adaptation strategies, in particular, to coordinate the insurance sector with disaster management risk reduction efforts.

Global Warming as a Security Threat

In 2007, under the leadership of the British, the United Nations Security Council held its first debate over the risks climate change poses to world security. The Foreign Office circulated a paper explaining why the debate was necessary. It warns of changes to the world's physical landmass and the likelihood of border and maritime disputes. In addition, the paper suggests there could be conflicts over scarce energy resources and security of supply of energy. Attention was drawn to an estimated 200 million environmental refugees who will flee their communities in search of greater security elsewhere. The British report is joined by reports coming from the U.S. military including the Center for Naval Analyses and the U.S. Army War College both of which argue that global warming presents significant national security challenges to the United States.[85]

A 2006 study released by the Naval War College called attention to the fact that the waters of the Canadian Arctic are becoming free of ice and therefore free to navigate. Security implications will arise that the United States must address including the increased threat from terrorist attack. In addition, the study calls for closer attention to defending U.S. interests in the region, including Arctic oil, though cooperative relations with Canada.[86]

In a larger study commissioned by the Center for Naval Analyses and undertaken by group of retired generals and admirals called the Military Advisory Board, the threat of security issues was examined. The report concluded:

> Climate change can act as a threat multiplier for instability in some of the most volatile regions of the world, and it presents significant national security challenges for the United States. Accordingly, it is appropriate to start

now to help mitigate the severity of some of these emergent challenges. The decision to act should be made soon in order to plan prudently for the nation's security. The increasing risks from climate change should be addressed now because they will almost certainly get worse if we delay.[87]

The report concludes that for national and international security, global warming adds to hostile and stressing factors. At the simplest level these include natural and humanitarian disasters on a large scale. These will contribute to political instability and failed states where governments are unable to cope with social demands for action. The report declared:

> Unlike most conventional security threats that involve a single entity acting in specific ways and points in time, climate change has the potential to result in multiple chronic conditions, occurring globally within the same time frame. Economic and environmental conditions in already fragile areas will further erode as good production declines, disease increases, clean water becomes increasingly scarce, and large populations move in search of resources. Weakened and failing governments, with an already thin margin of survival, foster the conditions for internal conflicts, extremism, and movement toward increased authoritarianism and radical ideologies. The U.S. may be drawn more frequently into these situations, either alone or with allies, to help provide stability before conditions worsen and are exploited by extremists. The U.S. may also be called upon to undertake stability and reconstruction efforts once a conflict has begun, to avert further disaster and reconstitute a stable environment.[88]

The report further warns that the U.S. and Europe may be called upon to accept large numbers of immigrant and refugee populations as they flee the anticipated natural disasters, droughts, food shortages, floods, and extreme weather events expected. The report recommends that the national security consequences of climate change be fully integrated into general security and military planning, that the U.S. should join in the international effort to stabilize climate, that the U.S. should help less developed nations to adapt to climate change, that the Department of Defense should adopt improved energy efficiency standards, and that the Department of Defense should assess the impact on military installations worldwide of "rising sea levels, extreme weather events, and other projected climate change impacts over the next 30 to 40 years."[89]

This report agrees with an earlier report put out by the Global Business Network, which advises intelligence agencies and the Pentagon, on the unrest that could be generated by climate change in heavily populated regions like Bangladesh as its sinking delta region becomes less habitable. The report looked at Somalia in the early 1990s as an example of what the U.S. confronts. Disruption there was driven by drought, which lead to societal collapse, humanitarian relief efforts, and U.S. military intervention. Other studies have shown the link between global warming and civil conflicts in places like Afghanistan, Nepal, Sudan, and Darfur.[90]

Conclusion

As this chapter has shown, climate change is a complex environmental issue that will have enormous economic, security, ecological, and social impacts. The scientific understanding of the role that greenhouse gases play for our climate dates back to the 19th century. It took years for the scientific community to come to a good understanding of the forces at work. That said, scientists today continue to fully explore the complexity and dynamism of the climate system.

Scientific projections of the consequences of global warming paint a frightening picture of likely outcomes. These include flood and droughts, glaciers melting with resultant loss of drinking water, extreme weather events, wild fires, and the spread of tropical diseases as northern latitudes warm. Plants and animal species will be given very short periods of time to adjust to the changing ecosphere and many of them will be lost in a great extinction.

Indeed, global chances clearly associated with increasing levels of GHGs in the atmosphere are being observed. Global temperatures have increased, glaciers are melting with astonishing speed, oceans are becoming more acidic, tropical diseases are on the move northward and into higher elevations, and extended droughts are impacting food production in many locations. These changes are bringing pressure to bear on those already surviving on the margin and creating the first waves of global warming environmental refugees.

The full extent of future climate changes the world may experience are still uncertain because of lack of understanding about how the large number of factors that play a role in the process of climate change may interact. Much remains to be fully understood including the function of feedback loops and the timing of climate change.

What is clear, however, is that the cost of inaction is far greater than the cost of swift action. Mitigation of GHG emissions though creation and deployment of better technologies, through energy efficiency, and through reduced demand is necessary. That said, we will not be able to avoid some of the effects of global warming even if we are successful in reducing emissions because of the amount of greenhouse gases already in the atmosphere and their long life. While mitigation remains a pressing concern, attention must also turn to how human settlements can best adapt to the climate changes that are now underway.

Those changes pose a real threat to the national survival of many states. Climate change is seen by military analysts as a threat multiplier for instability in the most vulnerable nations in the world. Global warming may be the trigger for mass human migrations, as economic and environmental conditions in fragile countries result in decline in the production of food and goods. Expanded demands for scarce resources may topple weak governments and generate internal conflicts that the United States and its allies may be drawn into to provide some measure of stability so that extremists are not able to take advantage of desperate conditions to gain power. It is in the best interest of all nations, and the United States in particular, to promote adaptation strategies so that the worst consequences of climate change are contained as best as is possible.

2

Climate Change Policy in the United States

From the Framework Convention to the Obama Administration

Early in his administration, President George W. Bush withdrew the U.S. from the Kyoto Protocol agreement arguing that the science was uncertain, that mandatory limits on greenhouse gas emissions would hurt the U.S. economy, and that it was unfair to exempt developing nations from mandatory reductions while expecting binding targets from developed nations. This stand reversed the U.S. position on climate change begun under George W. Bush's father, George H. W. Bush, when he was 41st president of the United States — a policy that was continued under President Bill Clinton. Both George H. W. Bush and Bill Clinton supported international engagement on the issue of climate change. Despite the stated policy position of the federal government under the George W. Bush administration, some progress was made in the U.S. between 2000 and 2008 to control GHG emissions. The steps forward were largely accomplished by the states acting alone or together in regional partnerships to redirect U.S. climate change policy after the default of the federal government.

After the election of President Barack Obama, the federal government reversed again. President Obama called for the United States to once more assume leadership on the issue of climate change. Early in his administration a number of steps were taken to steer the U.S. on the path toward climate leadership and domestic GHG emissions reduction. The historic economic stimulus bill passed early in the Obama administration contained key energy and environmental provisions to promote alternative energy and energy efficiency — a significant effort to deal with climate change. In his first address to a joint session of Congress, President Obama called for Congress to send him legislation imposing a market-based carbon control scheme for the U.S. The Obama administration made the expansion of renewable energy a centerpiece of his initial policy goals and adopted policies that would pave the way for the creation of a new green energy sector in the United States. Clear signals were sent to the international community that the United States would once again act in partnership with them to address the climate crisis.

This chapter begins with an overview of the international treaties and agreements that form the legal basis for GHG reductions and the U.S. position, over time, vis-à-vis these negotiations and agreements. The chapter then turns to a discussion of the role of the states and state-based regional alliances, highlighting efforts taken to enact policies dealing with climate change. Information gathered through a series of personal interviews conducted with state officials working on one or more of these regional alliances is presented. Some actions taken by states and the state-based regional alliances have raised legal and constitutional concerns. After discussing these, the chapter provides an assessment of why these state and regional efforts are significant, both for reducing GHG emissions and for laying the foundation for national policy. Within this context, the consequences of enacting climate change policy from the bottom up rather than the top down are evaluated. The chapter concludes with an introduction to the goals and early policy actions of the Obama administration.

The International Framework for Climate Change Policy

The Bush administration repudiated the Kyoto Protocol shortly after taking office in 2001. The Kyoto Protocol, an agreement among signatories to reduce GHG emissions to 1990 levels between 2008 and 2012, had been negotiated under the Clinton administration. The United States signed the treaty in 1998; however, President Clinton was not able to muster enough support in the Senate for ratification so he never submitted the treaty for consideration. The complete withdrawal of the Bush administration from this agreement could have dealt a death blow to the Kyoto Protocol because ratification was required by at least 55 countries accounting for at least 55 percent of the developed countries' 1990 emissions.[1] Despite the withdrawal of support by the U.S. and Australia, Russian ratification achieved the 55 percent threshold. The Kyoto Protocol went into effect February 16, 2005, with Russia as the 126th party to the agreement. Its importance, though, was clearly undermined by the fact that the world's largest GHG emitter, the U.S., was not a party to the agreement.[2]

The Kyoto Protocol grew out of an earlier series of international meetings and agreements among scientists and policy advisors. The first of these came in 1988 with the creation of the Intergovernmental Panel on Climate Change. IPCC, organized by the World Meteorological Organization and the United Nations Environment Program at the recommendation of the U.S., joined the National Academy of Sciences as an official advisor to the United States government on climate change issues. The IPCC represented almost all the world's governments and their climate experts.[3] In 1992 the United Nations Framework Convention on Climate Change was adopted at the Earth Summit which met in Rio de Janeiro that year. The United States signed and ratified the treaty. The UNFCCC required all parties to stabilize GHG concentrations in the atmosphere at a level that would not interfere with climate, with due regard to sustainable economic development. UNFCCC also required that parties create and publish an inventory of GHG emissions. A series of other meetings, called Conferences of the Parties (COP), followed the Rio Earth Summit. The COPs developed the legal framework for the treaty, put all UNFCCC parties on a schedule to reduce emissions, and negotiated a policy agreement that industrialized countries should be first to reduce their emissions while developing countries would be allowed to continue to develop without having to consider GHG emissions.[4] It was this last point that created conflict in the Congress and convinced President Clinton that if he took the treaty to the Congress for ratification, it would fail. Then, with the election of President Bush, the U.S. fully pulled out of the agreement saying the costs of reducing GHG emissions would hurt the economy and citing the unfairness of the agreement in so far as it let developing nations continue to pollute.

The withdrawal from the Kyoto Protocol was accompanied by a good deal of rhetoric from the administration calling into question the scientific accuracy of global warming. The administration repeatedly questioned whether there was sufficient evidence to conclude that global warming was really occurring, and if it was, whether it was the result of human activities rather than some natural climate shift. The Bush administration used these points to frame a debate that many who opposed any policy action on climate change supported. Environmentalists and those who supported a responsible assessment of the threat of climate change were discontented with the position of the Bush administration, not just because they disagreed with the U.S. withdrawal from the Kyoto Protocol, but because the administration tried to justify its position by attacking what most considered accurate and valid scientific evidence. The Bush administration's claim that the science was unsettled fit with the claims coming from the well organized industry-based anti-climate change lobby spearheaded by ExxonMobil and supported by many oil, coal, and fossil fuel-intensive companies.

The presence of a determined opposition to environmental advocacy is nothing new in American politics.[5] Since the 1970s, with the beginnings of mandatory regulations to deal with air and water pollution, the environmental opposition has been a formidable obstacle that those who favor environmental policy action have had to overcome. In the debate over of climate change and what, if any, measures should be taken to address it, the Bush administration became the champion of those who favored policy inaction. Early in the tenure of the Bush administration, these opponents included many from the business community that saw climate change legislation as yet another regulatory burden. Later this would change as the states and regions began implementing different plans in different geographic locations. The latter was seen as more of a burden to industry than a single mandatory national standard.

It is interesting to note that in 2001, the same year the Bush administration assumed office, IPPC scientists issued a strong statement of consensus regarding global warming and its causes. In their third draft report they concluded, as they had similarly done in their first and second draft, that it was much more likely than not that the planet was undergoing human-induced global warming. Finally in 2004, the Bush administration reluctantly gave up its sustained opposition to the world's scientists. It sent Congress an analysis that was accompanied by supportive cover letters from the Secretaries of Energy and Commerce as well as the President's Science Advisor. The analysis at long last accepted the scientific evidence that humans were causing global warming. The report confirmed that GHG emissions were the only explanation for the atmospheric warming observed over the past several decades. The Bush administration, however, proposed no mandatory policy actions to deal with GHG emissions[6] still arguing that the costs of reducing emissions was too high and that the United States should not be required to reduce emissions if developing countries were not also required to do so.

Rather than follow along with efforts being made internationally for the implementation of the Kyoto Protocol, the Bush administration called for a summit on climate change to be held in Washington in September of 2007. The purpose for the summit was to explore an alternative process for moving forward on the climate change issue. The conference was attended by only mid-level officials from 16 nations. Many of the European representatives feared that the Bush summit was an attempt to derail the UN-sponsored process that had culminated in the Kyoto Protocol.[7] Indeed, the parallel process the Bush administration was trying to set up relied entirely on voluntary reductions and continued non-cooperation with the mandatory reductions supported within the UN Kyoto process.

With the end of the Kyoto Protocol scheduled for 2012, the next round of UN-sponsored international talks to address climate change came with the COP in Bali, Indonesia held in December of 2007. The goal of the Bali meeting was to set the roadmap for negotiating a successor agreement to the Kyoto Protocol by 2009. The U.S. sent a representative but continued to raise issues about how strongly a successor agreement to Kyoto should demand GHG reductions on the part of developing nations, especially China. The United States insisted that no firm 2020 target numbers for GHG reductions appear in the preamble, and so a compromise was agreed to whereby the language used simply recognized the need for "deep cuts" in emissions. The bitterness towards the role of the U.S. in the proceedings was revealed by former U.S. Vice President Al Gore who told delegates that the United States was obstructing progress. Gore had arrived at the Bali COP after receiving the Nobel Peace Price along with the IPCC for their efforts to alert the world of the threat of climate change. Delegates at the conference saw two sides of the U.S.: the official delegates representing the Bush administration and American activists, like Gore.[8] The great divide in America over what to do about climate change was abundantly obvious to all.

In the end, the Bali Action Plan was agreed to by all parties but only after considerable drama that included booing and hissing by many delegates aimed at the U.S. delegation. The Bali Action Plan had no binding commitments, as required by the U.S. but did provide that the next two years of negotiation proceed on a two track path — one for those countries not committed to mandatory limits and one that builds on the Kyoto Protocol. In the end, the U.S. agreed to the two tracks to avoid the total breakdown of the meeting. The roadmap thus allowed for continued negotiations for mandatory reductions to succeed Kyoto in 2012. Those that favored the mandatory approach held out hope that with a new administration in Washington after 2008, the U.S. might shift its position.[9] It seems they were correct in this expectation for the Obama administration has shifted policy.

It should be noted that the U.S. federal government under the Bush administration did have some programs in place to address GHG emissions. Those that existed, however, were extremely limited and consisted entirely of voluntary approaches. For instance, the federal government programs Climate VISION and Energy STAR worked with industry to reduce GHG emissions voluntarily. These federal programs and clean energy R&D were coordinated by the Federal Climate Change Technology Program. The federal government also had the Federal Climate Change Initiative which had a goal of reducing the GHG intensity of the economy by eighteen percent (from 2002 to 2012). However, none of these federal efforts called for a mandatory cap on emissions and none directly sought to reduce the overall level of GHG emissions.[10] In fact the plan to reduce GHG intensity of the economy specifically allowed for continued growth in overall GHG emissions.

Engagement at the State Level

The default of the federal government under the Bush administration did not result in total inaction on the part of other governmental organizations. Concern about climate change had been growing at both local and state levels for many years. In several regions of the country the state and local response to the U.S. withdrawal from the Kyoto process was the trigger that moved them to policy action. With inaction at the federal level, leadership fell to the states.[11]

Environmental policies are implemented in the U.S. under the system of cooperative federalism which allows a system of dual sovereignty between the states and the federal government. States are considered sovereign and cannot be commandeered or taken over by the federal government. That said, the Supremacy Clause of the Constitution establishes that the federal government has the authority to preempt state laws when they are in conflict with federal laws. Congress may also explicitly prohibit states from issuing separate regulations especially when the regulations deal with products that will be sold in interstate commerce. For instance, the Clean Air Act specifically prohibits states from adopting standards to control emissions in new motor vehicles and the Energy Policy Conservation Act prohibits states from regulating automotive fuel economy. This does not mean, however, that states cannot have more stringent standards than a federal standard, only that they may not have regulations that are in conflict with federal standards or when Congress has directly prohibited the issuance of state regulations. The federal government, of course, can use a variety of inducements to get the states to enact policies that the federal government would like to see put in place. Most of these inducements are financial incentives or penalties that may be applied should the state not follow federal preferences.[12] For instance, the federal government may provide money to states and localities if they put into operation programs the federal government would like to see implemented. Conversely, sub-national jurisdictions may be penalized by the federal government by its withholding certain funds if the jurisdiction refuses to comply with federal dictates.

What happened at the state and local levels over the climate change issue was that enterprising civil servants with experience in related areas of environmental management such as recycling or air pollution moved into action when the federal government failed to act. They drew on their experience in other related areas to build networks and develop ideas that could work to reduce GHG emissions. Operating in the absence of federal action, they crafted innovative programs that could both reduce GHG emissions and protect the economic self-interest of the state at the same time. Concerns over quality of life issues also pressured governors to adopted green policies that would continue to attract businesses and investors to their state. Early adopters of climate change policy action saw such policy as tied to long term economic development as well as the immediate economic benefit of such things as protection of oceanfront development, tourism, water adequacy, biodiversity, or other environmentally sensitive features of state life. Those forging climate change policy at the sub-national level also considered the potential for cascading impacts or co-benefits from GHG reductions including such things as overall air pollution reduction, diversification of the energy supply, less traffic congestion, and stability of the regulatory framework for regulated firms.[13]

A number of states have taken individual climate policy action. In 1997, Oregon became the first state to regulate GHG emissions. In that year Oregon required new power plants to offset approximately 17 percent of their addition to GHG emissions either through improved efficiency or by purchasing offsets (reductions in GHGs achieved outside of the regulated sector, in this case power plants, such as by reforestation, landfill gas recovery, methane capture from farming operations, etc.).[14]

California, frequently a leader in environmental efforts, passed AB 32, the Global Warming Solutions Act of 2006. Recognizing the devastating economic and social impacts that climate change would have on California, such as an anticipated 90 percent loss of snow pack from the Sierra Mountains, California devised a state-based strategy for GHG reductions. AB 32 required that the state's emissions must be reduced to 1990 levels by 2020, a 25 percent reduction, and by 80 percent of 1990 levels by 2050. To accomplish this, a mandatory state-wide cap on GHG emissions will be phased in starting in 2012. The California Air Resources Board (CARB) is responsible for developing regulations and a mandatory tracking system to monitor GHG reductions.[15] These binding reductions are across all sectors, not just major sources such as power plants.[16]

Other states have enacted state-based programs to address the issue of climate change. In 2007, Iowa established a clean energy fund and created a new Office of Energy Independence. The goal of the effort is to achieve energy independence from foreign sources of energy by 2025. In addition, Iowa established the Iowa Climate Change Advisory Council which was charged with the mission of developing strategies for reducing GHG emissions in the state. A state-wide inventory and registry was also established.[17]

New Mexico, an energy producing state, set goals to lower state GHG emissions by 75 percent by 2050 and created the New Mexico Climate Change Advisory Group to forge a strategic plan to reach the goals.[18]

Minnesota's governor Tim Pawlenty signed the Next Generation Energy Act of 2007 into state law. The law established a goal for the state to cut its energy consumption by 25 percent by 2025. The law also obligates the utilities and electric associations to set energy efficiency and conservation improvement levels at 1.5 percent of their retail sales. The Act sets Minnesota's GHG reduction goals to 15 percent by 2015, 30 percent by 2025, and 80 percent by 2050. The legislation requires that a plan to reach these goals have a mandatory cap-and-trade system for CO_2 from power plants. In 2007, Minnesota also put into place a second law that focuses on building standards. By that law, any building that is constructed or maintained using state funds is required to consider using solar or geothermal heating and cooling systems when installing a new system or upgrading an old one.[19]

Massachusetts has restricted CO_2 emissions from its six existing coal-fired power plants. These facilities were given some latitude in how they reduce emissions but they are required to do so.[20]

Maryland engaged the climate change issue in 2007 by establishing the Maryland Green Building Council. The council was set up to advise the governor and legislature on using green building technologies in state facilities. The governor, by executive order, also established a Climate Change Commission which was charged with developing an action plan to identify Maryland's carbon footprint and suggest strategies for reducing emissions.[21]

Localities have also taken direct action to combat climate change. In June of 2005, the U.S. Conference of Mayors approved the U.S. Mayors Climate Protection Agreement. By signing the agreement, mayors pledge to reduce GHG emissions in their cities by seven percent below 1990 levels by 2012. These levels represent what the U.S. would have been required to do if the U.S. had become a signatory of the Kyoto Protocol.[22] Over 750 U.S. cities by the end of 2007 had signed the pledge. Localities are assisted in these efforts by a number of civil sector organizations including the Sierra Club and Environmental Defense.[23]

It is important to add that most states have some form of renewable portfolio standard (RPS) in place to encourage the development of renewable energy. While these RPS requirements were not generally instituted to respond to climate change issues, they serve that purpose in any event by reducing fossil fuel use, one of the leading causes of CO_2 emissions. Renewable portfolio standards vary state to state but generally they require utilities to diversify their energy portfolio to include a specific capacity from renewables. The percentage coming from renewables increases each year thus creating a stable market for clean energy technologies.[24]

Engagement at the Regional Level

As the states developed independent policies to deal with climate change, they began to reach out to their neighbors to form regional solutions. In most cases, these regional accords involve some mix of industry representatives, nongovernmental organizations (NGOs), university-based experts, and governmental organizations. They generally use data provided by national or international scientific groups such as the Intergovernmental Panel on Climate Change as well as scientific data gathered by local and regional organizations pertaining to climate change and other environmental issues. It is common for these regional groups to build on an already established foundation of local and regional expertise in environmental protection. Regional efforts often take the predictions provided by international organizations such as the IPCC regarding the overall impacts of climate change such as rising seas and increased storm intensity and then try to deduce from these global predictions the likely specific regional and local impacts.[25]

As these groups came together to create a larger advocacy block seeking to implement climate change policy at the local and regional levels, they were countered by a persistent opposition.[26] This opposition often took the form of regional industrial and economic actors objecting to GHG curbing efforts that they viewed as likely to negatively impact their interests. Such groups included automakers arguing against increasing Corporate Average Fuel Economy (CAFE) standards and developers lobbying against zoning that might block lucrative coastal development. While much of this opposition was active on the national scene as well, their influence in regional and state politics was powerful.

The earliest regional agreement, the Climate Change Action Plan, was established in 2001 by several New England states and Canadian provinces. Maine, New Hampshire, Vermont, Massachusetts, Rhode Island and Connecticut joined with the five eastern Canadian provinces of Nova Scotia, Newfoundland and Labrador, Prince Edward Island, New Brunswick, and Quebec in the agreement. This plan was a coordinated regional agreement to lower GHG emissions to 1990 levels by 2010 and 10 percent below 1990 levels by 2020. The parties to the agreement further pledged to eventually reduce their emissions to a level at which they would pose no threat to the climate. The plan was established based on "no regrets" measures, that is to say, using efforts that both reduce energy costs while at the same time lower GHG emissions. The agreement included provisions for establishing a standardized GHG emissions inventory, developing a plan for reductions, increasing public awareness, emphasizing conservation and energy efficiency, and exploring a market-based emissions trading scheme.[27]

To reach the commitments made in the Climate Change Action Plan, the New England Governors and Eastern Canadian Premiers subsequently implemented several programs. One of these programs was the Regional Greenhouse Gas Initiative (RGGI) which was initiated on December 20, 2005 by a memorandum of understanding (MOU) signed by the governors of Connecticut, Delaware, Maine, Massachusetts, New Hampshire, New Jersey, New York, and Vermont. RGGI was the first U.S. cap-and-trade program for power plant emissions of CO_2. RGGI was scheduled to begin by capping emissions at 2009 levels in 2009 and then reducing them by 10 percent by 2019. Maryland subsequently joined RGGI.[28] The District of Columbia, Pennsylvania, Rhode Island, and the Eastern Canadian Provinces, and New Brunswick are observers in the process.[29] RGGI focuses on electricity generating power plants only. These utilities will either have to reduce operations, invest in cleaner technologies, or buy offsets to meet their emissions reduction targets.[30] Figure 1 shows RGGI states and observers.

The RGGI agreement implementation phase began with the drafting of model regulations. These model regulations were subject to a 60 day comment period during which some minor changes were made. In particular, the participating states agreed to simplify the incorporation of offset credits into the plan, that is, credits earned by reducing GHG emission from another source such as by capturing methane gas from landfills or in another way such as by creating carbon sinks by planting trees. The governors of the participating states had until December 31, 2008, to pass the appropriate state legislation or issue regulations to achieve state approval of the RGGI model regulations.[31] For the RGGI states this means that they had make decisions about how they wanted to handle GHG emissions allowances and what they wanted to do with revenues generated by the sale of allowances.

The RGGI agreement equated one allowance with one ton of CO_2 emissions and established each state's limit. These allowances were to be allocated internally in the state. The RGGI agreement required states to sell at least 25 percent of its allowances and use the resulting revenues for public benefits or strategic energy purposes. How the states decided to allocate the remaining 75 percent of allowances was determined separately by each state. They could be given away for free or auctioned off for a profit but in either event the state regulators had to find a mechanism for deciding how many initial allowances a generator may have. According to RGGI, this could be done in several ways: by using the average level of historical emissions (grandfathering), by allocating allowances based on their need assuming the best available technology (benchmarking), or by allocating allowances based on the proportion of electricity generated each year (output-based). After the initial allocation, RGGI permitted generators to buy and sell allowances on the open market.

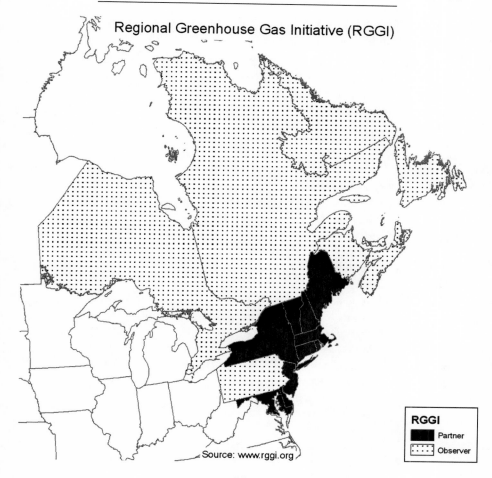

Figure 1

These choices benefit the generators and the entire state's population in different ways. For instance, giving away allowances provides for a smooth transition to a regulated system whereas auctioning allowances supplies a revenue stream to the government so that it can provide public benefits, for instance, by directly subsidizing energy bills for the poor or by investing in efficiency programs to reduce usage and thereby lower bills. Grandfathering tends to reward the most polluting plants, while benchmarking favors those plants that have already taken action to reduce emissions, while output-based allocation strategies tends to level the playing field while allowing for new power plants to enter the market.[32] As states implemented RGGI, they each had to make these decisions.

In 2003 Oregon, California, and Washington joined in the West Coast Governors' Global Warming Initiative (WCGGWI) and set the goal of coordinating policy across the three states. As a result of this agreement, these states agreed to collaborate on the purchase of hybrid vehicles for their fleets, increase by 1 percent per year retail sale of renewable energy, and expand the adoption of energy efficiency standards to those products not under federal regulatory control.[33] In October of 2006, the governors of New York and California announced plans to link California's GHG reduction programs to RGGI which in turn increased the potential for greater RGGI-WCGGWI cooperation.[34]

Population growth in the West is one of the greatest drivers of increased energy demand. To address the problem, in 2004 the Western Governors' Association (WGA) adopted the Clean and Diversified Energy Initiative to explore the feasibility of reaching a goal of generating 30,000 megawatts of clean energy by 2015 (solar, geothermal, biomass, wind, combined heat and power, and hydroelectric), a 20 percent improvement in energy efficiency by 2020, and a reliable transmission grid to meet growth expectations for the next 25 years. To plan for and facilitate reaching these goals, the WGA established the Clean and Diversified Energy Advisory Committee.[35] The WGA also promoted the use of alternative transportation fuels to replace insecure imported oil and had a separate initiative to address climate change with the goal of reducing anthropogenic GHG emissions through deploying clean energy sources and supporting regional carbon sequestration.[36] While the Clean and Diversified Energy Initiative did not have GHG reductions as its goal, reliance on clean energy did have the same effect. As issues associated with carbon emissions became more central to decision making, the West moved to develop other climate accords.[37]

The West developed a regional tracking system to meet state-based renewable portfolio standard requirements. The Western Renewable Energy Generation Information System (WREGIS) was begun in June of 2007 to allow for regional renewable energy certificate (REC) trading. Data in WREGIS includes the megawatt hours produced, fuel source, and facility location.[38] This system also provides valuable information to the Clean and Diversified Energy Initiative.

On February 28, 2006, Arizona and New Mexico entered into the Southwest Climate Change Initiative. This agreement fosters coordination between the states to reduce GHG emissions while promoting energy efficiency, new technologies, and clean energy sources. The expectation was that economic development would be fostered as much as climate change issues would be addressed.[39]

The Western Climate Initiative (WCI) was signed on February 26, 2007, by the governors of Arizona, California, New Mexico, Oregon, and Washington. The Western Climate Initiative was a joint effort to promote mitigation strategies while at the same time reduce GHG emissions. The emissions covered by the agreement include carbon dioxide, methane, nitrous oxide, hydrofluorocarbons, perfluorocarbons, and sulfur hexafluoride. Utah later joined WCI as did British Columbia and Manitoba. The WCI obligates parties to jointly set regional emissions objectives and to establish (by August of 2008) some type of a market-based system to meet those targets. Effective August of 2007, the emissions targets were set at 15 percent below 2005 levels by 2020. The WCI built on efforts already taken by separate states or provinces as well as the Southwest Climate Change Initiative and the West Coast Governors' Global Warming Initiative.[40] Figure 2 shows WCI partners and observers.

In a similar but less formal way, several Midwestern states joined in a voluntary regional initiative called Powering the Plains (PTP). This organization drew together alternative energy advocates, agricultural interests, state officials, and industry partners with the goal of devising ways to fight climate change while not impeding economic development. North and South Dakota, Iowa, Minnesota, Wisconsin and the Canadian Province of Manitoba were members. The group met four times a year to develop policy, strategies, and pilot programs to promote the region's economic development while also reducing the potential threats of climate change.[41] PTP focused on areas of the region's comparative advantage and sought to create a roadmap to a sustainable and carbon neutral future for the region. PTP laid the foundation for what would become the Midwest Greenhouse Gas Reduction Accord. PTP built a consensus between industry, agriculture, the energy sector and environmentalists regarding the path forward. By June of 2007 that consensus was reached and PTP staff began working with the Midwest governors. They proposed an energy summit, met with various states governors' staff, and created a steering committee of governors' staff. In the summer of 2007 working groups from 12 states in the Midwest region and Manitoba came together. The PTP roadmap became the political and conceptual starting point for the negotiation of a climate accord.[42]

In November of 2007 the governors of Illinois, Iowa, Kansas, Michigan, Minnesota, and Wisconsin signed the Midwestern Greenhouse Gas Reduction Accord (MGGRA). By signing this agreement, the states committed themselves to set GHG reduction targets within a year, to establish a cap-and-trade system to achieve reduction targets, and to join the Climate Change Registry to track, manage, and credit entities that reduce GHG emissions.[43] The governors also signed the Energy Security and Climate Stewardship Platform which consigned the states to a regional goal to "maximize the energy resources and economic advantages and opportunities of Midwestern states

Western Climate Initiative (WCI): Partners & Observers

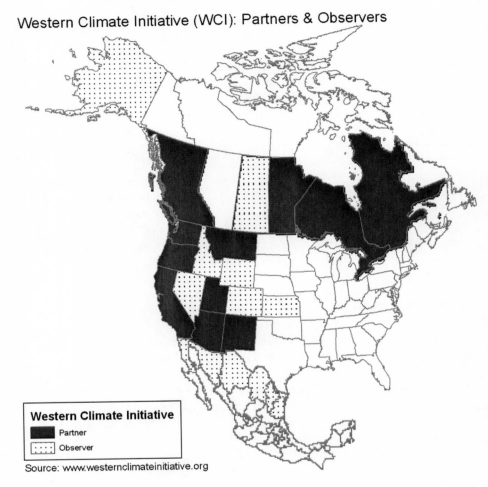

Western Climate Initiative

▪ Partner

⋮ Observer

Source: www.westernclimateinitiative.org

Figure 2

while reducing emissions of atmospheric CO_2 and other greenhouse gases."[44] In all, the accord was a broadly structured energy sector platform for measuring goals, setting targets for energy efficiency, renewable energy, biofuels, and carbon capture. The accord included this broad range of policy tools and emphasized more than just a cap-and-trade agreement. Because it emphasized energy efficiency and renewables it sought GHG emission reductions independent of the cap.[45] Figure 3 shows WGGRA partners and observers.

Finally, it is important to note that several of these regional agreements have Canadian and or Mexican partners. International arrangement between individual states and foreign countries are also under consideration. For

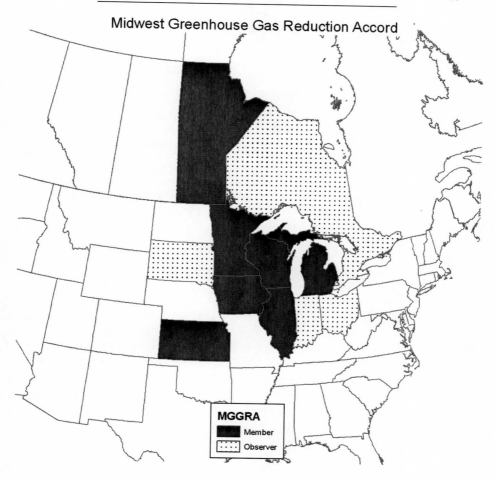

Figure 3

instance, New Jersey has displayed interest in entering into collaboration with the Netherlands to design and promote the use of an emissions banking system. New Jersey has also adopted the Netherlands "sustainability covenants" and is using them to commit signatories in its jurisdiction to GHG reductions. The signatories range from universities, colleges, religious organizations, to major utilities.[46]

Constitutional Concerns

Agreements among several states as well as accords between states and foreign nations are restricted by Article I, Section 10, of the Constitution which states:

> ***No state shall enter into any treaty, alliance, or confederation;*** grant let-
> ters of marque and reprisal; coin money; emit bills of credit; make any-
> thing but gold and silver coin a tender in payment of debts; pass any bill
> of attainder, ex post facto law, or law impairing the obligation of contracts,
> or grant any title of nobility.
>
> No state shall, without the consent of the Congress, lay any imposts or
> duties on imports or exports, except what may be absolutely necessary for
> executing it's inspection laws: and the net produce of all duties and imposts,
> laid by any state on imports or exports, shall be for the use of the treasury
> of the United States; and all such laws shall be subject to the revision and
> control of the Congress.
>
> ***No state shall, without the consent of Congress,*** lay any duty of ton-
> nage, keep troops, or ships of war in time of peace, ***enter into any agree-
> ment or compact with another state, or with a foreign power,*** or engage
> in war, unless actually invaded, or in such imminent danger as will not
> admit of delay [emphasis added].

While there has thus far been no test of the constitutionality of regional
alliances designed to fight climate change, it does seem likely that voluntary
nonbinding agreements might stand the test of constitutionality but that
mandatory binding agreements might require the prior consent of Congress.
The failure of the federal government during the Bush administration to
negotiate on the international level with other countries, led the states to
enter the debate. These state-foreign nation relationships also raise questions
of whether the states have exceeded their authority under the Constitution.[47]

Finally, there is concern that regional cap-and-trade system might be
unconstitutional because they may restrict interstate commerce which is con-
stitutionally protected through Article I, Section 8. Commonly called the
Commerce Clause, this provision of the Constitution gives Congress the
power to "regulate Commerce with foreign Nations, and among the several
States, and with the Indian Tribes." This clause has been historically interpreted as limiting the power of the states to regulate interstate commerce in
ways that either burden commerce or discriminate against out-of-state actors
that might want to be engaged in interstate commerce. Regional cap-and-
trade systems would generally restrict the amount of electricity imported into
the region from producers outside the region that rely on sources that generate GHG emissions.[48] When such limits come into effect, it is likely that
those constrained from market entry may challenge those restrictions in
court.

The Battle in the Courts

A series of battles between the states and the federal government over
regulation of GHGs played out in the courts in the last several years. Three

of these cases involve a requested waiver from California that would allow California and subsequently other states as well, to impose stricter air pollution standards than the federal government. The reason for this odd situation with California is that in the 1960s it had already implemented vehicle-emission standards. This was well before the federal government passed laws to do so. When the federal government did pass such legislation, all states were preempted from adopting separate vehicle emission standards, except for California, which was required to seek a waiver of preemption from the EPA in the event it wanted to impose higher standards. The Clean Air Act was later amended to allow other states to adopt California's standards but only after California received a waiver.[49]

In 2002, California passed a law that set limits on one source of global warming gases—automobiles. The bill empowered the California Air Resources Board to set standards for California's automobile fleet to achieve a cost-effective reduction in global warming pollution coming from automobile tailpipes. Specifically, the law required that all cars and light duty trucks sold in California beginning in model year 2009 have 22 percent reduced CO_2 emissions compared to emissions in 2002 and increasing to 30 percent by model year 2016.[50] Since 2002, eleven states have followed California's lead and set GHG emissions standards for passenger vehicles. Three states—California, Vermont, and Rhode Island—were sued by the automobile industry to block their efforts. The fourth case was brought by several environmental groups and the state of New York in an attempt to induce the EPA to impose GHG controls on new power plants. These cases all stalled in the courts awaiting the results of yet another case that had made its way to the Supreme Court.[51]

The Supreme Court ruled on April 2, 2007, in the *Massachusetts v. Environmental Protection Agency* that EPA had the authority under the Clean Air Act to regulate GHG emissions in new motor vehicles. The court further ruled that the EPA could not avoid its responsibility to regulate GHGs unless it could provide a scientific basis on which to do so.[52] The case had been brought by a group of states (California, Connecticut, Illinois, Main, Massachusetts, New Jersey, New Mexico, New York, Oregon, Rhode Island, Vermont, and Washington), local governments (District of Columbia, American Samoa, New York City, and Baltimore), and private organizations (Center for Biological Diversity, Center for Food Safety, Conservation Law Foundation, Environmental Advocates, Environmental Defense, Friends of the Earth, Greenpeace, International Center for Technology Assessment, National Environmental Trust, Natural Resources Defense Council, Sierra Club, Union of Concerned Scientists, and U.S. Public Interest Research Group).[53]

Massachusetts v. Environmental Protection Agency was embraced by environmental groups and many states that had committed themselves to regional agreements for GHG reductions. But EPA's subsequent actions served to illustrate the tensions between federal and state actors during the Bush administration. For instance, despite this ruling, the EPA did not move to bring CO_2 under regulation in granting a permit to Deseret Generation and Transmission for an expansion of a power plant near Vernal, Utah. As a result, House Oversight Committee Chair Henry Waxman on September 19, 2007, said his panel would investigate whether EPA was in violation of the Supreme Court's ruling.[54] The EPA argued, however, that the Massachusetts ruling indicated that EPA must go through a full rulemaking process before it could regulate CO_2 as a pollutant and insisted that CO_2 cannot be regulated through the prevention of significant deterioration permitting process which applied in the Deseret case.[55]

With the Supreme Court ruling in *Massachusetts v. Environmental Protection Agency*, California urged to the EPA to take up its 2005 request for a waiver to limit greenhouse gas emissions from vehicles. California threatened to file legal action if EPA did not respond to its request for a waiver. When EPA did not act, California filed a law suit on November 8, 2007, to force a decision from the EPA.

The Supreme Court decision in *Massachusetts v. Environmental Protection Agency* also allowed the other pending cases to begin to move through the courts. U.S. District Judge William Session ruled against automakers in September 2007, saying that Vermont could regulate GHG emissions from vehicles. Likewise, the case against California by automakers was decided by U.S. District Judge Anthony Ishii, who ruled that the state had the right to control air pollution. Neither of these cases, however, could be enforced with out the waiver approval from the EPA.[56]

The decision on California's request for a waiver was not long in coming. Only hours after the Congress passed and the President Bush signed into law the Energy Independence and Security Act on December 21, 2007, EPA Administrator Stephen L. Johnson denied California's waiver request. Johnson announced that the new law, which raised CAFE standards to 35 MPG by 2020, made the California waiver unnecessary because the primary way California would reduce GHG emissions from automobiles would be by imposing higher fuel economy standards. Indeed, if the waiver had been granted, the California standard would have required 36 MPG by 2016[57] a more stringent standard than the one passed by Congress. California and fifteen other states filed suit against the Bush administration for denial of the waiver on January 3, 2008, marking the next round in the five year battle between the states and the federal government under the Bush administration over who has the right to regulate GHG emissions.[58]

When the Obama administration took office, however, one of the first acts of the new president was to order EPA to reconsider its prior denial of California's waiver. Saying that it was time for the federal government to work with the states and not against them, the Obama administration set a new tone. Action by the Obama administration may pave the way for more stringent regulation of GHG emissions from auto tailpipes instituted at the state level.

State and Regional Policy versus National Policy

With climate change being a global issue, several questions immediately rise to the surface: Do state and regional efforts matter? Can they be effective in combating climate change? What do these regional agreements tell us about future climate change policy?

The answer to the first two questions is yes. The United States is the world's largest emitter of GHGs. In 2005, the U.S. emitted 6,431.935 million metric tons of CO_2 equivalent.[59] This represents a 16 percent increase since 1990. While many other countries have been cutting their emissions, the U.S., not a party to the Kyoto protocol or any other binding international agreement, continues to increase its emissions. With no federal mandatory cap in place, national emissions could continue to grow unabated. State regulations and regional agreements, however, have begun the process of providing a cap, at least regionally. Since the three major regional agreements as well as the independent actions of California account for vast areas of the U.S., such agreements can have impact. Figure 4 displays the regional alliance partners to reduce greenhouse gas emissions. The map shows that vast portions of the United States are included in such efforts.

Connecticut, Delaware, Maine, Maryland, Massachusetts, New Hampshire, New Jersey, New York, and Vermont fall under RGGI. Even though RGGI only caps power plant emissions, these emissions will be substantial contributors to climate change. At 2004 levels, electric power generation emissions alone for these states amounted to respectively 8.6, 5.91, 4.53, 30.42, 23.67, 7.71, 18.9, 52.98, 0.02 million metric tons for a total of 152.74 million metric tons.[60] In 2004, these combined emissions exceeded the GHG emissions put out by a number of European countries including Austria (which emitted 74.2 million metric tons equivalent), Belgium (146.4), Czech Republic (142.3), Denmark (66.68), Finland (62.4), Greece (132), Hungary (74.7), Iceland (5.4), Ireland (68.4), Norway (29.38), Sweden (64.2), and Switzerland (52.2).[61]

Likewise, those states that are party to the WCI include Arizona, California, New Mexico, Oregon, Utah, and Washington. The WCI requires part-

Figure 4

ners to reduce all GHG emissions 15 percent below 2005 levels by 2020. If one only considers emissions from fossil fuel combustion, in 2004 these states emitted respectively 96.16, 393.83, 58.32, 42.5, 64.38, 84.9 million metric tons for a combined total of over 740 million metric tons.[62] In that same year, these combined state emissions exceeded those of Australia (523.3), France (495.4), Italy (473.9), Spain (373.6), and approached those of Canada (828).[63] Finally, the Midwest Greenhouse Gas Reduction Accord states of Illinois, Iowa, Kansas, Michigan, Minnesota, and Wisconsin together accounted for over 787 million metric tons of CO_2 in 2004 just from the burning of fossil fuels.

If all 2004 capped emissions for states that are members of one of the three major regional accords were added together, the total sum would be nearly 1,700 million metric tons — a number that quite significant for global reductions. These annual emissions account for 26 percent of all U.S. emissions for 2004. The emission levels occurring in these states are the equivalent of 43 percent of the emission of the entire EU. So, while state regulations and regional agreements have their limitations, if fully implemented they could substantially reduce global emissions. The limitations are substantial, however. These include the likely potential of legal challenges to regional agreement, the persistence of uncertainty while legal challenges make their way through the courts, and inconsistent standards from region to region (which is not good for business). A single national program to reduce GHG emissions would solve these problems. With the Obama administration calling for Congress to pass a national program, perhaps one will be forthcoming in the near future.

What do these regional agreements tell us about the future design of a national climate change policy? To answer this question it is useful to first understand that each regional agreement has strengths and weaknesses and that to a certain extent they built on each other. When the federal government does establish a national program to regulate GHG emissions, it is likely that a federal program will be built around the state and regional programs already in place. This means that the design mechanisms the states and regions used to implement their programs will likely have lasting influence on any federal program. There are differences in the regional plans. Some, like RGGI, regulate only power generators while others, such as California's regulations and the WCI seek to control emissions from all sectors. The issue of whether the allowances will be given away or auctioned is also one that needs to be worked out. In the end, the implementation differences between plans may create significant problems for those companies that operate in areas governed by multiple programs. Firms tend to prefer one national standard rather than a variety of different standards. Recent corporate calls for a national standard for GHG emissions attest to the need for certainty on the part of the firms.

RGGI showed that regions could exercise leadership and move forward without the federal government.[64] RGGI set a standard for other potential programs in so far as it focused on generation rather than on consumption. RGGI focused on reducing GHGs from power plants generating electricity within the region rather than on overall energy consumption. Designing the program in that fashion has consequences. First, states that make some of their income by exporting energy outside of the regional agreement area face equity issues. Exporters are in the position of having to hold up a larger share of GHG reductions than their direct energy use would suggest if the agreement was based on consumption rather than generation. A cap on generation also poses the problem of leakage. Some states will import power from power plants outside of the region that may be dirtier, thus undermining RGGI's goals.[65] On the other hand, starting by regulating power plants makes sense in so far as power plant managers are skilled at reporting emissions and thus the likelihood of getting reliable, high quality data that can be used to track progress is high. If RGGI were to later expand to other generators, or to switch to an economy-wide consumption measure, tracking data may not be so reliable.[66] RGGI's provision of auctioning allowances also set a precedent. The revenues gained through auctions can be directed toward energy efficiency and technology development thus lowering the overall cost of energy.[67] However, if allowances become too costly too quickly, energy prices could increase.[68] Finally, the RGGI design allowed for the use of offsets as part of the calculation of emissions.[69]

The WCI includes a diverse set of states, some of which are coal states, some resource extraction states, and some rooted in agriculture. The diversity represented by these states brought a full range of perspectives and issues to the table, making WCI a good model for a potential national accord.[70] WCI also showed the importance of political leadership. It was the executive leadership of governors, Canadian officials, and senior staff that was crucial in bringing these partners together.[71]WCI also expanded beyond RGGI by developing a multi-sector cap-and-trade mechanism rather than just focusing on power plants.[72] Meaningful reductions in GHGs will require such a multi-sector approach. The WCI also incorporated a sense of the need for adaptive management. Because this is the first time an accord of this dimension has been negotiated without the assistance of a federal mandate to do so, the parties charted new territory. WCI personnel are aware that they must engage in constant evaluation and make changes when indicators show a lack of success.[73] WCI also paved new directions by examining the potential of energy efficiency, electric vehicles, and other innovations that might keep demand for energy down while being reasonable about the need for secure energy supplies for the region.[74] Finally, WCI took serious the need for cost effectiveness in policy designs while acknowledging the costs of doing nothing to address climate change.[75]

The Midwest Greenhouse Gas Reduction Accord built on the other regional agreements and went further than any of the other agreements had. By establishing a broad based program that went far further than just a cap-and-trade system to include energy efficiency, biofuels, carbon capture, transportation, renewables and renewable portfolio standards, the accord expanded the policy design.[76] Perhaps part of this can be explained by the way the Midwest accord was developed. Beginning with PTP's coalition of industry, agriculture, environmentalists, and energy sector actors, the Midwest accord represented the diverse interests of the region. It also drew on the consensus-based process established during PTP's discussions.[77] In their effort to understand climate issues, this broad coalition traveled to Europe where they came to appreciate the European long timeframe approach to the issue. They returned to the U.S. with a consensus that they needed to frame a climate accord with a 50 year reach. That long term vision is innovative and important for U.S. policy making which frequently looks no farther out than the next election.[78]

Given the ambiguity of constitutional and legal issues, many court challenges may be forthcoming. If the courts find that the states have overstepped their constitutional authority, state and regional plans could be tossed out. These legal challenges may take a considerable period of time to sort out, leaving state and regional climate change policy in considerable uncertainty and disarray for some time to come. If the regional agreements do stand the test of legal challenges, inconsistent standards from region to region will remain a significant weakness. The business community would most certainly prefer one national standard rather than having to operate under multiple regional standards. A single national program to reduce GHG emissions, designed with the knowledge gained from earlier state and regional efforts, would be a better solution. Hopefully Congress will look to these regional programs as they draft national legislation.

The Obama Administration's Agenda for Energy and the Environment

President Obama, while running for the presidency in 2008, said that under his administration the U.S. will enter an economy-wide cap-and-trade system for controlling GHG emissions. Initial actions taken by the administration seem to suggest intention to treat climate change seriously including the appointment of Carol Browner to serve as White House Energy and Climate Czar and the appointment of individuals to key posts with records that call for action on climate change. These include Nancy Sutley as head of the Council on Environmental Quality, Steven Chu as Secretary of Energy, and Lisa Jackson as Administrator of the EPA. In addition, Secretary of State Hilary Rodham Clinton appointed Todd Stern as her special envoy for climate change. He will serve as the country's lead climate negotiator at the United Nations and in other international summits.[79]

In his Inaugural address, the president mentioned the threat that climate change posed for the U.S., several times saying that "each day brings further evidence that the ways we use energy strengthen our adversaries and threaten our planet" and "we will harness the sun and the winds and the soil to fuel our cars and run our factories" and "with old friends and former foes, we'll work tirelessly to lessen the nuclear threat and roll back the specter of a warming planet."[80]

The White House web page, posted on Inauguration Day, listed the president's agenda and prominently displayed the agenda for energy and the environment. The position expressed by the Obama administration was:

> The energy challenges our country faces are severe and have gone unaddressed for far too long. Our addiction to foreign oil doesn't just undermine our national security and wreak havoc on our environment — it cripples our economy and strains the budgets of working families all across America. President Obama and Vice President Biden have a comprehensive plan to invest in alternative and renewable energy, end our addiction to foreign oil, address the global climate crisis and create millions of new jobs.[81]

To achieve these goals, the Obama administration pledged to invest $150 billion within a decade to encourage the private sector to build a clean energy future, to engage in conservation efforts to save on oil use, to increase fuel efficiency and energy efficiency standards, and to find ways to put a million plug-in hybrid cars on the road by 2015. In addition, the Obama administration pledged to a goal of 10 percent of U.S. electricity to come from renewable sources by 2012, and 25 percent by 2025. Finally, Obama called for the implementation of an economy-wide cap-and-trade program to reduce greenhouse gas emissions 80 percent by 2050. Additional goals include the development of clean coal technology and a commitment to make the U.S. a leader on climate change. [82]

Within weeks of taking office, President Obama provided not only his agenda but also some significant action on climate change and energy policy. First, President Obama directed EPA head Lisa Jackson to review EPA's prior rejection, issued under the Bush administration, of California's request for a waiver to set strict limits on tailpipe emissions to reduce greenhouse gases. The tone of the directive left little doubt that the Obama administration's goal was the reversal of the Bush administration's position.[83] In remarks given at the time of the order, President Obama said:

> [T]he federal government must work with, not against, states to reduce greenhouse gas emissions. California has shown bold and bipartisan leadership through its effort to forge 21st century standards, and over a dozen states have followed its lead. But instead of serving as a partner, Washington stood in their way. This refusal to lead risks the creation of a confusing and patchwork set of standards that hurts the environment and the auto industry. The days of Washington dragging its heels are over. My

administration will not deny facts, we will be guided by them. We cannot afford to pass the buck or push the burden onto the states. And that's why I'm directing the Environmental Protection Agency to immediately review the denial of the California waiver request and determine the best way forward. This will help us create incentives to develop new energy that will make us less dependent on oil that endangers our security, our economy, and our planet.[84]

In a memo issued to EPA employees immediately after assuming the post of Administrator, Lisa Jackson highlighted her five top priorities for action and first on the list was reducing greenhouse gas emissions. She said:

The President has pledged to make responding to the threat of climate change a high priority of his administration. He is confident that we can transition to a low-carbon economy while creating jobs and making the investment we need to emerge from the current recession and create a strong foundation for future growth. I share this vision. EPA will stand ready to help Congress craft strong, science-based climate legislation that fulfills the vision of the President. As Congress does its work, we will move ahead to comply with the Supreme Court's decision recognizing EPA's obligation to address climate change under the Clean Air Act.[85]

In the same memo, Administrator Jackson emphasized that EPA must use the best available science to inform its actions and that when expert advice is

suppressed, misrepresented or distorted by political agendas, Americans can lose faith in their government to provide strong public health and environmental protection. The laws that Congress has written and directed EPA to implement leave room for policy judgments. However, policy decisions should not be disguised as scientific findings. I pledge that I will not compromise the integrity of EPA's experts in order to advance a preference for a particular regulatory outcome.[86]

The second policy action coming from the Obama administration was the issuance of a directive to the Department of Transportation to begin drawing up regulations to implement a 2007 law that mandated higher fuel efficiency standards for automobiles and light trucks by 2020. The Bush administration had not issued any rules to implement the 2007 law. To avoid losing the time that drafting new regulations takes, President Obama issued an order that a temporary rule should be put in place by March of 2009 so that automobiles sold beginning in 2011 will be affected.[87] Before signing the order President Obama said:

[W]e must ensure that the fuel-efficient cars of tomorrow are built right here in the United States of America. Increasing fuel efficiency in our cars and trucks is one of the most important steps that we can take to break our cycle of dependence on foreign oil. It will also help spark the innovation needed to ensure that our auto industry keeps pace with competitors around the world. We will start by implementing new standards for model year 2011 so that we use less oil and families have access to cleaner, more efficient cars and trucks. This rule will be a down payment on a broader and sustained effort to reduce our dependence on foreign oil. Congress has passed legislation to increase standards to at least 35 miles per gallon by 2020. That 40 percent increase in fuel efficiency for our cars and trucks could save over 2 million barrels of oil every day — nearly the entire amount of oil that we import from the Persian Gulf.[88]

In the statement that accompanied the signing of these orders, the president set a new direction for U.S. policy:

No single issue is as fundamental to our future as energy. America's dependence on oil is one of the most serious threats that our nation has faced. It bankrolls dictators, pays for nuclear proliferation, and funds both sides of our struggle against terrorism. It puts the American people at the mercy of shifting gas prices, stifles innovation and sets back our ability to compete. These urgent dangers to our national and economic security are compounded by the long-term threat of climate change, which if left unchecked could result in violent conflict, terrible storms, shrinking coastlines and irreversible catastrophe. These are the facts and they are well known to the American people — after all, there is nothing new about these warnings. Presidents have been sounding the alarm about energy dependence for decades. President Nixon promised to make our energy — our nation energy independent by the end of the 1970s. When he spoke, we imported about a third of our oil; we now import more than half.

Year after year, decade after decade, we've chosen delay over decisive action. Rigid ideology has overruled sound science. Special interests have overshadowed common sense. Rhetoric has not led to the hard work needed to achieve results. Our leaders raise their voices each time there's a spike in gas prices, only to grow quiet when the price falls at the pump. Now America has arrived at a crossroads. Embedded in American soil and the wind and the sun, we have the resources to change. Our scientists, businesses and workers have the capacity to move us forward. It falls on us to choose whether to risk the peril that comes with our current course or to seize the promise of energy independence. For the sake of our security, our economy and our planet, we must have the courage and commitment to change.[89]

President Obama assumed office at a time of terrible economic turmoil. The housing bubble had burst, the banking system was in the worst crisis since the Great Depression, credit markets were frozen, the economy had entered a recession in 2007 and millions of jobs had been lost. Along with having to honor his campaign pledges, he also confronted the worst economy in half a century. As the Obama administration sought to address the financial crisis with an economic stimulus package meant to stop the loss of jobs and the downward spiral of GDP, he did so by building the economic stimulus package he would submit to Congress at least partially around a new energy agenda. Elaborating his new policy, Mr. Obama said:

It will be the policy of my administration to reverse our dependence on foreign oil, while building a new energy economy that will create millions of jobs. We hold no illusion about the task that lies ahead. I cannot promise a quick fix; no single technology or set of regulations will get the job done. But we will commit ourselves to steady, focused, pragmatic pursuit of an America that is free from our energy dependence and empowered by a new energy economy that puts millions of our citizens to work. Today, I'm announcing the first steps on our journey toward energy independence, as we develop new energy, set new fuel efficiency standards, and address greenhouse gas emissions. Each step begins to move us in a new direction, while giving us the tools that we need to change. [W]e must take bold action to create a new American energy economy that creates millions of jobs for our people. The American Recovery and Reinvestment Plan before Congress places a down payment on this economy. It will put 460,000 Americans to work, with clean energy investments and double the capacity to generate alternative energy over the next three years. It will lay down 3,000 miles of transmission lines to deliver this energy to every corner of our country. It will save taxpayers $2 billion a year by making 75 percent of federal buildings more efficient. And it will save working families hundreds of dollars on their energy bills by weatherizing 2 million homes. This is the boost that our economy needs, and the new beginning that our future demands. By passing the bill, Congress can act where Washington has failed to act over and over again for 30 years. We need more than the same old empty promises. We need to show that this time it will be different. This is the time that Americans must come together on behalf of our common prosperity and security.[90]

Within the first month of being in office, the Obama administration was able to successfully push through Congress an economic stimulus bill, the American Recovery and Reinvestment Act of 2009, aimed primarily to address the severe recession gripping the country. That bill nevertheless contained key provisions to fulfill President Obama's agenda for energy and the environment. Of the historic $787 billion bill, more than $45 billion focused on energy efficiency and alternative energy programs and tax breaks. The bill included $13 billion to make federal buildings and public housing more energy efficient and to weatherize as many as a million residential homes. More than $10 billion was provided to modernize the electricity grid by applying digital technology to create a "smart grid"—an interactive electrical network that is decentralized, reliable, efficient, capable of fully utilizing all sources of renewable energy, and responsive to consumer demands. Also included in the bill was $20 billion for further development of renewable energy power, $18 billion for a variety of environmental projects, and $2 billion for R&D on carbon capture and storage. The bill also provided tax credits of up to $7,500 for purchasers of plug-in hybrid cars.[91]

In his first speech given to a joint session of Congress on February 24, 2009, President Obama called for Congress to send him legislation that places a market-based cap on GHG emissions. Speaker of the House Nancy Pelosi has said that she wants a vote on climate change legislation by December of 2009 and Senate leader Harry Reid has called for legislation in the Senate no later than the summer of 2009. As the Democrats move to draft and pass climate change legislation, a powerful lobby has emerged. Analysis of Senate disclosure lobbying forms for 2008 reveals that more than 770 companies had hired more than 2,340 lobbyists to influence federal policy on climate change in 2008 and spent more than $90 million. The number of lobbyists on climate legislation has increased over 300 percent in just 5 years. These lobbyists do not represent the narrow interests of key power producers from the oil, gas, coal and electricity utilities along with a small number of environmental groups. Rather, these lobbyists represent the U.S. Chamber of Commerce and the National Association of Manufacturers—two of the largest and most powerful industry groups. Also included in the list of those attempting to influence climate legislation are USCAP, numerous alternative energy companies, Wall Street banks like Goldman Sachs and JP Morgan Chase, and private equity financial organizations that will likely manage carbon markets. Lobbyists represent cities, public transit organizations, universities, and others that hope to gain from the revenue that will likely be generated when carbon allowances are sold.[92]

The presence of such a large group of lobbyists shows that climate change has taken its rightful place in Washington and that the era of doing nothing is over. More importantly, climate change has been transformed from just an environmental issue to an energy and national security issue as well. The active presence of so many interests, however, will mean that passing legislation will be a very complex process and many compromises will have to be made along the way. Some are concerned that pressure brought to bear by lobbyists seeking lower levels of regulation may result in watered down legislation that will not provide sufficient GHG emissions reductions to avoid the climate tipping point—beyond which there will be no hope of averting the worst impacts from climate change. Such sentiments have been expressed by leaders from the IPCC. A scientific meeting held in Copenhagen in March of 2009 focused on fears that the world's politicians are being too timid on climate action and that climate changes may strike more quickly and harshly than expected.[93] James Hansen, in an open letter to President Obama, warned that the influence of many interest groups may cause a delay in climate action that will push the Earth past its tipping point. That tipping point is widely seen as 2012.[94]

President Obama's first budget specified some of his goals more clearly. In that document he asked Congress to develop and economy-wide emissions reduction program to reduce GHG emissions to 14 percent below 2005 levels by 2020 and 83 percent below 2005 levels by 2050. The administration asked that this be done through the creation of a cap-and-trade program with 100 percent auction of allowances to ensure that polluters would not be grandfathered in and that there be a revenue stream created to provide public benefit funds that will be used to support the goals of reducing GHG emissions.[95]

Conclusion

U.S. climate change policy has shifted enormously since the signing of the Framework Convention on Climate Change. The national opposition to mandatory regulation of GHG emissions which began during the Clinton administration became more adamant during the Bush administration. Indeed, the Bush administration first tried to cast doubt on global warming as a real phenomenon. After consensus in the scientific community forced President Bush to accept global warming as real and human activity as its cause, he then used the uncertainty associated with the extent of impacts climate changes would have on the globe to staunchly oppose action. The Bush administration's full withdrawal of the U.S. from the Kyoto process served to undermine global progress.

The actions taken on the part of the states and regions to impose restrictions on GHG emissions built policy from the bottom up. Beginning with a narrow, energy production sector approach and then widening to an economy-wide scheme, state and regional agreements made progress. During the eight years of the Bush administration, no national policy was forthcoming but America did move forward in crafting climate change policy. The states and regions came together and framed agreements that would begin the reduction of greenhouse gas emissions— even without national leadership.

The election of Barack Obama signaled a clear reversal of Bush administration policies on both climate and energy. Mr. Obama said it plainly:

> We will make it clear to the world that America is ready to lead. To protect our climate and our collective security, we must call together a truly global coalition. I've made it clear that we will act, but so too must the world. That's how we will deny leverage to dictators and dollars to terrorists. And that's how we will ensure that nations like China and India are doing their part, just as we are now willing to do ours.
>
> It's time for America to lead, because this moment of peril must be turned into one of progress. If we take action, we can create new industries and revive old ones; we can open new factories and power new farms; we can lower costs and revive our economy. We can do that, and we must do that. There's much work to be done. There is much further for us to go.
>
> But I want to be clear from the beginning of this administration that we have made our choice. America will not be held hostage to dwindling

resources, hostile regimes, and a warming planet. We will not be put off from action because action is hard. Now is the time to make the tough choices. Now is the time to meet the challenge at this crossroad of history by choosing a future that is safer for our country, prosperous for our planet, and sustainable.[96]

Within one week of taking office, the Obama administration signaled a full reversal of U.S. climate change policy as it had been handled under the Bush administration. America once again assumed a world leadership role in addressing global warming and its consequences. The successful passage of the economic stimulus bill containing huge provisions for renewable energy and energy efficiency within a month of taking office and the call for Congress to pass market-based climate change legislation showed that a new policy was underway.

3

The Challenge of the Post–Kyoto Accord

The meeting that took place late in 2007 in Bali, Indonesia, marked the beginning of the negotiations for a post–Kyoto accord. The rift between the Bush administration and the other nations nearly ended the conference on a sour note, but grudgingly the U.S. delegation agreed to the general Bali framework of moving forward with a next generation of the Kyoto accord. That said, then-president George W. Bush continued to pursue a parallel process for developing an alternative international agreement on voluntary GHG reductions for all the world's countries and he further announced in the spring of 2008 that the U.S. would continue to let its GHG emissions rise till 2025. Central to the split between the Bush delegation and other nations attending the Bali conference was adherence on the part of most countries to the principles of differentiated responsibility and the need to take precautionary action. These two principles conflicted with the Bush administration's call for fairness and emphasis on economic costs when uncertainties exist. This chapter will explore these differences in some detail because they are at the very heart of any possible post–Kyoto agreement. The social justice concerns of the developing nations insisting on their right to develop first and join the global GHG cleanup effort later are critical to understand. If, however, demands for differentiated responsibility keep large polluters like the U.S. out of an international agreement, as they did during the Bush years, one clearly must question the soundness of the accord. The Kyoto Protocol was fundamentally flawed in that manner as well as in others.

The Obama administration announced a shift in U.S. policy toward climate change in 2009, vowing to make the U.S. a leader in climate change policy. Nevertheless, influential policy actors in the U.S. continue to question the fairness of differentiated responsibility as it is structured under the Kyoto Protocol. Perhaps more importantly, a growing number of analysts are questioning the wisdom of not differentiating obligations for developing nations that have achieved substantial levels of poverty eradication over the past decades—China, India, and Brazil—from those developing nations at the earliest stages of development. Scientists increasingly warn that without the participation of China, India, and Brazil the reduction of GHG emissions that must be reached to avert global climate crisis will not be achievable.

To fully understand the challenge of a post–Kyoto accord, the Kyoto Protocol itself needs to be carefully critiqued. This chapter provides such a critique. The Kyoto Protocol put in place a specific set of policy mechanisms for the implementation of the agreement. One of these was the cap-and-trade system established for member nations. As discussed in chapter 2, several U.S. states and regions have adopted Kyoto-like mechanisms to reduce their GHG emissions and the Obama administration has pledged to put one in place for the entire U.S. The EU has established its own emission trading scheme. How well are these mechanisms working? It is likely that the next generation agreement will build on what currently exists, so it is important to explore the efficacy of Kyoto's implementation and outcomes to date. This chapter addresses these issues as well.

Finding ways to overcome obstacles that prevent countries from engagement in a post–Kyoto accord that will produce significant GHG emission reductions within the next several decades is critical to the future of the planet. This chapter outlines the major obstacles that must be overcome to move forward with a post–Kyoto accord.

Differentiated Responsibility

The idea that there should be different responsibilities for developed and developing nations regarding their obligations to reduce greenhouse gas emissions was at the root of the disagreement between the Bush administration and most of the world's countries regarding the design of the Kyoto Protocol. The notion of differentiated responsibility, however, was not invented at Kyoto. Rather it harkens back to a long tradition in UN environmental agreements that stretch back to the 1972 Stockholm Convention on the Human Environment. This was the first international meeting to focus on the issue of the global environment. The meeting was highly influenced by the publication by the Club of Rome, a global think tank, of the book *Limits to Growth* which questioned whether the Earth could sustain itself given the pressures of population growth and rising demand for resources.[1] The Stockholm Declaration, the written document that came out of the Conference, provided the first statement of differentiated responsibility between developing and developed nations. Proclamation 4 states:

In the developing countries most of the environmental problems are caused by under-development. Millions continue to live far below the minimum levels required for a decent human existence, deprived of adequate food and clothing, shelter and education, health and sanitation. Therefore, the developing countries must direct their efforts to development, bearing in mind their priorities and the need to safeguard and improve the environment. For the same purpose, the industrialized countries should make efforts to reduce the gap [between] themselves and the developing countries. In the industrialized countries, environmental problems are generally related to industrialization and technological development.[2]

This proclamation was accompanied by Principles 9 and 10 of the Declaration which state:

Environmental deficiencies generated by the conditions of under-development and natural disasters pose grave problems and can best be remedied by accelerated development through the transfer of substantial quantities of financial and technological assistance as a supplement to the domestic effort of the developing countries and such assistance as may be required.

The environmental policies of all States should enhance and not adversely affect the present or future development potential of developing countries, nor should they hamper the attainment of better living conditions for all, and appropriate steps should be taken by States and international organizations with a view to reaching agreement on meeting the possible national and international economic consequences resulting from the application of environmental measures.[3]

The United Nations Conference on the Human Environment was the first of a series of international meetings on the global environment to incorporate the concept that developing nations needed to develop before they could really concentrate on environmental problems. Indeed, the major environmental problems of developing nations were thought to come from under-development. For example, poor farmers in South American developing nations lack fertile land and adequate agricultural technology to produce acceptable crops, so year after year they burn down huge sections of the tropical rain forests to convert it for crop use. These new lands, however, are marginal and yield crops only for a year or so, and then the cycle repeats. In the end, the farmers are no better off and the rain forest, along with all its precious biodiversity, is damaged. In this scenario, the causal link between poverty and environmental degradation is clear. Another example of poverty leading to environmental deterioration is the poaching of endangered animals in Africa by local people desperate for a source of income. Rhino populations have been decimated due to demand for its horn and local poachers all too willingly provide the horn for a price. The idea raised by the Stockholm Declaration was that environmental ruin could be avoided if the pressure of poverty was eliminated and so development was given high priority.

In the two decades after the Stockholm meeting, most industrialized nations put in place strong environmental enforcement regimes. As awareness and knowledge of environmental problems grew, most developed nations came to place a high priority on a clean environment. This created a conflict for the developing world, which consistently argued that the developed world had gotten wealthy polluting and it was fundamentally unfair for the developed world to suggest that developing nations should shift their priority from development to environmental protection. The result of this dialog was a report from the World Commission on Environment and Development that was presented to the General Assembly in 1987. The Brundtland Report, named after Gro Harlem Brundtland who chaired the committee, argued against the notion that economic development must result in environmental deterioration. Instead, the report provided the concept of sustainable development — development that meets the needs of the present without compromising the ability of future generations to meet their needs.[4]

The concepts of differentiated responsibility and sustainability were strongly supported at the United Nations Conference on Environment and Development (also called the Earth Summit) held at Rio de Janeiro in 1992. Two important documents came out of this conference, which was attended by over 170 nations. These were the Rio Declaration and Agenda 21 which provided principles and strategic details for the implementation of global sustainable development. The Rio Declaration first reaffirmed the Stockholm Declaration and then went on in Principle 7 to say:

> States shall cooperate in a spirit of global partnership to conserve, protect, and restore the health and integrity of the Earth's ecosystem. In view of the different contributions to global environmental degradation, States have common but differentiated responsibilities. The developed countries acknowledge the responsibility that they bear in the international pursuit to sustainable development in view of the pressures their societies place on the global environment and of the technologies and financial resources they command.[5]

The Rio Declaration's Principle 6 also acknowledged the "special situation and needs of developing countries" and Principle 3 assured developing countries the "right to development." Principle 11 acknowledged the need for states to enact environmental legislation but added that "standards applied by some countries may be inappropriate and of unwarranted economic and social cost to other countries, in particular developing countries."[6] Agenda 21, so named because it spelled out the agenda for the 21st century, was an action plan for the implementation of sustainable development. Agenda 21 and its goals were reaffirmed at the World Summit on Sustainable Development held in Johannesburg, South Africa, in 2002.[7]

The concept of differentiated responsibility was included in the 1992 United Nations Framework Convention on Climate Change which clearly stated that

> the Parties should protect the climate system for the benefit of present and future generations of humankind, on the basis of equity and in accordance with their common but differentiated responsibilities and respective capabilities. Accordingly, the developed country Parties should take the lead in combating climate change and the adverse effects thereof.[8]

The United States is among the signatories of the United Nations Framework Convention on Climate Change and is obligated under it to provide an annual report to the United Nations with an inventory of its GHG emissions as well as efforts taken to reduce emissions. The treaty, however, does not obligate nations to specific targeted emission levels rather it states the goal that nations will return to 1990 levels in the most cost effective manner. The treaty also obligates some developed nations, including the United States, to provide financial and technological assistance to developing nations so that they can reduce their own emissions as well. The treaty acknowledges

> the largest share of historical and current global emissions of greenhouse gases has originated in developed countries, that per capita emissions in developing countries are still relatively low and that the share of global emissions originating in developing countries will grow to meet their social and development needs.[9]

The Kyoto Protocol to the Framework Convention on Climate Change was adopted in 1997. It followed the well established precedent of differentiated responsibility by obligating developed countries to reduce their GHG emissions by approximately 5 percent between 2008 and 2012. The primary difference between the Framework Convention on Climate Change and the Kyoto Protocol is that the Convention encouraged developed countries to reduce their emissions while the Protocol established mandatory binding reductions. In keeping with the concept of differentiated responsibilities, the Kyoto Protocol applies only to developed countries. Those countries and the emissions reduction commitment are provided in Annex B of the Protocol. The United States, for instance, is listed in Annex B as having to reduce its emissions to 93 percent of the amount emitted in the base year of 1990, a seven percent reduction. No developing countries are listed in Annex B.

The Protocol does provide ways in which developed nations can help developing nations reduce their emissions while at the same time receiving credits for such efforts that count toward their own mandatory reduction targets. The Kyoto Protocol's Article 12 provides for a Clean Development Mechanism (CDM) specifically established to help developing countries attain sustainable development while also giving developed nations an alternate path to emissions reductions. Under the Clean Development Mechanism developed countries can receive credits for projects undertaken in other countries, hopefully in developing countries, and apply these credits to their commitments.[10] These CDM efforts, however, are voluntary. CDM does introduce some flexibility into the ways in which developed countries can meet their goals while at the same time encouraging developing nations to develop sustainably.

Precautionary Action

The idea that countries should be willing to bear the burden of costs associated with precautionary policy actions taken to avert untoward environmental outcomes while the state of scientific understanding is uncertain was the basis of another key disagreement between the Bush administration and most of the world's countries regarding the design of the Kyoto Protocol. Yet, just as the concept of differentiated responsibilities did not begin with Kyoto, neither did the "Precautionary Principle." The idea that nations should take action, even in the event of scientific uncertainty, if the probable consequences of not acting rapidly are profoundly negative was fully enunciated in the Rio Declaration. Principle 15 of the Declaration states:

> In order to protect the environment, the precautionary approach shall be widely applied by States according to their capabilities. Where there are threats of serious or irreversible damage, lack of full scientific certainty shall not be used as a reason for postponing cost-effective measures to prevent environmental degradation.[11]

The United Nations Framework Convention on Climate Change also obligates Parties to the precautionary principle:

> Parties should take precautionary measures to anticipate, prevent or minimize the causes of climate change and mitigate its adverse effects. Where there are threats of serious or irreversible damage, lack of full scientific certainty should not be used as a reason for postponing such measures, taking into account that policies and measures to deal with climate change shall be cost-effective so as to ensure global benefits at the lowest possible cost.[12]

Since the Kyoto Protocol is an extension of the United Nations Framework Convention on Climate change, the mandate that countries should adhere to the precautionary principle clearly applies to actions taken under Kyoto as well.

Differences in attitude toward the precautionary principle, especially between the U.S. during the Bush years and Europe, are at odds with overall cultural approaches. In the U.S. there is a general acceptance of the novel making Americans less likely to be concerned when new products appear on the market. The perspective is one of acceptance in the face of the unknown or uncertain and rejection only when there is clear proof of a problem. For Europe, tradition generally rules perception so that in the face of the unknown, there is rejection until certainty is proven. Comparing and contrasting general social perceptions towards genetically modified (GM) food confirms these differences. GM food is widely rejected in Europe while it is widely accepted in the U.S. Approaches toward the science of climate change, though, are inconsistent with these cultural norms. The U.S. under the Bush administration demanded absolute scientific proof to accept the claims of human-caused climate change necessitating action while Europe accepted the precautionary principle and sought to move forward with CO_2 reductions irrespective of some scientific uncertainty. The answer to this seeming riddle rests with the differing views of cost and fairness.

Cost and Fairness

After agreeing to the Kyoto Protocol with its emphasis on precautionary action and differentiated responsibility, developed countries had to ratify it. Because the Kyoto Protocol's emissions cuts apply to all sectors, powerful industrial actors began to speak out against the burden this agreement would place on industry. The Kyoto Protocol was eventually ratified by the appropriate number of countries and went into effect in February of 2005. In the U.S. though, the ratification process did not go smoothly. The U.S. had signed the Kyoto Protocol when it was drafted in 1997; however, President Clinton was not nearly as enthusiastic about the treaty as was Vice President Al Gore. Feeling the pressure of industry and other opposition forces, senators made their concerns known to the Clinton White House. Clinton never submitted the Kyoto Protocol to the Senate for ratification. The opposition was based largely on two grounds: first, Kyoto was not fair because it exempted developing nations from emissions cuts and second, that implementation of such a treaty would hurt the economy.[13] These two objections would be used during the 8 years of the Bush administration to keep the United States out of the agreement.

After President George W. Bush took office in 2001, he announced to the world that the U.S. would withdraw from the Kyoto Protocol — that while he was in office he would not submit the treaty for consideration of ratification. Three reasons were given. First, it would hurt the economy. Second, it was not fair to let China and other developing nations opt out of mandatory carbon restrictions. These two reasons were ones that echoed industry's concerns and resonated in the Senate. The final reason offered, however, was a clear rejection of the precautionary principle. That reason was that the science was not certain enough to move forward with what was expected to be a very expensive environmental program.

Whether implementation of the Kyoto Protocol by the U.S. would have hurt the economy is a question that can be answered differently, depending on what variables are considered. The Bush administration did not factor in the costs of doing nothing. Rather, the administration assumed that adaptation to a changing climate would be cost-free. As noted in chapter 2, the states did not make that same assumption and did take action because of the threats they anticipated to their state economies, infrastructure, and resources. The Bush administration did not look at the potential for growth of "green jobs" as a new industry developed to propel the world into a reduced carbon future. The administration instead looked at the costs of transforming traditional industries and rejected out of hand such costs. Undoubtedly they were heavily lobbied by utilities, oil, gas, and coal interests as well as by automakers and other transportation sector interests such as railroads with their heavy ties to coal. Two lobbies that saw a potential gain from a global warming trend, the nuclear industry and biofuels, already had the support of the administration on the grounds of security and energy independence more than out of concern for climate change.

It is interesting that the Obama administration took completely the opposite view on the economic prospects of climate change. Instead of seeing it as a cost, the Obama administration saw it as an opportunity to create a new sector of "green" energy jobs and a way to guarantee American competitiveness well into the 21st century. The Obama administration also linked solving the problem of climate change not only to job creation and economic growth but also to reducing the harmful energy dependence on imported oil. President Obama rejected the view of his predecessor that doing nothing was an option. Seeing climate change as a major threat to the economy and the nation's resources changed the calculation. These differences in perspective allowed President Obama to reverse course on climate change immediately after coming to office.

The fairness argument made by the Bush administration and others is more difficult to understand, especially given the long history of acceptance of differentiated responsibility in United Nations agreements accepted by the United States. It is also important to note that rejection of the Kyoto Protocol on the basis of its lack of fairness was not just the position of the Bush administration. The Senate, under the Clinton administration, shared that view. The fairness concern was tied to the economic one in the sense that members of Congress and the Bush administration felt that the U.S. economy would suffer from the creation of an uneven playing field if cuts were mandatory for the U.S. and not mandatory for developing countries, China in particular.

The fairness argument needs to be examined in two ways. One way is to consider total emissions by country, which is indeed the way Congress and the Bush administration approached the issue. When looked at from this perspective, in the late 1990s the total emissions of China rivaled those of the U.S. and could only be expected to grow in the future. Requiring that all major polluters be part of an agreement that might have negative economic impacts might not be seen as unreasonable from this point of view. If, however, per capita emissions of GHGs is the measure used then clearly the developing world has a great distance to go to catch up with the U.S. and other developed nations. The United Nations agreements are based on per capita emissions, thus justifying the developing world's need to continue to develop even if in doing so they raise their GHG emissions.

The final argument offered by the Bush administration was that the climate science was not certain enough for the U.S. to act in a precautionary manner. This argument was strongly supported and widely spread by economic interests that feared they would be on the losing side should carbon regulation take form. The opposition of big oil, coal, and industry took the form of well funded lobbyist groups and anti-science skeptics. Groups such as the Global Climate Coalition, founded by ExxonMobil, the American Petroleum Institute and other energy, automotive, and industrial companies heavily lobbied Congress and the Bush administration against GHG emissions restrictions.[14] Other groups such as the Competitive Enterprise Institute, George Marshall Institute, Oregon Institute of Science and Medicine, Science and Environmental Policy Project, Greening Earth Society, and the Center for the Study of Carbon Dioxide and Global Change concentrated on discrediting the scientific evidence pointing to climate change.[15] Perhaps no effort to discount the science of global warming was larger than that of ExxonMobil, which reportedly funded more than 40 groups that focused on distorting public understanding of climate change science $16 million between 1998 and 2005.[16] With these misinformation efforts underway, the Bush administration added to them by publicly raising doubts as to the veracity of global warming. It was not until 2004 that the Bush administration sent an environmental analysis to Congress accepting the scientific evidence that humans were causing global warming.[17] Nevertheless, the administration argued for finding ways to adapt to rising temperatures rather than setting on a path of mitigation by curbing emissions.

The Obama administration came to office pledging to return to the days when science informed government. President Obama stated very soon after coming to office that the era of denial was over. Mr. Obama confirmed that he accepted the view of the world's scientists—that global warming was a human-caused climate crisis facing the planet—and that he would lead to help find solutions. How this shift in attitude will affect the negotiation of a post–Kyoto accord is not yet fully clear but what is clear is the Obama administration will not use debates over the veracity of scientific claims to delay a treaty.

The Kyoto Protocol: Implementation and Compliance

The Kyoto Protocol was intensely debated before the final draft was accepted. Central to the debate was the percentage decrease in GHG emissions that each member state must attain. The final targets were 8 percent for the European Union (EU), 7 percent for the U.S., and 6 percent for Japan. The EU was treated as bubble so that individual countries had different responsibilities. For instance, Germany and Denmark were obligated to cut 21 percent, Great Britain to cut 12 percent, while other EU countries were allowed to increase their emissions. The U.S. did not become a party to the Protocol and did not participate in GHG reductions. For those states that did become parties to the agreement, some were required to reduce emissions while others were allowed increases in emissions. Figure 1 shows the assigned amounts of reductions or increases over the 2008–2012 commitment period.

The key contentious issue in drafting the Kyoto Protocol, however, was the inclusion of various flexibility mechanisms desired by the U.S. While the EU countries thought of these mechanisms as loopholes, they eventually went along when they realized the cost of carbon reduction and in an effort to keep the U.S. as a party to the agreement.[18] The Kyoto Protocol has three flexibility mechanisms built in to allow countries to meet their obligations. These are emissions trading, the clean development mechanism, and joint implementation (JI).

Annex B countries, those that have GHG reduction targets assigned in the treaty, have their allowable emissions expressed as "assigned amounts units" or AAUs. Those nations that have AAUs left over can sell their AAUs on a newly created carbon market. The Kyoto Protocol also allows for trading of commodities other than AAUs. These include removal units (RMUs) generated by land use, land use change and forestry (LULUCF), emission reduction units (ERU) generated by joint implementation projects, and certified emissions reduction (CER) that come from clean development mechanism activity.[19]

Land use and land use changes impact the emission of GHGs. Sinks, like forests, reduce the overall emissions. Under the Kyoto Protocol, those countries assigned Annex I status in the United Nations Convention on Climate Change, can include in the calculation of their emissions land use and land

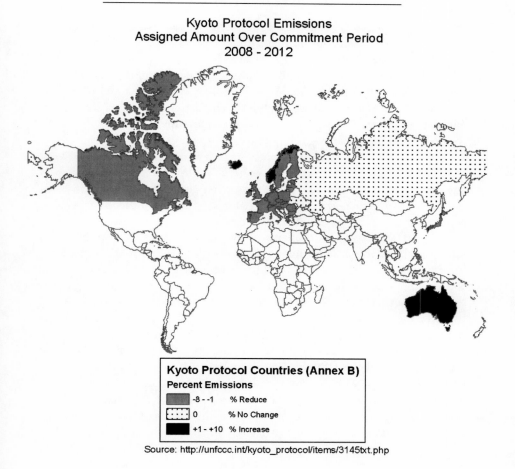

Kyoto Protocol Emissions
Assigned Amount Over Commitment Period
2008 - 2012

Kyoto Protocol Countries (Annex B)
Percent Emissions

-8 - -1   % Reduce
0   % No Change
+1 - +10   % Increase

Source: http://unfccc.int/kyoto_protocol/items/3145txt.php

Figure 1

use change. Establishing new forests (afforestation), renewing established forests by replanting or reseeding (reforestation) and clearing of forests (deforestation) can be included in emissions calculations along with crop-land management, grazing land management and revegetation. When GHG emissions are reduced because of LULUCF activities, an Annex I country can issue ERUs as part of meeting its targets. Using the CDM (discussed below) Annex I nations can get credit for afforestation and reforestation LULUCF projects conducted in non–Annex I nations as well. Also, under the joint implementation mechanism (discussed below) Annex I countries can get ERUs for activities that create more sinks in another Annex I country.[20]

The Clean Development Mechanism is established under Article 12 of the Kyoto Protocol. The CDM allows Annex B countries (the developed nations with reduction commitments under Kyoto) to get credit for projects undertaken in developing countries. The idea is that the CDM allows for sustainable development in developing countries while helping developed countries meet their emissions reduction goals. When a project is undertaken, the CERs produced can be counted as emission reductions for the nation undertaking the project. These projects have to be mutually agreed upon by both countries and may involve both public and private parties.[21]

The joint implementation mechanism is defined in Article 6 of the Kyoto Protocol. JI allows Annex B nations to get credit for projects undertaken in any other Annex B country that reduces GHG emissions. These reductions can come from either sinks or actual reductions and earn ERUs that can be applied to the country's target.[22]

To participate in the mechanisms, Annex I counties have to meet certain eligibility criteria. These include having ratified the Kyoto Protocol; having calculated their assigned amount of tons of CO_2 equivalents for the accounting of AAUs; having in place a national system for estimating emissions within their territory, having in place a national registry to create and track the movement of RMUs, CERs, ERUs, and AAUs; and annually reporting emissions and removals to the Secretariat.[23]

In addition to the national registries of each of the 37 Annex B parties, the Secretariat of the United Nations Framework Convention on Climate Change keeps a CDM registry for creation of CDM credits and issuing them to national registries. The registries are designed to be the backbone of the carbon trading market by matching buyers with sellers and transferring credits. Each registry is expected to act through the International Transaction Log (ITL) which is under creation and will be administered by the Secretariat of the United Nations Framework Convention on Climate Change. The ITL became active in November 2007 with the CDM registry and Japan's national registry. Other parties are planning to go live with the ITL when they meet data exchange standards necessary for electronic transaction processing. The ITL's role is to verify registry transactions and make sure that trading parties are following the rules according to Kyoto Protocol. If parties are not, the ITL will not permit the transaction. In 2012, when the Kyoto commitment period is over, the ITL will compare the AAU holdings of each Annex B country with its emissions record to determine if the party has met its commitment. The EU emissions trading scheme (EU ETS) sits outside of this ITL framework but is accepted by the United Nations as in compliance with Kyoto. Between 2005 and 2008 the EU ETS used the Community Independent Transaction Log (CITL) to monitor trades. In 2008, however, the CITL connected to the ITL which directly monitors transactions.[24]

Compliance, under the Kyoto Protocol, is monitored by the Compliance Committee. It has two core units: the 10 member facilitative branch and the ten member enforcement branch. The facilitative branch's mission is to provide advice and assistance to parties seeking to meet their commitments. The enforcement branch is charged with putting in force consequences for Annex I parties not meeting their commitments either to reduce emissions or to provide appropriate reporting of inventories. The Compliance Committee handles questions referred to it by any party or by expert review teams. These teams were established by Article 8 of the Kyoto Protocol to review and provide input on reports submitted by parties regarding their emissions. If the enforcement branch concludes that a party exceeds its assigned amount, then it must declare the party in non-compliance and demand that the party make up for the difference in reductions during the second commitment period (after 2012), plus an additional reduction of 30 percent. The enforcement branch also has the authority to require that the party submit a compliance action plan and to suspend privileges to the party to engage in emissions trading. The enforcement branch has 35 weeks to respond to questions received regarding implementation.[25]

Kyoto Protocol Critique

The success of the Kyoto Protocol rests on several key items. First, of course, is whether the parties comply with their commitments to reduce GHG emissions. Underlying that, though, is a concern that the data used to verify those commitments is accurate. In addition, the effectiveness of the design and implementation of the accord needs to be considered, including an assessment of the ability of the Protocol to enforce compliance. Finally, the Kyoto Protocol should be critiqued based upon how successful it was, globally, in reducing GHG emissions and stabilizing the climate system.

Early assessments of whether or not parties to the Kyoto accord will meet their obligations vary. The EU-15, or those states that were part of the EU prior to 2004 and who are the largest block of Kyoto member states, will probably meet their 2012 reduction targets of reducing emissions 8 percent below 1990 levels. In 2007, a report by the European Environmental Agency (EEA) projected that if EU-15 states implement all additional policies in their reduction plans they will meet or exceed their targets. The member states projections show that existing policies and actions will reduce EU-15 GHGs by 4 percent below 1990 levels. If planned but not yet implemented measures are implemented, the EEA expects an additional 3.9 percent decrease. Finally, the EEA anticipates that use of the CDM and JI projects will offset emissions by another 2.5 percent and notes that 2.9 billion Euros have been budgeted for these projects. In all, the EEA 2007 report indicated that the EU-15 might achieve an overall 11.4 percent reduction. In addition, all new EU member states expect to meet their targets. Finally the EEA expects that the EU ETS will bring significant reductions between 2008 and 2012.[26] Other Kyoto parties are not proceeding as well. For instance, while Canada is reducing its emissions, the drop still leaves it well behind its Kyoto goals of reducing to 1990 levels between the years of 2008 and 2012. Canada's emissions in 2006 were 22 percent above 1990 levels.[27]

In so far as emissions trading within the EU ETS will impact the success of Kyoto, it is important to note that the decision to give most allowances away for free and to provide too generous a number of allowances will have an adverse impact. The result of these decisions was that EU ETS at the beginning drew a very low price for allowances and this in turn provided no real incentive to reduce emissions.[28] The Russian Federation and Ukraine pose the special problem of "hot air" trading which may result in fewer reductions in emissions than would be the case without trading. Hot air trading results when a party to the Protocol is allocated more allowances than their economy can actually use. They can then sell these AAUs without undertaking any reductions. Both Russia and Ukraine have stabilization targets under Kyoto based on 1990 levels but have experienced large economic downturns since 1990, leaving them with a great deal of AAUs to sell.[29] The EU ETS carbon market continues to exist under great uncertainty. The market could be affected by Russia's decision of whether or not to sell its estimated excess 800 million tons of AAUs before the end of the first commitment period. These AAUs exceed the total number of AAUs for all the other Kyoto parties. If Russia sold them, the carbon market would be flooded, and would likely collapse. World Bank officials, however, think that Russia will bank their allowances at least until the mandatory reductions of the post–Kyoto treaty are negotiated.[30]

The flexibility mechanisms built into Kyoto are somewhat problematic. One question is whether the transaction costs associated with using either JI or CDM outweigh the benefits. That is, there are high costs associated with identifying partners and projects to undertake that may exceed the benefit. If the same efforts were directly applied to carbon reduction, more gains might be achieved.[31] Some critics, like the World Wildlife Fund, argue that the environmental impact of emissions reduction projects in developing nations has been minimal. After studying 800 such projects they concluded that "one out of five emission reduction credits sold under the Kyoto Protocol's Clean Development Mechanism lack environmental integrity."[32] They say that 40 percent of the projects resulted in no extra GHG reductions, that is, that the projects would have been undertaken regardless of the emissions trading.

Additionally they contend that emissions reduction projects undertaken have not been assessed well and they call for the use of Gold Standard certification, a carbon-offset quality rating system developed by World Wildlife Fund and other environmental nongovernmental organizations. In essence, the concern is that projects undertaken under the CDM provide a loophole for developed nations so that they can meet their targets without reducing their own emissions.

The sanctions associated with non-compliance with Kyoto are questionable. For instance, if a country misses its targets in the first commitment period, it must make up for the slack in the next period plus an extra 30 percent. The sanction also includes being barred from selling emissions permits in the next period. Some countries have argued that these sanctions adversely affect them, even if they themselves are in compliance, by pushing up the price for AAUs on the carbon market. If a country plans to meet its targets through the purchase of some additional AAUs and if the price is driven up by sanctions that remove some players from the market, an indirect negative consequence falls on the purchasing country. This could be very problematic if a country such as Russia with large numbers of AAUs to sell was sanctioned.[33]

The failure of the Kyoto Protocol to include two of the world's largest polluters, the United States and China, is a significant issue. The United States argued under the Bush administration that it would not join an agreement that does not include the developing world (especially China and India) but those nations argue for differentiated responsibility. India firmly opposes any commitment to reduce GHG emissions in a post–Kyoto accord and will press the developed world not only for clean technologies but also for intellectual property rights to those technologies. India continues to argue that its per capita emissions are amongst the lowest in the world and represent just 4 percent of U.S. per capita emissions, just 8 percent of U.K. per capita emissions, and just 10 percent of Japan's per capita emissions.[34] China, on the other hand, has pledged to join in a post–Kyoto agreement although also expresses caution about mandatory cuts to the emissions of developing countries based on the fact that it is the developed world that is responsible for current atmospheric levels. China has stated only its willingness to study ways and measures to reduce GHGs emissions. With China surpassing the U.S. in emissions, commitment to merely study the issue is problematic. How the Obama administration will negotiate these issues is not yet clear.

The final assessment criterion to ask of the Kyoto Protocol is will it bring down global GHG emissions. China and the U.S. account for about half of global GHG emissions and neither country is part of the mandatory reductions required by Kyoto. This fact, in and of itself, is a considerable argument for a negative response. But if the EU and other Kyoto member states are successful in lowering their emissions, that will provide some help.

The Post-Kyoto Accord's Major Obstacles

There are major obstacles to overcome in a post–Kyoto accord. The 2007 Bali Climate Declaration by Scientists stated that the necessary goal of a post–Kyoto agreement must be to limit warming to no more than 2 degrees Celsius above the pre-industrial global temperature. This will require that GHG emissions be reduced by 50 percent of their 1990 levels by the year 2050. To accomplish this, scientists concur that global emissions must peak and then begin to decline in the next 10 to 15 years[35] if not sooner.

At the Bali meeting, which was the beginning of the process to draft a post–Kyoto agreement, the United States and China, the two largest polluters, refused to commit to mandatory reductions in a post–Kyoto agreement. China remains focused on what it considers its primary policy goal — economic development and the eradication of poverty. The U.S. delegation insisted that no firm targets be part of any language coming out of Bali.[36] While the U.S. under the new leadership of the Obama administration will likely change the U.S. position adopted under the Bush administration, it is still difficult to see the way forward if China remains entrenched in its position. The EU and its allies argued at the Bali meeting that they endorse the view of scientists that emission must begin to fall in the next 10 to 15 years. They want industrialized countries to agree to cut their emissions 25 to 40 percent by 2020 and for major developing nations (particularly China, India, and Brazil) to agree to firm targets in the future.[37]

The issue of developing nations accepting targets is contentious. Given the long history of differentiated responsibility in past United Nations accords, this issue will have to be revisited. There are differences between developing nations that must be brought into focus. South Korea, for example, has an annual per capita income of $17,000 where as Togo's per capita income is 20 times less. The concept of differentiated responsibility must be applied more reasonably. That is, it should not apply only to developed and developing nations but rather it should be applied within groups of developing nations as well. Those that are well on their way to development, like China, India and Brazil, must recognize that they need to do more than far poorer developing nations. That may not be so easy to do in democratic countries, such as India, where politicians have taken stands against accepting targets.[38]

The failure of the Kyoto Protocol to include developing countries in emissions reductions is a serious one. Annual emissions of developing countries are growing so rapidly that even if the industrialized countries meet all their goals under the Kyoto Protocol, the goal of reducing emissions enough to avoid a global climate crisis will not be achieved. One approach that is under consideration is contraction and convergence (C&C). Under a C&C method, emission permits are equitably distributed to all countries and all countries are expected to be part of the emissions reduction regime. Permits are allocated using per capita emissions as the base. The total number of permits issued is based on overall emissions contraction over time with per capita emissions converging over time. During this transition period, emission allowances converge from the status quo to equal per capita emissions.[39]

Developing countries might be encouraged to participate in a post–Kyoto agreement if they are given incentives to stop deforestation. Such a program emerged in concept at the Bali meeting. REDD, which stands for reducing emissions from deforestation and forest degradation, allows developing countries to earn carbon credits if they set targets for deforestation reductions and they exceed those targets. The credits could be sold on the carbon market. It is anticipated that industrialized countries would want to purchase these credits to help them reach their emissions reduction targets, thus earning participating developing nations billions. Since deforestation accounts for about 20 percent of global carbon emissions, such a program will be critical to a post–Kyoto agreement. In 2007, the World Bank pledged $160 million to support a pilot project to test the viability of such a regime.[40]

Access to technologies that can keep emissions down is critical for developing countries. This has major implications for trade policy. The developed world will be able to find new markets for technologies but developing countries will negotiate for financing, intellectual property rights, and technologies.[41] At the Bali meeting, China argued that developing nations should have access to state-of-the-art renewable energy technologies at reduced costs. The U.S. delegation, however, stated that U.S. companies do not want to sell their new technologies at low-cost. U.S. officials also expressed concern about intellectual property rights, fearing that once China and other developing countries get cutting-edge technology they will reverse engineer and illegally copy the innovation.[42] It is unclear what position the Obama administration will take on these matters, however, a post–Kyoto agreement will require that issues associated with innovation and technology transfer be worked out.

The post–Kyoto agreement that is due to be negotiated in Copenhagen in the end of 2009 must include measures that will encourage private capital to flow in the direction of combating climate change. Public resources are small in comparison to private sector wherewithal. The public resources that do exist need to leverage private investment in green technology. Three central problems need to be addressed to accomplish this. New technologies have to earn a return on investment, the perception of risk in the emerging market needs to be addressed, and the size of the green market has to be global. The post–Kyoto agreement must create investment opportunities so that the private sector will make the adequate investments to solve the problem.[43]

A post–Kyoto agreement will have to solve the thorny problem of carbon equalization and trade. The EU Commission began considering implementing a carbon tariff on non–Kyoto countries in 2008. The scheme requires that goods produced in Annex I countries that are not parties to Kyoto, like the U.S., would have a tariff imposed on them when imported into the EU. The EU is also considering imposing such a tariff on industrial developing countries such as China, India, and Brazil. The U.S. also considering imposing such a tariff on Chinese and Indian goods imported into the U.S. under several bills introduced but stalled in Congress.[44] Any such a tariff might fall into trouble with World Trade Organization (WTO) agreements and will certainly be challenged. The post–Kyoto accord must find a way to reconcile WTO rules with the new multilateral environmental agreement.

Finally, a post–Kyoto agreement will have to deal with the fact that energy use is increasing and that by 2030 energy-related emissions are forecast to be 60 percent higher than in 2004. Dealing with the climate crisis requires more than just slowing the growth rate of emissions; it requires emissions reductions. Kyoto may be a good starting point but the reductions mandated by the Protocol, even if met, will not produce the emissions reductions that scientists tell us must be made to achieve climate stabilization. A post–Kyoto agreement must address increased energy use and significantly greater reductions.[45]

Conclusion

This chapter has shown that two framework concepts underpin global climate change negotiations and treaties: differentiated responsibility and the precautionary principle. Each began to develop decades ago and each has been included in all United Nations conventions to date. The idea of differentiated responsibility originated in the 1972 Stockholm Convention on the Human Environment and has carried through to the Kyoto Protocol. The right to development and the special needs of the developing nations have been persistently guaranteed. Likewise, the precautionary principle traces its roots back to the Rio Declaration and continues in the language of the Kyoto Protocol.

The recent rejection on the part of the Bush administration of both the precautionary principle and the concept of differentiated responsibility on the basis of cost and fairness poses dilemmas for the negotiation of the successor treaty to the Kyoto Protocol. The least troubling of these is rejection of the precautionary principle. The Bush administration did finally acknowledge the scientific claim of anthropogenic causes of climate change and the Obama administration fully supports scientific opinion. The rejection of the concept of differentiated responsibility on the grounds that it is unfair remains a major barrier to achievement of a successor treaty. It is not yet clear how the Obama administration will balance the need to respect the arguments of developing countries that they should be judged on per capita emissions with the need to get China and to a lesser extent India and Brazil to reduce their staggering emissions. Total national emissions present a clear problem. The problem of global warming cannot be solved without the active participation of developing countries, at least those that currently produce the largest total national emissions. China and India certainly must be a meaningful part of the next accord that will mandate the next round of emissions reductions.

Finding ways to reduce deforestation in developing countries and providing them access to clean technologies are both critical steps in the right direction. The problem is massive and government action alone will not be able to forge a solution. Private capital must be part of the solution. Finding ways to encourage its use is crucial. Finally, nations must come to an agreement on carbon equalization and trade. The post–Kyoto accord must be able to deal with the rules for world trade while at the same time enforce the next multilateral environmental agreement.

4

Science and Anti-Science

The debate over whether or not to do anything about global warming has been central to the making of climate policy in the U.S. Beginning with the signing of the Kyoto Protocol by the Clinton administration, carrying through the entire eight years of the Bush administration, and into the Obama administration a policy dispute raged. Many interest groups opposed U.S. ratification of the Kyoto Protocol. Many opposed any sort of mandatory regulations of GHG emissions— whether by international treaty or domestic law. Some opposition groups used the tactic of devaluing the science behind global warming as a primary tool to support their agendas. This chapter focuses on these efforts.

One group of influential actors in the policy debate argued that the scientific base was too weak to take any policy action. This view was strongly supported and widely spread by economic interests that feared they would be on the losing side should carbon regulation take form. The opposition of big oil, coal, and many industries produced well funded lobbyist groups willing to use anti-science skepticism to slow or stop potential regulation. Groups such as the Global Climate Coalition, founded by ExxonMobil and temporarily joined by other energy, automotive, and industrial companies heavily lobbied Congress and the Bush administration against GHG emissions restrictions. The Global Climate Coalition was influential in Bush administration decision making on withdrawal from the Kyoto Protocol and policy positions on a successor treaty.

A number of third-party organizations were also influential in the debates. These groups were organized largely as nonprofit organizations and based their opposition to GHG emissions regulation on some mix of general opposition to regulation and scientific skepticism regarding the veracity of global warming and its causes. Many drew large portions of their funding from ExxonMobil. These groups included the American Petroleum Institute, the Competitive Enterprise Institute, the George Marshall Institute, the Oregon Institute of Science and Medicine, the Science and Environmental Policy Project, the Greening Earth Society, and the Center for the Study of Carbon Dioxide and Global Change among others. Along with ExxonMobil and a host of political forces, they concentrated on discrediting the scientific evidence pointing to human induced global warming.

Politicians, political supporters, and political strategists had much to do with the climate change debate that continued through most of the Bush administration. There were two groups that dominated the discussion and each had different albeit overlapping reasons for doing so. One group was comprised primarily of anti-science conservatives. This group, largely comprised of fundamentalist Christians, founded most of their anti-science position on arguments against evolution. The crossover to skepticism about global warming was relatively easy in the midst of the dispute with science and scientists rooted in the evolution issue. The other major group consisted of conservative Republicans who used the tactic of attacking scientific evidence to defeat what they saw as unnecessary regulation that would stifle the economy. They cynically used their positions to introduce doubt into public opinion through an assault on what they called "unsound science."

A sometime unwitting but powerful player in the anti-science debates was the media. On the pretense of equal and balanced reporting, they created an inaccurate perception that there was major dispute among climate scientists regarding the causes of global warming. By pairing a legitimate scientist one on one with a skeptic, they promoted the illusion that there was an equal divide in scientific opinion. Some media outlets, most notably those aligned with the conservative Republican message, acted as bullhorn to promote doubt over the scientific evidence.

This chapter explores the role that these actors played in the U.S. policy debate and the wider role that science, science skeptics, and misinformation played in framing the U.S. climate change debate. The chapter begins with a review of the processes that scientists use to determine fact and how climate science applies these principles. The groups that participated in the debate are separately discussed including ExxonMobil, third party anti-science organizations, anti-science conservatives and deregulatory Republicans, and the media. How these groups all came together to create the perfect storm of misinformation is explored. The chapter discusses the silencing of the anti-science crescendo toward the end of the Bush administration as clear evidence of global warming and its impacts became widely apparent. How and why the public changed its view on the importance and consequences of global warming are explored. Much of the view of the public toward climate change is the result of the information received largely from the media. The role of the media in transmitting scientific information is explored. The chapter ends with a discussion of the commitment of the Obama administration to "restore science to its rightful place."[1]

Determining Fact through Scientific Method

Philosophers of science have provided a great deal of literature that distinguishes ways of knowing achieved through science from other ways of acquiring knowledge. Human inquiry into the way the world works takes many forms. Knowledge can be gained in a variety of ways including from tradition and from authorities. People who wish to understand a particular phenomenon can turn to the past and seek explanations rooted in a particular culture that itself firmly accepts certain basic concepts about how the world works. Gaining knowledge about the world through tradition may have definite advantages for it saves us from having to rediscover each Spring, for instance, that Spring is the best time to plant. Knowledge from tradition, however, can also mislead us if the traditional source of knowledge is incorrect. The widely held misconception that the world was flat was derived from tradition. Some of the knowledge we have about the world is also gained from authorities. Like knowledge acquired from tradition, this may be both an advantage and a disadvantage. Accepting information about the way the world works from reputable authorities saves us from the need to discover all knowledge ourselves but if we accept interpretations of experts who later turn out to be incorrect we would have been mislead.[2] One often used source of knowledge from authorities comes from religious authorities where the guiding principle is belief or faith, not empirical observation.

Human inquiry that is rooted in scientific method has several characteristics that differentiate it from knowledge flowing from tradition or authority. First, science seeks to explain and predict natural phenomenon. The key questions for scientific inquiry are why and how. Thus scientific explanation is rooted in theory, not belief, philosophy, or ideology. Not all questions can be approached using the scientific method. Scientific questions, or hypotheses, must be testable and must be able to be found false. Questions that cannot be tested — "Is there a God?" — are not suitable for scientific inquiry. Second, knowledge gained from scientific investigation is based on empirical observation that normally involves experimentation. Typically, although not always, scientific experimentation occurs in a laboratory setting where variables can be controlled so that a causal agent can be identified. Experimentation involves randomly selecting subjects into groups and controlling conditions so that only one group receives the treatment that is in question. If the treatment group reacts differently than the control group, the treatment is determined to have caused the effect. Experimental methods thus employed eliminate bias and ensure that the treatment variable under scrutiny is the agent causing observed differences between the experimental and control groups. When the issue of scientific inquiry cannot be sequestered in a laboratory for study, finding scientific explanation becomes more challenging. Third, scientific knowledge is cumulative, that is, one breakthrough builds on the next. Fourth, science is open and subject to peer review examination so that errors that may be in the work will be discovered. In this way, science is self-correcting since replication of experiments, openness, and peer scrutiny eventually will debunk unsound findings.

Climate science shares the characteristics denoted above but climate science is not an experimental science. Not all sciences are experimental. Astronomy, for instance, one of the oldest and most developed branches of science is not an experimental science either. Lacking controlled experimentation, climate science must proceed outside of the laboratory using a three step process. First, climate scientists must show that climate has changed with some level of statistical certainty. Second, they must argue that this change is consistent with computer models that simulate human-induced changes in climate. Finally, they must demonstrate that no rival hypothesis (such as natural climate cycles) could account for the observed change.[3] This is difficult to do. Indeed, it took decades for climate scientists to develop accurate models with adequate detail and complexity to allow a scientific consensus on the anthropogenic causes of climate change to emerge.

Those interest groups that opposed taking policy action to curb GHG emissions skillfully used the slow emergence of this consensus to their advantage. They also used a feature of typical scientific discourse to raise doubts about the certainty with which scientists made their claims. As scientists investigate a phenomenon, they raise controversial ideas and hypotheses that are vigorously debated. Expert disagreement typically dominates the dialog for some period of time before all the evidence is weighed and consensus is reached. Once reached, the controversy dies down and researchers set their sights on the next piece of the puzzle. Little continuing emphasis is placed on resolved issues. Those interest groups that opposed climate policy action chose to focus on the expert disagreement rather than the arrived at consensus, thus falsely giving the impression to the general public that there was considerable disagreement within the ranks of climate scientists when in fact no such discord existed. The debate and dialog was part of the normal process of inquiry through scientific method.

ExxonMobil, the Global Climate Coalition, and the Global Climate Science Team

A number of organizations and individuals opposed taking any policy action to reduce GHG emissions. They took their stands for a variety of reasons. Some undoubtedly sincerely disagreed with the evidence being presented by climate scientists and remained skeptics. Others opposed policy action, not because they did not concede that human actions were changing the atmosphere and propelling climate change, but because they believed any action taken would be harmful to their economic interests. Politicians could be swayed by the promise of campaign contributions to listen to the appeals of opponents.

Perhaps the most powerful force against the recognition of humanly-induced climate change and the need to reduce GHG emissions was ExxonMobil, the world's largest publically traded oil and gas company. In 2007, ExxonMobil had revenues in excess of $390 billion and profits of more than $40 billion.[4] Lee Raymond, ExxonMobil's CEO until 2006, set an uncompromising tone regarding climate change during his thirteen years as CEO both through opposition to caps on emissions and through denial of the scientific consensus on climate change. Raymond's replacement, Rex Tillerson, maintained Raymond's stand. In 1989, ExxonMobil and the American Petroleum Institute (which was twice chaired by Lee Raymond) formed the Global Climate Coalition. Other energy, automotive, and industrial companies also joined the Global Climate Coalition. The Coalition's mission was to oppose policy action on climate change. ExxonMobil and the Coalition argued that global warming was a natural phenomenon and that human actions were not contributing to it.[5] The strategy drew on tactics pioneered by the tobacco industry in the 1960s— to promote doubt and uncertainty in the mind of the public that human actions were not contributing to global warming.[6]

With the signing of the Kyoto Protocol in 1997, British Petroleum, Shell, DuPont, and Texaco accepted the scientific consensus that climate change was caused by human activities and withdrew from the Global Climate Coalition. Their withdrawal was also an acknowledgement of criticism they had received from European environmentalists. By 1999 Ford Motor Company also pulled out.[7] The departure of these members marked the beginning of the decline of the Global Climate Coalition, which subsequently disbanded in 2002. Many of the withdrawing members publically acknowledged the dangers of global warming. The Coalition, however, claimed success on its web page suggesting that with the abandonment by the Bush administration of the Kyoto Protocol, the Coalition had achieved its goals.[8]

In 1998, ExxonMobil put together a task force called the Global Climate Science Team (GCST). Among its members were Randy Randol, ExxonMobil's chief environmental lobbyist; Joe Walker, the American Petroleum Institute's public relations point person; and Steven Milloy, the head of Advancement of Sound Science Coalition, a nonprofit organization originally created by Philip Morris in 1993 to raise doubts about the relationship between second hand smoke and disease.[9]

The GCST created a Global Climate Science Communications Action Plan at a workshop in 1998. A six page memo forwarded to the team by Joe Walker, summarized the Action Plan. Under the header "Situation Analysis" the memo incorrectly stated the scientific consensus on climate change by arguing that it is not in fact "known for sure whether (a) climate change actually is occurring , or (b) if it is, whether humans really have any influence on it. Despite these weaknesses in scientific understanding, those who oppose the [Kyoto] treaty have done little to build a case against precipitous action on climate change based on the scientific uncertainty."[10] The memo went on to suggest strategies and tactics. One of these was the creation of a national media relations program to "inform the media about uncertainties in climate science; to generate national, regional and local media coverage on the scientific uncertainties...." To implement this, the GCST was to "identify, recruit and train a team of five independent scientists to participate in media outreach. These will be individuals who do not have a long history of visibility and/or participation in the climate change debate. Rather, this team will consist of new faces who will add their voices to those recognized scientists who already are vocal. [They will] develop a global climate science information kit for media including peer-reviewed papers that undercut the 'conventional wisdom' on climate science."[11] The memo included tactics for the distribution of a steady stream of opinion editorials and tailored information to science writers in major media outlets as well as strategies to convince major television news journalists to question the scientific foundations of the Kyoto Protocol. All in all, the memo detailed a plan to call into question the scientific knowledge-base of climate science which had already been vetted through scientific peer review.

The Global Climate Science Communications Action Plan, under the header "National Media Program Budget —$600,000 Plus Paid Advertizing" laid out plans to undercut "the prevailing scientific wisdom" by establishing a "Global Climate Science Data Center ... in Washington as a non-profit educational foundation with an advisory board of respected climate scientists. It will be staffed initially with professionals on loan from various companies and associations with a major interest in the climate issue."[12] The staff was to have expertise in such areas as media relations, grassroots organization and campaign organization. The memo argued that funding levels for the Global Climate Data Center should be high enough to ensure that it could succeed and that it could fund research contracts to provide "a complete scientific critique of the IPCC research and its conclusions."[13]

The final pages of the Global Climate Science Communications Action Plan outlined a lobbying plan to "inform and educate members of Congress, state officials, industry leadership, and school teachers/students about uncertainties in climate science."[14] In particular, the plan targeted the National Science Teachers Association and pledged to work with that group to develop school materials that supported GCST's position on climate change policy, that is, that no action should be taken. Walker's memo also specified measures that would be used to assess their success. These measures included shifts in baseline public opinion and government official opinion, tracking the percent of media articles that raised questions about the accuracy of climate science's projections regarding global warming, the number of members of Congress exposed to their materials, the "number of radio talk show appearances by scientists questioning the 'prevailing wisdom' on climate science," the number of students and teachers reached, and the number of science writers briefed that subsequently included doubt about climate science in their writings.[15] Walker wrote that "victory will be achieved when average citizens 'understand' (recognize) uncertainties in climate science; recognition of uncertainties becomes part of the 'conventional wisdom.'"[16] Included in Walker's victory scenario was that the media would also come to recognize uncertainties in climate science and would be sure to include the opinion of skeptics in reporting. Finally, Walker proclaimed that victory would be achieved when "those promoting the Kyoto treaty on the basis of extent science appear to be out of touch with reality."[17]

Oil companies were extremely effective in directly affecting climate change policy during the Bush administration. White House documents show that ExxonMobil and ConocoPhillips executives participated in Vice President Cheney's Energy Task Force which established the goals for U.S. energy policy under the Bush administration.[18] A memo to Under Secretary Dobriansky, prepared to brief her prior to a visit from representatives of ExxonMobil's Global Climate Coalition, revealed that the Bush administration rejected the Kyoto Protocol in part because of input from the Global Climate Coalition.[19]

Third Party Anti-Science Actors

In subsequent years, ExxonMobil followed the action plan closely. It shifted its strategy to supporting independent third-party groups that supported its position on not regulating GHG emissions.[20] Between 1998 and 2004 ExxonMobil spent over $16 million to fund organizations that focused on creating public uncertainty regarding the scientific consensus of humanly-caused climate change. ExxonMobil attempted to create a counterbalance to the legitimate science so as to spread doubt and slow political process that might lead to regulation. Initially, the company targeted well known conservative and anti-regulatory organizations such as the American Enterprise

Institute, the Competitive Enterprise Institute, and the Cato Institute. Later ExxonMobil widened its list of organizations to include many less well known groups such as the American Council for Capital Formation Center for Policy Research, the George C. Marshall Institute, the American Legislative Exchange Council, and the Committee for Constructive Tomorrow. Between 1998 and 2005 ExxonMobil funded these and other organizations with nearly $16 million for climate change issues or outreach.[21] While Exxon-Mobil funded these groups that shared its aversion to GHG regulations, it simultaneously tried to project a better image by funding genuine climate science research. For instance, in 2003 ExxonMobil pledged more than $100 million in funding over a decade to Stanford University for climate research.[22]

A 2007 Union of Concerned Scientists report traced many of these third-party organizations funded by ExxonMobil and disclosed that they published the works of a small and overlapping group of individuals, some of them scientists, who discounted the consensus in the scientific literature on climate change. The report further alleged that many of these organizations included the same individuals as board members and scientific advisors. In tracing just eleven of the names most prominent among the third-party organizations, the Union of Concerned Scientists report revealed numerous overlaps. Two individuals are reported to be affiliated with eleven ExxonMobil funded anti-climate change groups, another with nine, another with six, and three with five. Each of the eleven is affiliated with multiple ExxonMobil funded groups. This extent of overlap tends to suggest that these vocal individuals used multiple outlets to magnify their impacts.[23] A review of just a few of these third-party organizations that ExxonMobil provided more than $1 million a year in funded to is informative.[24] Most of these third- party organizations are modest in size but highly vocal in the global warming dialog.

The Competitive Enterprise Institute (CEI) was originally founded in 1984 to "advance the principles of free enterprise and limited government."[25] Holding to a deregulatory ideology, CEI weighed in early as a global warming skeptic. As late as 2008, CEI included material in its "We Call It Life" series that is part of its global warming issues page that mocks the scientific consensus on global warming. The text to a brief video available on the CEI site reads:

> You've seen those headlines about Global Warming.
> The glaciers are melting. We're doomed!
> That's what several studies supposedly found.
> But other scientific studies found exactly the opposite:
> Greenland's glaciers are growing, not melting;
> The Antarctic ice sheet is getting thicker, not thinner.
> Do you see any headlines about that?
> Why are they trying to scare us?

Global warming alarmists claim the glaciers are melting
because of the carbon dioxide from the fuels we use.
Let's force people to cut back, they say.
But we depend on those fuels
To grow our food,
move our children,
light up our lives.
And as for carbon dioxide,
It isn't smog or smoke.
It's what we breathe out and plants breathe in.
Carbon dioxide.
They call it pollution.
We call it life.[26]

The site contained a global warming frequently asked questions page which blatantly mischaracterizes IPCC statements regarding the urgency of mitigating GHG emissions. The CEI states: "Alarm over the prospect of the Earth warming is not warranted by the agreed science or economics of the issue." The CEI posted the following statement: "There is no 'scientific consensus' that global warming will cause damaging climate change."[27]

The George Marshall Institute (GMI) is another third-party group that was funded by ExxonMobil. Also founded in 1984, the GMI stated it was dedicated to improving the use of science in public policy making. Despite the overwhelming scientific consensus on global warming, the GMI argued that "the global warming debate isn't likely to cool off anytime soon, with experts disagreeing about its causes, and even its existence."[28] In addition to denying the existence of global warming, the GMI tried to project the image that they were victims of attempts to be silenced: "There is something odd about the ferocious amount of energy expended suppressing any dissent from orthodoxy on climate change." At the same time they launched attacks on recognized science and on one of the world's best known and respected climate scientists: "In the past year a number of expert U.S. scientists have been conducting a public investigation which raises large question marks over the methods used to arrive at NASA's figures" and "NASA's James Hansen proclaimed that people who spread 'disinformation' about global warming should be tried for crimes against humanity. Such a blatant attempt to curtail scientific inquiry and stifle free speech seems inexcusable."[29] Such efforts to discredit mainstream science and scientists were standard fare for the GMI.

In 1998, the GMI partnered with the Oregon Institute of Science and Medicine in a scientists' petition drive which sent thousands of scientists across the U.S. a mass mailing asking them to sign a petition calling on the government to reject the Kyoto Protocol. The mailing included an article formatted to look like one that might appear in the journal of the National Academy of Sciences (NAS), a prestigious peer-reviewed scientific publication. The article discounted the scientific evidence of global warming. However, the article had not been peer reviewed nor accepted for publication in the NAS journal. The NAS later released a statement disavowing any connection to the petition or the article and stating its support for the scientific proof of global warming.[30]

Anti-Science Conservatives and Deregulatory Republicans

It was not just a handful of third-party rogue skeptics that rejected the scientific claim of anthropogenic causes of global warming. One group that was at the core of George W. Bush's constituency were conservatives with a deregulatory agenda. One of the central themes of the Bush administration was the need for continued deregulation. Echoing the deregulatory rhetoric of the Reagan years, President Bush pushed for policies that sought to create markets unfettered by regulations. The problem of climate change and the Kyoto Protocol suggested that solutions lay in regulating GHG emissions. This group of deregulatory Republicans was not interested in ushering in more regulation. One clear way out of having to sanction more regulations would be to discount the certainty of climate change by undercutting the science and to argue that before any policy action should be taken, more study should be undertaken.

Many studies have shown that conservatism is negatively related to pro-environmental attitudes primarily because pursuit of environmental protection typically involves some form of government action that restricts economic libertarianism. The conservative movement saw attempts to regulate GHG emissions as particularly threatening because it would likely involve a binding international treaty that they feared would hurt economic growth and the free market while at the same time threatening national sovereignty and their agenda for continued deregulation.[31] In a study of fourteen conservative think tanks active in the 1990s, McCright and Dunlap analyzed hundreds of documents and publications pertaining to global warming for content and found that 71 percent attempted to discredit the scientific evidence for global warming. These conservative think tanks emphasized the uncertainty of climate science and described it with terms such as contradictory, flawed, murky, junk science, and tabloid science. The think tanks frequently attacked the claim that any scientific consensus on global warming existed and often denied the fact of a warming world. These think tanks often characterized the scientific claim of global warming as suspect because of supposed hidden agendas held by climate scientists. Some went so far as to suggest that the IPCC was a political as opposed to scientific organizations and alleged that the IPCC edited its reports to create the image of scientific consensus while suppressing the views of scientific skeptics.[32]

Another core group that comprised part of George W. Bush's base of support was fundamentalist Christian conservatives. These conservatives strongly supported many facets of President Bush's conservative social agenda that included opposition to abortion and hostility to stem cell research. Fundamentalist Christian conservatives differed from many Christians in their position on science and its role in faith. Former president Jimmy Carter, an evangelical Christian, framed one of the differences between evangelical Christians and fundamentalists as rooted in a different interpretation of what could be learned from science. Carter, like many Christians associated with mainstream denominations, sensed no divide between science and religious belief. Christian fundamentalists, however, by accepting the literal truth of the Bible, are placed in a position of having to reject the teachings of science which they interpret as in direct conflict with a literal reading of the Bible.[33]

The schism was first popularized in the Scopes case in 1925 which was a test of Tennessee's Butler Act, which made it illegal for any state-funded school to teach a theory which denied the correctness of the Biblical explanation of divine creation. The widely publicized case marked the beginning of the controversy between the teaching of the theory of evolution, a theory that widely underpins modern understanding of the life sciences, and the literal belief in the story of creation depicted in the Bible. After the Scopes case, fundamentalists returned to their traditional isolation from politics, but with the rise of the Moral Majority under Jerry Falwell, political lobbying became a central focus of the fundamentalist agenda. Moral Majority was ended in 1989 but its successor, the Christian Coalition under the leadership of Pat Robertson, continued the emphasis on political engagement to achieve the movement's aims. Those goals included the elimination of legal abortion, resistance to stem cell research, protections for the "traditional family," opposition to rights for homosexuals, and a demand for the teaching of a viable alternative to the theory of evolution in schools. This alternative at various times was suggested under different names including creationism, creation science, and intelligent design. Regardless of their names, they rely on the biblical explanation for human life being created separately from other life species and with a divine creator. This differs from evolution which links all life forms together and suggests that species change over time, including the human species. Fundamentalist Christians see a conflict between science and their views on the nature of creation. Because they possess a natural suspicion of science in general, they were a likely group to accept challenges to the science of global warming.[34]

In the run up to the 2004 election, Republicans were quite willing to use denial of climate change science as a response to demands for policy action. A controversial 2003 memo from Republican strategist Frank Luntz warned Republicans that they were vulnerable on environmental issues and that they should change their tactics. In pages 131 through 146 of the lengthy memorandum, Luntz laid out the approach that should be taken. On global warming Luntz stated: "Voters believe that there is *no consensus* about global warming within the scientific community. Should the public come to believe that the scientific issues are settled, their views about global warming will change accordingly. Therefore, *you need to continue to make the lack of scientific certainty a primary issue in the debate....*" The memo cynically went on to assert that "*the scientific debate is closing [against us] but not yet closed. There is still a window of opportunity to challenge the science* (italics in original)."[35]

In advising Republicans on how to generally approach the global warming issue, Luntz encouraged Republicans to cling to arguments for "sound science" even when it was clear from the tone of the memo that any such plea was a deliberate excuse for delay in GHG regulations despite clear scientific evidence. Luntz urged the use of language deliberately selected to slow action, telling Republicans to argue: "We must not rush to judgment before all the facts are in. We need to ask more questions. We deserve answers. And until we learn more, we should not commit America to any international document that handcuffs us either now or into the future."[36]

The combination of the deregulatory Republicans and the fundamentalist Christians created a large group within the Bush administration's constituency that was keen to use doubt of science to deny, delay, or obscure the facts about global warming. Within the operations of the administration these efforts played out in different ways. One was the editing of EPA scientific reports about climate change to emphasize doubt and uncertainty in the scientific findings. Suppression of scientific reports was not restricted to EPA. Dr. James Hansen's reports and speeches were changed by NASA officials to emphasize the uncertainty of climate science. Such actions were rather remarkable considering Hansen's long history with the issue. Hansen complained about the editing and garnered headlines when a political appointee in NASA's Public Affairs Office threatened Hansen with retribution if he continued his complaints. Undeterred, Hansen took his objection about the politicization of science to the media. When it was revealed that the Public Affairs official had lied about having a university degree on his resume, he was fired. NASA subsequently established standards that its scientists could speak officially to the public and press on issues of only of science but when they advocated policy, they would have to do so as ordinary citizens and not as NASA scientists.[37]

The Bush administration took other actions as well. NASA's mission statement was formally changed in 2006 to remove the phrase "to understand and protect our home planet" thereby shifting the orientation of research undertaken in the agency. To the distress of many NASA scientists the change was made without consulting the agency's 19,000 employees or informing them of the change in advance.[38] In the Alaskan division of the Fish and Wildlife Services (FWS), biologists and other scientists traveling in the Arctic were censored by the Bush administration. As the issue of whether the polar bear should be put on the endangered species list was being considered, FWS scientists were told they could not discuss climate change, polar bears, or sea ice unless they were specifically authorized to do so.[39] In 2007, the White House's Office of Management and Budget (OMB) cut the written testimony given by the head of the Centers for Disease Control (CDC) to a Senate committee investigating the health risks associated with global warming. The language cut included the only statements in the written testimony that concluded that climate change was a serious health concern.[40]

Public Opinion, the Media, and the Climate Change Debate

Beginning in the 1930s, there was some public recognition that the weather was changing but there was little concern associated with observations that the weather was warming and few people associated such changes with human activities. Slowly, scientists and science journalists began to educate the American public that climate change was underway, that it might affect life on Earth sometime in the distant future and that it was associated with human activities. Recognition of these facts grew slowly. In the 1970s, the question of whether the climate was warming became a wider public concern as general interest in the newly emerging environmental movement grabbed wide public attention. The issue became muddled as a series of scientific studies and popular scientific reports called attention to the chance that a new Ice Age was approaching. Scientists gradually came to consensus that the cooling phenomenon being observed was a temporary one caused by the presence of aerosols in the atmosphere. Scientists predicted that by the 1990s the aerosols would drop out of the atmosphere and result in a return to global temperature increases. This prediction proved to be correct.[41]

The public was only minimally aware of climate change and its causes before several focusing events occurred in the late 1980s. After the public debate over a new Ice Age had died down in the 1970s, the press paid very little attention to climate change. According, it is not surprising that in 1986, when asked by a national polling organization, if they has heard or read anything about the greenhouse effect only 39 percent of the public said they had.[42]

After the summer of 1988, however, public opinion changed dramatically. That summer the environment was increasingly in the news due to the severe heat wave and violent weather patterns that affected most of the U.S.

On one very hot day in the summer of 1988, Senator Tim Wirth, the Democrat from Colorado, chaired a hearing on climate change and invited several prominent scientists to testify. The hearing received wide press coverage and NASA scientist James Hansen's testimony lead the headlines. His testimony concluded that global warming was underway. This was the first time a respected government scientist has been so definite and vocal about climate change. The result of the wide press coverage and expert testimony drew the public's attention to the issue.[43] By September of 1988, 58 percent of Americans said they had heard of or read about the greenhouse effect.[44]

Public opinion, however, had to navigate the fierce political debate that ensued regarding risks, the extent of scientific certainty, and costs of action (or inaction). Efforts by industry later joined by the Bush administration to deny global warming and to deter action were influential.[45] The media played a critical role in shaping information dissemination to the public in this politicized time. Media actions taken during this period focused heavily on attempts to personalize, dramatize, and narrate the story. This significantly influenced the media content and diminished emphasis on authority and true balance of scientific opinion which led to a great deficiency in the media coverage of the climate change issue between the years of 1988 and 2005.[46] Conservative Web sites claiming to debunk the phenomenon of global warming dominated the Internet for two decades. These sites included industry supported ones such ones as *www.CO2science.org* and *www.junkscience.com*. In 2004 several scientists launched a site to provide scientific evidence that human actions are the primary cause of global warming. This site was co-organized by Gavin Schmidt of NASA, speaking as an individual citizen under NASA's newly adopted rules for appropriate scientific conduct adopted during the Bush administration.[47]

The media played a powerful role in the debate over the science of climate change and created several inaccurate perceptions about global warming. First, they confused the issue by suggesting that there was a major dispute among climate scientists regarding the causes of global warming. This was done largely by pairing legitimate scientists one on one with skeptics, thus they promoted the illusion that there was an equal divide in scientific opinion when such division simply did not exist. Second, in framing the issue the way they did, the press did not use science as the basis for explanation of the facts. Rather the press treated the issue as one of opinion. The media frequently gave voice to those who argued they did not "believe" in global warming when scientific fact and observation is not a matter of faith or belief.[48]

The impact that climate change skeptics had on the public opinion through media outlets has been studied, at least for the print media. When comparing the number of articles in the print media that referred to either a legitimate climate scientist or a well known skeptic, the pattern that emerges is that legitimate scientists lost ground throughout the 1990s. By the end of the decade, legitimate scientists were being referenced with no greater frequencies than skeptics.[49] The press continued both these practices until 2005 when they finally began treating climate change as a scientific phenomenon supported by scientific consensus. This was a real failure on the part of the media.

It was not until 2005 that the U.S. media began to report the issue clearly, giving much less time to the few scientists voicing skepticism about the issue. Around the same time a series of films, television dramatizations, and odd weather events focused public attention on the adverse outcomes associated with global warming. The 2004 movie *The Day After Tomorrow* depicted a rapid and severe shift in U.S. weather. Millions of people watched Al Gore's documentary *An Inconvenient Truth*; Perhaps no media effort was bigger than it — won an Academy Award for best documentary in 2007. The companion book was a best seller, and reached number 1 on the *New York Times* best seller list. Gore's movie had its supporters and detractors within the scientific community. Some scientists feared that Gore went too far in painting the consequences of global warming with too much certainty. The well known skeptic of dire climate predictions, Dr. Richard S. Lindzen, wrote an opinion piece for The Wall Street Journal calling Gore an alarmist. Others leading scientists strongly supported Gore's efforts, including NASA's James Hansen. Hansen disputed Gore's interpretation that Hurricane Katrina could be tied to global warming but overall supported Gore's representation of scientific fact in the movie.[50] Conservatives seized upon the debate to once again raise the issue of unsound science.

World weather events were influential in influencing public opinion. The U.S. public paid attention to the 2003 European heat wave but it was Hurricane Katrina in 2005 that really had an effect. While few scientists were willing to directly link that specific hurricane to climate change, the public was. They compared abstract scientific predictions of more severe weather to the press coverage of Hurricane Katrina and suddenly global climate change became a far more concrete phenomenon. For the public, the hurricane dramatized what scientists had long been saying.[51]

The bulk of the U.S. population has moved to an understanding that climate change is both real and caused by human actions. Polls taken as early as 1992 show that 68 percent of Americans held that view. That number declined to 57 percent in 1994, however; a trend likely promoted by conservative think tank efforts to boost skepticism about global warming. When asked again in the early 2000s, a greater number of the public was willing to accept scientific evidence. ABC news polls taken in 2005 show that 23 percent of Americans said they were totally convinced that that global warming is actually happening, while another 36 percent said they were mostly convinced. An Ohio State University and ABC News Poll taken in 1997, 1998, 2006, and 2007 asked respondents if they thought that temperatures have been increasing over the past century. The responses show a 76 percent, 80 percent, 85 percent and 84 percent yes answer. The shift in the importance of the issue is clearly visible among the U.S. public. The proportion of Americans who say that global warming is either personally extremely important or very important shifted from 27 percent in 1997 to 52 percent in 2007.[52] Finally, when ranking the importance of global warming as an environmental problem, by 2007 global warming took the top spot with 38 percent ranking it as the most important environmental problem over water pollution (14 percent), air pollution (13), garbage and landfills (10), loss of the ozone layer (7), endangered or vanished species (3) acid rain (1), and other environmental problems (7).[53]

Most Americans say they have accepted the idea that some action should be taken on climate change but that acceptance needs to be qualified. By 2007, the majority of Americans agreed with scientists that the globe is heating up, that human actions are causing the warming, that warming will generally be bad for life on Earth, and that some action should be taken. In 2005, two thirds of the public stated that actions taken to avert global warming would make the economy more competitive, compared to less than one third of the public who thought that efforts to reduce GHG emissions would hurt the economy.[54] The public's expression that it is willing to take action on climate change may be an overstatement, however, for when respondents were asked difficult questions about their willingness to undertake the extent of GHG reductions that scientists say will be necessary to avert climate crisis, public perception changes. For instance, while public opinion surveys generally show that the public understands that climate change poses significant risks, they also show that the public generally feels that reductions in GHG concentrations can be deferred until substantial economic harm is observed (not forecast). This wait-and-see attitude erroneously assumes that climate change, once underway, can be quickly reversed when harm is observed. Such attitudes demonstrate widespread misunderstanding of the problem and the necessity of timely responses.[55]

Conclusion

In his Inaugural Address, President Obama pledged to "restore science to its rightful place" thus signaled a new direction.[56] The mistrust with which

science and scientists had been treated before and during the Bush administration would not continue under the Obama administration. By the close of
the Bush administration, the heated debate about the actuality and causes of
global warming had largely dissipated. While a few naysayers continued their
arguments, the scientific position on climate change formed the basis of a consensus that dominated public opinion and media representations of global
warming. It is amazing that, despite the evidence, the debate seriously raged
for so many years in the U.S. This was so for several reasons.

First, the economic stakes were high. The financial consequences of taking action to reduce GHG emissions would have immediate short-term consequences on big oil, coal, and many industries. They responded by producing
well funded lobbyist groups that used anti-science skepticism to slow or stop
potential regulation. Following the play book forged by the tobacco industry years earlier, they used the tactic of introducing doubt into public discussions of global warming. ExxonMobil's Global Climate Coalition heavily
lobbied Congress and the Bush administration against GHG emissions restrictions. They developed action plans to turn the press and public opinion
against legitimate scientists by deliberately introducing uncertainty into the
dialogue. The Global Climate Coalition was successful in influencing the Bush
administration's decision making on withdrawal from the Kyoto Protocol.
They were influential in driving positions on a successor treaty to Kyoto as
well as in helping to forge the overall administration's approach to energy and
the environment. The Bush administration lost some of its own top appointees,
like Christine Todd Whitman, who would not remain in an administration
so dominated by Vice President Cheney's energy vision, and by extension, the
energy vision of ExxonMobil along with other oil, gas and coal producers.

Second, a number of conservative third-party organizations were
influential in the debates. These groups based their opposition to GHG emissions regulation on some mix of general opposition to government regulation and scientific skepticism regarding the veracity of global warming and
its causes. The American Petroleum Institute, the Competitive Enterprise
Institute, the George Marshall Institute, the Oregon Institute of Science and
Medicine, the Science and Environmental Policy Project, the Greening Earth
Society, and the Center for the Study of Carbon Dioxide and Global Change
were well funded by ExxonMobil. They concentrated on discrediting the scientific evidence pointing to human induced global warming.

Third, anti-science conservatives and deregulatory Republicans easily
went along. Fundamentalist Christians focused most of their anti-science
energy on fighting the teaching evolution in schools or at least they wanted
some form of creationism to be taught alongside evolution. They argued for
students to have a choice but never grasped the essential conditions that make

science scientific. For fundamentalist Christians, active in Republican circles, the crossover to skepticism about global warming was relatively easy. Conservative Republicans who used the tactic of attacking scientific evidence to defeat what they saw as unnecessary regulation that would stifle the economy also went along. They used their positions to introduce doubt into public opinion. Political appointees of the Bush administration used their power to join these efforts. Scientific reports were edited to remove valid scientific conclusions and to introduce uncertainty. The freedom of government employees to speak out on issues associated with climate change was curtailed. Agency mission statements were quietly rewritten so that research emphasizing global warming would be more difficult to justify.

The media provided a venue for anti-science skeptics to be heard far out of proportion to their representative numbers in the scientific community. On the affectation of equal and balanced reporting, the media created a false perception in the mind of the public that there was a broiling dispute among climate scientists regarding both the existence and causes of global warming. By failing to explain to the public the scientific process of open discussion and debate that eventually results in scientific consensus, the press painted the picture that scientific debates were never ending. By allowing the dialog to be debated on the basis of belief rather than evidence the press reduced a scientific phenomenon to mere opinion. By offering skeptics equal time with legitimate climate scientists, the press created the illusion of a fifty-fifty split among scientists, when the reality was that the overwhelming mass of scientists were in agreement on both the existence and causes of global warming Media outlets aligned with the conservative Republican message provided air and press time for the party line.

Polls show that American public opinion shifted substantially after 2005. Prior to that, the ferocious political debate over risks, the extent of scientific certainty, and costs of action (or inaction) fueled public uncertainty. Bush administration and industry efforts to deny global warming and to deter action were influential and the media played a critical role in shaping information dissemination to the public while these debates raged. Media reporting significantly underemphasized the authority of science and balanced reporting which distorted the media coverage of the climate change. It was not until 2005 and after that the U.S. media began to clearly report the issue, giving much less time to the isolated skeptics and finally reporting scientific reports accurately. A series of influential films and dramatic weather events — particularly Hurricane Katrina — focused public attention on the adverse outcomes associated with global warming. After 2005 the tide of public opinion shifted as the public accepted long-held scientific opinion. Public willingness to fully accept the urgency of scientific forecasts, however, remains in doubt.

5

Morals, Ethics, and Religion in the Policy Debate

Advocates for taking policy action to reduce GHG emissions frequently rely on appeals to morality, social justice, or religious duty. The U.S. environmental movement has a long history of appealing to ethics and values to motivate action. The environmental plea for action on climate change took root within organized religious groups as well, in some cases splitting them. The debate hinged on themes such as fairness, justice, social responsibility and obligation.

The secular-leaning wing of the moral and ethical movement was typified by the efforts of Vice President and Noble Prize winner, Al Gore and his many followers. In the late 1990s and first decade of the new millennium, they orchestrated a national campaign depicting climate change as an urgent global crisis and moral issue. Al Gore's efforts were critical in moving the center of attention for the general public from an emphasis on economic losses to a concern for moral values and social responsibility. Gore mobilized teams of activists to go into communities and present his slide show that served as the basis of his Academy Award–winning documentary, *An Inconvenient Truth*. The emphasis was placed not only on the physical effects that would likely result from global warming but also on the moral and ethical consequences of a failure to act.[1]

Secular backers of climate action focus on a number of ethical problems embedded in the climate change issue. They argue that not tackling the issue of global warming would simply result in the shifting of burdens created by one generation to the next, a transfer they conceive of as immoral. In a similar fashion, these advocates contend that a failure to act on the part of the developed countries would result in the unprincipled transfer of the problem to the developing countries, where climate change outcomes are forecast to be far more severe. Unfairness plays a critical role in their viewpoint, not only in shifting the problem to future generations or more impoverished nations, but also because elemental fairness dictates that the polluter should pay for the cleanup. The idea that plants and animals (human settlements and other species) in one geographic location would have to confront the brunt of climate change's negative consequences because of a mere accident of being in an unfortunate location, strikes these advocates as patently unjust. The notion that human life and communities will be disrupted is taken as important but equally so is the prediction of massive species extinctions. They ask: What right does humankind have to inflict such global damage? Secular advocates of taking action to fight global warming point to the limits of growth in a finite world. The moral imperative, they argue, is for population growth control along with responsible consumption which will result in a smaller carbon footprint for the human species.

The religious participants in the U.S. moral discussion include various faith traditions including Christians (both Protestants and Catholics), Jews, Muslims, and Buddhists as well as members of less well-know spiritual societies. Each of these faith traditions emphasizes the interconnectedness between humans and the natural world within a spiritual context that derives meaning for humans within the universe. Many of these religious groups call for an end to the rampant materialism and consumerism they argue plagues the world and for a return to responsible consumption. They emphasize the obligation to care for the poor and they trouble over the fact that global warming's most severe consequences will fall on those least able to respond or adapt.

Christians comprise the largest faith group in the U.S. with Protestants constituting the majority of Christians and Catholics the minority. Protestants are divided into many mainline and evangelical denominations. Catholics and most mainline Protestant denominations support taking action to address climate change. Protestant evangelicals split on their view toward global warming. Many evangelicals joined the advocates of climate action by promoting what they came to call "Creation Care." Others allied with those who opposed climate change action. These religious opposition groups echoed Republican claims of scientific evidence too doubtful on which to base costly programs. They anchored many of their positions in Dominion and End Days theology. They argued that a focus on climate action was incorrect because it would dilute religious opposition to abortion and what they called the "gay agenda" (gay rights and same-sex marriage).

This chapter examines the nature and reasons behind these positions. It begins with a discussion of the role of personal versus collective action. Following this, the foundations of both the secular and religious moral and ethical claims for action on climate change are discussed. The chapter concludes with a discussion of religious opposition to moral engagement on global warming.

Personal or Collective Action

Central to the ethical and moral approach to global warming is the question of to what extent actions undertaken should be personal. That is, should those who believe climate change is a threat take personal actions that will result in a changed lifestyle to reduce their personal carbon footprint? Or should they demand that governments, public and civic organizations, and businesses to make the changes necessary to combat global warming? Or should the solution involve some mix of both public and private action. These are key questions. The answers make a good deal of difference in likely outcomes.

Personal action involves individual efforts to reduce GHG emissions. For instance, individuals could replace incandescent light bulbs in their homes with compact fluorescent bulbs which use much less electricity and therefore produce fewer emissions. If a person chooses to do so, he or she then bears the cost for the action. Since compact fluorescent bulbs cost more in the short run than do incandescent bulbs, taking personal action imposes a penalty on the person undertaking such action. Short-term losses might be recouped later through lower energy bills, but an individual must be willing and able to take a short-term penalty first. The decision to take action is not a single one. One has to consider timing, extent, and consequences. How many bulbs should be replaced? Should action be postponed until an incandescent burns out and needs replacement to avoid waste (of the still good incandescent)?

Individuals can engage in a variety of other behaviors to reduce their personal GHG emissions. Such actions might include purchasing a hybrid or fuel efficient car, reducing the number of miles driven, or abandoning automobile use all together by riding a bicycle or using mass transit. Travel in airplanes can be reduced. Solar panels can be installed on roofs. Thermostats can be set higher in summer and lower in winter. Appliances can be replaced with energy efficient models. Houses can be insulated and weatherized. Unnecessary lighting can be shut off. Consumption of products whose manufacture and sale produces GHG emissions can be reduced. Since meat production produces a large volume of GHG emissions, individuals can reduce their meat consumption or become vegetarians. Like the example of replacing incandescent bulbs with compact fluorescents, each of these decisions will involve consideration of timing, extent, and consequences. To what extreme should individuals go to reduce their own carbon footprint?

Individuals can also opt for offsetting, rather than reducing, their GHG emissions. This is typically done by paying a premium price for "green" energy or by purchasing carbon offsets directly from a marketer. Terrapass, Carbonfund.org, and other nonprofit organizations are dedicated to selling offsets and using the funds to support their GHG emissions reduction programs (reforestation, reduction of deforestation, renewable energy, energy efficiency improvements, etc.). Sustainable Travel International works with major airlines to allow customers to purchase offsets at the same time as ticket purchase. Individuals who travel can pay to offset their individual GHG emissions from the trip. Purchasing offsets or paying a premium price for "green" energy can only be done by those with sufficient assets. The key question persists. To what extreme should individuals go to reduce their own carbon footprint?

Some argue that personal efforts alone will not be successful. This is owed to the fact that not all individuals can or will make the choice to reduce their GHG emissions sufficiently to provide a solution to the climate change problem. Action, they suggest, must be collective and to achieve uniform collective action government, public and civic organizations, and businesses must be involved. For instance, while a relatively small group of automobile purchasers sent a signal to automakers that they had a preference for fuel-efficient hybrids and were willing to pay a premium price to own one, U.S. automakers were slow to move. Rather, they pinned their hopes of profits on gas guzzlers, fuel-inefficient trucks, and SUVs. Only government mandates for greater fleet fuel efficiency resulted in a change from the automakers. In a similar fashion, corporations, public and civic organizations can be urged to take action to reduce their GHG emissions if the government requires such reductions. Those who favor the collective approach do not necessarily discount the effectiveness of a personal moral commitment to individual action. Rather, they suggest that only collective action, organized in large part in response to public policy actions, will get all the forces of society moving in the right direction.

Foundations of the Secular Moral and Ethical Claim for Action on Climate Change

Fairness, justice, and equity play a large role in providing a foundation for the secular moral and ethical claims for taking action on global warming. Concern for fairness and equity spans several issues. One of the most discussed is the clear unfairness of expecting the poor countries (the global South), who have only modestly contributed to current levels of GHG emissions, to share the burden of reducing those levels. Recognition of this is embodied in the expression of differentiated responsibilities under the Kyoto Protocol and is common to most UN declarations. Those who argue for taking action on climate change recognize that any moral and ethical approach to reducing GHG emissions must take into account the need for poverty reduction. They argue that those responsible for the current level of greenhouse gases in the atmosphere are responsible for the cleanup. This is only fair as the developed countries (the global North) in large part became wealthy by using the energy sources that have created the climate change problem. This in large part is seen as a social justice issue or as one of international distributive justice.[2] As UN General Assembly President Srgjan Kerim said in 2007, "Beyond the impact on ecosystems, economics and communities, we have a moral obligation to our fellow human beings."[3] These sentiments were echoed by President Obama in his inaugural address when he said, "We can no longer afford indifference to the suffering outside our borders, nor can we consume the world's resources without regard to effect."[4]

The unbalanced distribution of negative consequences from global warming falling on the less developed countries will exacerbate the existing poverty gap in North-South comparisons, making justice a core concern.[5] Some argue that the wealthy industrialized states should pay compensation to the less developed countries—that the developed countries owe an "ecological debt" to the less developed countries. Paying this ecological debt will be the mechanism used to restore balance and distributive justice.[6]

Fairness is also central to the argument that there should be no shifting of the burdens from those that created the problem to innocents. With climate change this happens in two ways. First, there may be an intergenerational shift. The generation that benefited from activities that resulted in GHG emissions should be the one that also bears the burden of reducing emissions. They should not be permitted to pass along to future generations the job of dealing with dangerous levels of greenhouse gases. Intergenerational burden-shifting is seen as patently irresponsible. Fairness and distributed justice demand that the current generation should protect the environment for future generations.[7] Second, with climate change there is a likelihood of geographic shifting. That is, people in regions not responsible for GHG emissions may feel proportionally higher negative impacts than will those in regions generating the emissions. It is clearly not fair that the continent of Africa will see some of the worst climate impacts when the people of Africa did the least to contribute to the problem. Those who argue for taking action to address GHG emissions argue that these shifts of burdens must be addressed.[8]

As Vaclav Havel so clearly enunciated, we must develop "a consciousness of the commonality of all living beings and an emphasis on shared responsibility."[9] This consciousness must evolve out of a profound understanding of the connectedness of all life and must include more than an engineering approach focused on developing and deploying new technologies. Rather the new consciousness must insude education on ecological princi- ples and circumspection of what it means to behave responsibly.[10] Similar sentiments were expressed by Al Gore in response to receiving the Nobel Peace prize in 2007 for his work to alert the world of the dangers posed by climate change. Mr. Gore stated: "The climate crisis is not a political issue. It is a moral and spiritual challenge to all of humanity. It is also our greatest opportunity to lift global consciousness to a higher level."[11]

Environmental policy in the U.S. and internationally has long been based on the premise that the polluter should pay for the cleanup. This concept is rooted in a fundamental decent and principled axiom that if one engages in an activity which results in negative consequences, it is the obligation of who- ever created the negative outcomes to restore the situation. Since efforts to reinstate the environment to a pre-pollution condition typically take expert skills that may not be possessed by the polluter, having the polluter pay for the restoration is generally considered a reasonable way to deal with the prob- lem. One should clean up one's own mess, however, if that is not possible than one ought to pay to have it cleaned up.

Radical environmental activists have, for decades, held the position that humans are only one animal on the planet and that we have no more right to life than do other species. This belief is not shared by most environmen- talists, who would accept the notion that humans are the dominant species on the planet. That said, the belief that humans have an obligation to pro- tect other species is a widely held value. Climate change threatens to bring with it a massive extinction of numerous species. Many feel action is neces- sary to prevent such an extinction event out of our moral obligation to other species. When considered in this way, the moral and ethical question becomes, to what extent should the standing of other species be weighed against a human-centered approach?[12]

Recognition of the limits to growth on a finite planet presents the case for ethical action to responsible consumption and a smaller environmental footprint. This view of the limits to growth dates back to the very beginning of the environmental movement when the Club of Rome released the results of a computer model predicting severe consequences of continued popula- tion growth and sustained consumption patterns. While the report was widely challenged, few environmentalists disagreed with the assumption that humans have an ethical obligation to avoid an unsustainable future by changing their actions.[13] The issue of climate change raises this dimension once again to the fore as changes in consumption patterns and population increases seem to threaten the global future. Some argue that the roots of the environmental crisis of our time lies in unrestrained capitalism and its emphasis on economic growth above all else. In a political context, unrestrained capitalism empowers social actors who care little for environmental consequences while others who do care are excluded from decision-making circles. This again raises the issue of fairness, justice, and equity.[14]

Foundations of the Religious Claim for Action on Climate Change

Religious claims for action on climate change vary by religion although most of the major world's religions share a reverence for the Earth and a sense of human responsibility to care for it. In its most general form, religion can be seen as an orientation to the universe and our human role in it. Religion is a means whereby humans undertake certain practices that transform themselves and their communities within the framework of the wider cosmos. Religious ritual practice and ethical norms create systems in which humans can become embedded in a world of meaning and responsibility. Religion may assist people to be in relation to both the natural world and to better understand their place in the universe.[15]

The U.S. is primarily a Christian nation, although other religions are practiced. According to the Central Intelligence Agency (CIA), in 2007 the U.S. population was comprised of the following religious groups: Protestant (51.3 percent), Roman Catholic (23.9 percent), Mormon (1.7 percent), other Christian groups (1.6 percent), Jewish (1.7 percent), Buddhist (0.7 percent), Muslim (0.6 percent), other or unspecified religious groups (2.5 percent), unaffiliated (12.1 percent), and none (4 percent).[16] The Pew Forum on Religion and Public Life conducted a survey of 35,000 adult Americans in 2007 and reports similar findings. Pew found that of the 78.4 percent of Americans that are Christians, 51.3 percent are Protestants, 23.9 percent are Catholics, and 1.7 percent are Mormons. Protestants are divided into a large number of different groups or denominations that can be depicted in the three general categories. Of the Protestants, 26.3 percent attend evangelical churches, 18.1 percent attend mainline Protestant churches, and 6.9 percent attend historically Black churches. Pew reports the same percentages of Jewish, Buddhist and Muslim worshippers as does the CIA and confirms the growing number of Americans unaffiliated with any religious organization (over 16 percent).[17]

While fewer than 1 percent of Americans claim Buddhism as their faith,[18] Buddhist religious traditions join with other world religions in promoting spiritual, ethical, and moral ecological values. Buddhist environmentalists argue that the mindful awareness of the universality of suffering should produce compassion and empathy for all life. This compassion extends beyond human life and includes animals, plants, and the Earth itself. The Buddhist ethic focuses on the actions and behaviors of humans. Buddhist ecologists think that human actions directly affect the natural world. Buddhists believe that human greed and desire led to the division and ownership of the land which in turn promotes violence, conflict, and destruction. Buddhists believe that the universe is an interconnected and interdependent cooperative. For contemporary Buddhists, like the 14th Dalai Lama of Tibet,[19] a sense of responsibility rooted in compassion is at the core of an environmental ethic. According to this ethic, humans must not only take compassionate responsibility for other humans but also for all plants, animals, and the planet itself.[20] His Holiness the Dalai Lama offset his carbon emissions produced during his 2007 world tour and speaks with conviction about protecting forests and wildlife. He says that a clean environment is a basic human right and calls on us to pass on a healthy world to future generations.[21]

Islam, like Buddhism, is a belief system held by less than 1 percent of Americans[22] but like Buddhism it teaches reverence for the natural world. Islam instructs that the universe exists to sustain the process of life. In the Qur'an, humans are seen as the custodians of the natural world and nature is anchored in the divine. Humans are viewed as superior to other creatures, not because they enjoy any greater authority or control over nature, but because humans are accountable before Allah. Islam teaches the central doctrine of self-injury which provides the source for the Islamic position on ecology. Humans are thought to be part of nature rather than separate from it and are subject to the laws of nature just as are other life forms. Muslims believe that humans should act in league with other life forms to bring balance to the natural world. According to the doctrine of self-injury, to damage or destroy the balance of the natural environment is to damage or destroy oneself. Such behavior is seen as suicidal.[23] Islamic environmentalists, such as Fazlun Khalid, argue that as guardians of Allah's creation humans should act as stewards of the environment and maintain the interconnected balance of natural systems.[24]

Jewish religious tradition, a tradition followed by nearly 2 percent of Americans,[25] focuses on the complexity of creation and commands that humans should not destroy any part of creation. Judaism's view of the environment sees God as the center and originator of creation and the unifying force of the universe. Creation is seen as a self-contained but dynamic system where every human action affects the balance and rhythm of life. Commandments given in the Hebrew Bible (also known as the Christian Old Testament) teach humans to restrain their destructive or destabilizing influence on the universe. Jewish tradition teaches that human are a part of life, but not its center. Humans should be careful not to think they can control and rule the universe. The stories of the Hebrew Bible, or Old Testament, show the relationship between incorrect community behaviors and environmental disasters including floods, droughts, and storms. Deuteronomy 28:15–24 states that adverse weather changes are a sign of divine punishment while Deuteronomy 11:11–17 and 28:1–12 state that pleasant sun and shade, clean streams, and gentle rain are symbols for lives filled with correct actions. The Hebrew Bible also prohibits harming fruit-bearing trees even during war and these environmental protections are expanded by Talmudic law to include the air, land, and water.[26]

Active Jewish leaders, like Rabbi Warren Stone, participated in the negotiation of the Kyoto Protocol as United Nation's delegates.[27] In 2001, the Coalition on the Environment and Jewish Life released a statement that called for an end to delay on action on global warming and for an action plan to reduce anthropogenic interference with the atmosphere. The Coalition aided in the creation of the Interfaith Climate and Energy Campaign, an organization that helps people of faith to have their views on climate change heard by elected officials and other governmental decision makers. The United Synagogues of Conservative Judaism sponsors a program called Green Sanctuaries with the goal of promoting green building.[28]

With over 78 percent of Americans in their number, Christians represent by far the largest religious group in the United States. Because of their overwhelming size, understanding the religious claim for action on climate change requires an in depth understanding of how Christians respond to the issue. The wide variety of theological positions and church leaders within the American Christian community has resulted in differences in response to ecological issues. Responses have varied from deep spiritual embrace of the environmental movement to rejection of it. Views toward taking action on climate change also vary by religious group.

A small number of American Christians are Orthodox Christians and follow the leadership of the Ecumenical Patriarch, currently Bartholomew I.[29] The majority of U.S. Christians are either Roman Catholics (about 24 percent) or Protestants (about 51 percent).[30] Roman Catholics follow the leadership of the Pope, currently Benedict XVI,[31] and the hierarchical structures established in the United States for church leadership including the Conference of Catholic Bishops. Bartholomew I, also known as the Green Patriarch, is leader of 300 million Orthodox Christians worldwide. The Patriarch is the winner of the U.S. Congressional Gold Medal and the Sophie Prize for leadership in environmental protection and sustainable development. He basis his stand to protect the environment on the notion of stewardship — that to harm the environment is to diminish divine creation.[32] In 2001, Ecumenical Patriarch Bartholomew I released a statement on climate change, asserting that there was sufficient scientific evidence of global warming to move forward with climate change action.[33]

The Roman Catholic Church has a long track record on climate issues. Going back to 1991, a statement by the U.S. Conference of Catholic Bishops addressed the climate crisis calling it a moral challenge. The statement called for an examination of how humans use and share natural resources, the impacts on future generations, and how we live in harmony with creation. The statement called attention to references to the poor in the Bible and affirmed that it is the poor that suffer most from environmental decline.[34] By 2001, the Catholic Church was taking firm stands on climate change. A statement released by the U.S. Conference of Catholic Bishops in that year confirmed the church's position that significant scientific evidence exists to take action on climate change and called on the Catholic faith tradition of social justice to address those that are most likely to be the greatest victims of climate change.[35] They stated:

> At its core, global climate change is not about economic theory or political platforms, nor about partisan advantage or interest group pressures. It is about the future of God's creation and the one human family. It is about protecting both the human environment and the natural environment. It is about our human stewardship of God's creation and our responsibility to those generations who will succeed us.... As People of faith, we believe that the atmosphere that supports life on earth is a God-given gift, one we must respect and protect. It unites us as one human family. If we harm the atmosphere, we dishonor our Creator and the gift of creation.[36]

In 2006, Pope Benedict XVI called for a commitment on the part of Catholics to care for creation. In 2007, the Pope used his first address to the United Nations to warn about the dangers of global warming and added protection of the environment as a moral cause for all Catholics.[37] In 2007, in a statement given for the Symposium on Religion, Science and the Environment organized by Orthodox Patriarch Bartholomew I, Pope Benedict XVI said:

> Preservation of the environment, promotion of sustainable development and particular attention to climate change are matters of grave concern for the entire human family. No nation or business sector can ignore the ethical implications present in all economic and social development. With increasing clarity scientific research demonstrates that the impact of human actions in any one place or region can have worldwide effects. The consequences of disregard for the environment cannot be limited to an immediate area or populous because they always harm human coexistence, and thus betray human dignity and violate the rights of citizens who desire to live in a safe environment.... The relationship between individuals or communities and the environment ultimately stems from their relationship with God. When man turns his back on the Creator's plan, he provokes a disorder which has inevitable repercussion on the rest of created order.[38]

In turn, in 2007, John L. Carr, the secretary of the Department of Social Development and World Peace of the the U.S. Conference of Bishops, provided testimony to the U.S. Senate explaining its approach to climate change, an approach that rests on the three basic tenets of "prudence, the pursuit of the common good, and the duty to stand with and for the poor and vulnerable."[39] The U.S. Conference of Bishops argued:

> Prudence is not simply about avoiding impulsive action, picking the predictable course, or avoiding risks, but it can also require taking bold action weighing available policy alternatives and moral goods and taking considered and decisive steps before the problems grow worse. Prudence tells us that we know that when a problem is serious and worsening it is better to act now rather than wait until more drastic action is required.... The debate over climate change is too often polarized by powerful stakeholders seeking to advance their own agendas and interests and using or misusing science for their own purposes. However, the universal nature of climate change requires a concerted and persistent effort to identify and pursue the common good on climate with an attitude of we are all in this together.... Our response to climate change should demonstrate our commitment to future generations. We believe solidarity also requires that the United States lead the way in addressing the issue and in addressing the disproportionate burdens of poorer counties and vulnerable people. [40]

In support of these positions, the U.S. Bishops' Conference is working with the Catholic Coalition on Climate Change with the goal of bringing together grass roots gatherings in a number of states to encourage dialog among public officials, business and labor leaders, environmental activists and the public. Various efforts are being undertaken in communities under the Climate Change Justice and Health Initiative of the U.S. Conference of Catholic Bishops.[41]

Protestants are fragmented into many denominations that are typically clustered into several groupings based largely upon core beliefs. Mainline or mainstream Protestants are those that belong to the several denominations typically thought of as long-established and with a mix of liberal, moderate, or conservative viewpoints or theologies. Mainline churches are generally inclusive, welcoming of different viewpoints, and largely have supported the rights of women (especially for ordination) and gays, although those issues are often divisive. Most mainline churches view the Bible as the word of God but are open to interpretations of the text. They generally do not believe in Biblical inerrancy or that the Bible as written is without error or contradiction. Mainline churches are known for their focus on social justice, efforts to end poverty and racism, and support for actions that produce positive changes in the world. About 18 percent of American Protestants attend mainline churches.[42] Among these mainline Protestant denominations are American Baptists, Congregationalists, Methodists, Presbyterians, Episcopalians, Lutherans, Quakers, the United Church of Christ, and the Disciples of Christ.

Most mainline churches are part of the National Council of Churches and have submitted written statements to that body regarding climate change and actions that need to be taken. The Eco-Justice Program of the National Council of Churches and the National Religious Partnership for the Environment were organized in large part to educate the public regarding climate change issues. The National Council of Churches' Eco-Justice Working Group used Earth Day to focus the efforts of member congregations on protecting creation. In 2005 the National Council of Churches organized a conference on stewardship issues associated with climate change called "Tending the Garden, Cultivating the Commons."[43] Many of the mainline Protestant churches are also making efforts to take environmental action on their own. For instance, an organization called Interfaith Power and Light (originally called Episcopal Power and Light) encourages the building of eco-friendly religious places of worship.[44] Quaker Earthcare Witness is a spiritually centered movement of Quakers that seeks to join together the long-held Quaker concern for social justice and equity with concern for the environment.[45]

About 26 percent of American Protestants are evangelical Protestants.[46] Evangelicals believe in the need for a personal conversion experience to Christianity or the need to be "born again" and the inerrant truth of the Bible. Evangelicals are generally social conservatives. They reject homosexuality as an acceptable lifestyle and do not support the ordination of women. One of the largest evangelical groups is the Southern Baptist Convention, which has over 16 million members and represents over 42,000 churches.[47]

Evangelicals are often called fundamentalists but a distinction should be made. Fundamentalists originally were evangelicals who differed in their view of taking action in the world. Historically, fundamentalists were separatists and did not involve themselves in civic activities. Fundamentalism is a 20th century American movement tied to the revivalist tradition within evangelical Protestantism that opposed modernity and the cultural change associated with it. Where modern theology tended to explain life and religion in terms of natural developments, fundamentalists stressed supernatural explanations and divine control. During the 1920s in America, fundamentalists were very active in trying to control evangelical congregations and the wider culture. When these efforts failed, they became increasingly separatist, but continued to have influence on the many conservative evangelical organizations with which they had contact. Some of these took on some or all of key fundamentalist characteristics including divinely guaranteed inerrancy of Scripture, divine creation as opposed to evolution, and a millennialist approach to explaining historical change in terms of divine control.[48]

Beginning in the 1970s in the U.S., there was a movement that began among some of these fundamentalists to re-involve themselves in civic activities, a movement generally associated with the Supreme Court banning prayer in public schools. As the movement grew under the leadership of fundamentalists like Jerry Falwell, more and more fundamentalist Christians became active in political life. By the 1980s the movement had grown in influence and power, playing a key role in electing Ronald Reagan to the presidency. These politically active fundamentalist, or Right Wing Christians as they are typically called, played a critical role in the two elections of George W. Bush to the White House. With their ascendency, the link between the Republican Party and the fundamentalist Christian coalition was firmly established. But not all evangelical leaders were willing to go along with the Bush administration's inaction in respect to global warming.

Action on climate change among evangelicals began with a Declaration of the Care of Creation initially released by the Evangelical Environmental Network (EEN) and Creation Care Magazine in 1994. The document was based on the Bible verse "the Earth is the Lord's and the fullness thereof" (Psalm 24:1) and stated:

> As followers of Jesus Christ, committed to the full authority of the Scriptures, and aware of the ways we have degraded creation, we believe that biblical faith is essential to the solution of our ecological problems. Because we worship and honor the Creator, we seek to cherish and care for the creation. Because we have sinned, we have failed in our stewardship of creation. Therefore we repent of the way we have polluted, distorted, or destroyed so much of the Creator's work. Because Christ God has healed our alienation from God and extended to us the first fruits of the reconciliation of all things, we commit ourselves to working in the power of the Holy Spirit to share the Good News of Christ in word and deed, to work for the reconciliation of all people in Christ, and to extend Christ's healing to suffering creation. Because we await the time when even the groaning creation will be restored to wholeness, we commit ourselves to work vigorously to protect and heal that creation for the honor and glory of the Creator — whom we know dimly through creation, but meet fully through Scripture and in Christ. We and our children face a growing crisis in the health of the creation in which we are embedded, and through which, by God's grace, we are sustained.[49]

After describing the degradations of creation as misuse of the land and water pollution, deforestation, species extinction, and alteration of the atmosphere, the Declaration details the actions that need to be taken saying:

> First, God calls us to confess and repent of attitudes which devalue creation, and which twist or ignore biblical revelation to support our misuse of it.... Second, our actions and attitudes toward the earth need to proceed from the center of our faith, and be rooted in the fullness of God's revelation in Christ and the Scriptures. We resist both ideologies which would

presume the Gospel has nothing to do with the care of non-human creation and also ideologies which would reduce the Gospel to nothing more than the care of that creation. Third, we seek carefully to learn all that the Bible tells us about the Creator, creation, and the human task.... Fourth, we seek to understand what creation reveals about God's divinity, sustaining presence, and everlasting power, and what creation teaches us of its God-given order and the principles by which it works.... Therefore we call upon all Christians to reaffirm that all creation is God's; that God created it good; and that God is renewing it in Christ.... We urge individual Christians and churches to be centers of creation's care and renewal, both delighting in creation as God's gift, and enjoying it as God's provision, in ways which sustain and heal the damaged fabric of the creation which God has entrusted to us.... We make this declaration knowing that until Christ returns to reconcile all things, we are called to be faithful stewards of God's good garden, our earthly home.[50]

The EEN, in coalition with Creation Care Magazine, also sponsored the campaign *What Would Jesus Drive?* The purpose of the campaign was to raise awareness regarding the impacts of SUVs and other fuel-inefficient vehicles and their role in climate change.[51] Begun by the Reverend Jim Ball, an evangelical Christian minister and one-time director of EEN, the campaign began when he drove a Toyota Prius from Texas across the Bible Belt to alert evangelical churches along the way to the threat of global warming. Ball would also be influential in another effort.[52]

In February of 2006, a group of 86 evangelical Christian leaders signed a statement calling on fellow evangelicals to take action against climate change.[53] In the Statement of the Evangelical Climate Initiative (ECI) titled "Climate Change: An Evangelical Call to Action," the Evangelical Environmental Network provides reasons why Christians should take immediate action to address climate change. They extend the creation care logic and argue the moral obligation to protect God's creation as commanded in Genesis 1:26–28. They also call attention to the fact that the consequences of climate change will be hardest felt by the poor and as Christians, they have a responsibility to aid the poor.[54] This argument is rooted in justice. For evangelical Christians, the role of justice is exemplified by the full identification of Jesus with humanity, its woes and travails. In the Bible, Jesus tells his followers to care for the sick, hungry, and thirsty and in Mathew 25:40 Jesus reminds his followers "just as you did it to one of the least of these ... you did it to me." Poverty and the poor were of particular interest to Jesus. While the duty to care for the weakest among us is fully established in the Old Testament, these evangelicals believe the ministry of Jesus renews that demand.[55] The statement calls for federal legislation to reduce GHG emissions and the Evangelical Climate Initiative calls for mass action to influence public officials, education in churches, and educational events at Christian colleges and universities.[56] One of the strong supporters is Rick Warren, best-selling author of *The Purpose-Driven Life*, and founder and senior pastor of evangelical Saddleback Church in Lake Forest, California. Saddleback Church is the fourth largest church in the United States.[57] Pastor Warren was also called upon by President Obama to be one of the spiritual participants in his inauguration.

In 2007, a further effort was undertaken when a group of evangelicals from the National Association of Evangelicals (NAE) met with scientists from Harvard Medical School and produced a statement entitled "An Urgent Call to Action: Scientists and Evangelicals Unite to Protect Creation." The statement said that "reckless human activity has imperiled the Earth" and that "we share a profound moral obligation to work together to call our nation, and other nations, to the kind of dramatic change urgently required in our day."[58] The statement was sent to President George W. Bush, House Speaker Nancy Pelosi, congressional leaders, and national E\evangelical and scientific groups and urges changes in values, lifestyles and policies to address the worsening problem of global warming.[59]

Foundations of Religious-Based Opposition to Climate Action

Not all evangelicals supported the Evangelical Climate Initiative's "Climate Change: An Evangelical Call to Action" or the "Urgent Call to Action: Scientists and Evangelicals Unite to Protect Creation." Both promoted controversy and discord not only because of the message being sent but also because of concern regarding who should speak for evangelicals.

In January of 2006, some evangelical leaders who opposed action on climate change signed a letter addressed to the National Association of Evangelicals asserting that climate change was not a consensus issue among evangelicals. The signers included Charles Colson, of Prison Fellowship Ministries, James Dobson, of Focus on the Family, and Richard Land, president of the Ethics and Religious Liberty Commission of the Southern Baptist Convention. The letter asked the NAE not to take a stand on global warming and not to allow any of its staff members to do so. The opposition organized into a group that came to be called the Interfaith Stewardship Alliance.[60]

The Interfaith Stewardship Alliance responded to "Climate Change: An Evangelical Call to Action" with an open letter to the signers. They expressed opposition to the idea that there was scientific consensus on human induced climate change and drew on much of the misleading anti-science literature (discussed in the last chapter) to make their point. Indeed, eight of the signers belong to six organizations that have received over $2 million from ExxonMobil between 2003 and 2006.[61] They argued that no action should be taken on climate change because it would be both ineffective and vastly too expensive. They also argued that the true moral issue was that of poverty and that any action taken on climate change would further restrict money available for poverty-reduction efforts. [62] The Interfaith Stewardship Alliance was later renamed the Cornwall Alliance. In response to criticism raised by these opponents, NAE president Ted Haggard did not sign "Climate Change: An Evangelical Call to Action."

NAE continued to run into conflict. Following Ted Haggard's resignation as the result of a sex scandal, questions were raised about the role of NAE vice president for governmental relations, Reverend Richard Cizik as an advocate for climate change action. The Interfaith Stewardship (Cornwall) Alliance, James Dobson, and others protested Cizik's announcement of "An Urgent Call to Action: Scientists and Evangelicals Unite to Protect Creation" saying that Cizik had no right to speak for the NAE. Dobson called for Cizik's resignation.[63]

This opposition was joined by Jerry Falwell, influential founder of the Moral Majority, who took the side of Dobson and the Interfaith Stewardship (Cornwall) Alliance. Falwell stated:

> I believe the Church must quickly get serious about denouncing the accelerating effort to promote the alleged catastrophic human-caused global warming.... There's no need for the Church of Jesus Christ to be wasting its time gullibly falling for all of this global warming hocus pocus. We need to give our total focus to the business of reaching this world with the Gospel of Jesus Christ and stop running down meaningless rabbit trails that get our focus off of our heavenly purpose.[64]

Falwell's position was echoed by other evangelical leaders, including the controversial John Hagee. Pastor Hagee has built a huge evangelical organization, called the John Hagee Ministries, and has strong ties to leading Republicans including former Texas congressman Tom DeLay. DeLay, cofounder of Coalition for a Conservative Majority, was House Majority leader but stepped down from his post in January of 2006 after he was indicted on criminal charges of conspiracy to violate Texas campaign finance laws.

Hagee's belief is a form of Christian fundamentalism and apocalypticism that exists within American evangelicalism. This dispensationalist theology looks for the forthcoming end of time and the end of the continuation of the Earth as we know it. In this belief system, the true believers will be taken immediately to heaven in the "rapture" while the "left behind" will suffer for seven years. The Battle of Armageddon will be fought; Christ will win and reign for a thousand years on a newly created Earth. In such a theology, dominion over the earth is interpreted as power over rather than stewardship for creation, as Earth as we know it will not be here for very long anyway. Any concern for the planet is therefore unnecessary.[65] Not surprisingly, Hagee condemned the Evangelical Climate Initiative and opposed taking any action to combat climate change."[66]

Many Christian fundamentalists share Hagee's belief that concern for the Earth is irrelevant. Many actually welcome environmental destruction because they see it as a sign of the coming End Time. This is not a small group of Christians. Rather they constitute a group of nearly 50 million believers, a subset of the nearly 100 million U.S. evangelical Protestants.[67]

Conclusion

As this chapter has shown, those who advocate taking policy action to reduce GHG emissions frequently rely on appeals to morality, social justice, and religious obligation. The key debates center on premises such as fairness, distributional justice, social responsibility, poverty, stewardship, and obligation to humanity. Both secular and religious advocates base their arguments on these concepts.

Secular advocates of climate action argue that failure to deal with the issue of global warming will result in the shifting of burdens created by one generation to the next. Such an intergenerational transfer is viewed as immoral. These advocates demand action on the part of the developed world for failure would result in the morally wrong transfer of the problem to the undeveloped nations, whose main focus must remain on poverty eradication. Fairness dictates that the polluter should pay for the cleanup, and the polluter is largely the developed world. The religious participants in the climate change policy debates include various faith traditions including Protestants, Orthodox, Catholics, Jews, Muslims, and Buddhists. Each of these faith traditions emphasizes the interconnectedness of humans and the natural world. Many of these religious groups call for an end to materialism and a return to responsible consumption. They emphasize the obligation to care for the God's creation. They are deeply concerned that global warming's most severe consequences will fall on those who did not cause it and have little capacity to survive the climate crisis. Not all religious groups, however, support taking action on climate change. As this chapter has shown, large groups of fundamentalists reject action because they think it will dilute religious opposition to issues such as abortion and same sex marriage. Many simply think the issue is irrelevant for their theology focuses on the end of the Earth in the near future. But these views are not static.

In 2008, in a significant shift away from a 2007 resolution passed by the Southern Baptist Convention that expressed skepticism about climate change and rejected taking action, 44 Southern Baptist leaders signed "The Southern Baptist Declaration on the Environment and Climate Change." Among the signers were the current and past two presidents of the Convention who stated that they believed their past denominational engagement of climate change issues had been too timid. The new declaration states that the prior response of the Southern Baptist Convention to global warming might be seen by the world as "uncaring, reckless, and ill-informed."[68] The Declaration's three main points are: that humans must care for creation and take responsibility for human contribution to environmental degradation, that there is enough evidence to suggest it is prudent to act on climate change, and that Southern Baptist principles demand environmental stewardship.[69] With this shift, America's largest Protestant body joined the many that out of moral, ethical or religious conviction support taking action on global warming.

6

Mechanisms for Regulating U.S. Greenhouse Gas Emissions

The United States is one of the world's largest emitters of greenhouse gases. These emissions involve a number of contributing gases including carbon dioxide, methane, nitrous oxide, chemicals used to replace ozone depleting substances, sulfur hexafluoride, and perfluorocompounds. Carbon dioxide is by far the largest contributor to the emissions accounting for nearly 85 percent of total GHG emissions and 80 percent of the overall global warming potential of all U.S. releases. Almost all emissions of carbon dioxide are associated with fossil fuel use in transportation or use for heating, cooling, lighting, and various manufacturing processes by commercial and industrial organizations or residential housing units.

A great deal of carbon dioxide is produced from the generation of electricity. Energy use is the key producer of GHG emission in the U.S. Eighty six percent of total U.S. GHG emissions can be traced to energy use. Methane comes predominately from animal husbandry, landfills, and natural gas systems. Nitrous oxide emissions come primarily from agricultural practices. Sulfur hexafluoride releases come from electricity transmission. Perfluorocompounds come from manufacturing. Land use, land use changes, and forestry affect level of GHG emissions as well. This chapter explores the sources of those emissions and trends over time.

Having an inventory of greenhouse gas emissions is the first step in analyzing how to cut releases. Tracking emissions can be a problem as the methods used must be systematic and accurate. The IPCC and the U.S. EPA have established standards to accomplish accurate reporting. These standards and a number of registries currently in use are discussed. Tracking emissions is the first step to regulating emissions but regulation raises a number of questions. The first of these is whether regulation should be voluntary or mandatory. The Bush administration split with signers of the Kyoto Protocol over this issue, demanding that regulations be voluntary only. The Obama administration has called for a mandatory cap-and-trade system throughout the United States. The states and regions have moved forward to establish a variety of voluntary and mandatory regulatory schemes to reduce GHG emissions. This chapter discusses these as well as the system established by European countries to comply with their obligations under the Kyoto Protocol that resulted in the creation of international carbon markets.

While cap-and-trade market-based schemes are the dominant mechanism being used to reduce GHG emissions, some analysts caution against them. They suggest that a carbon tax is the better way to regulate emissions. This chapter considers the arguments for a carbon tax approach in addition to the use of cap-and-trade. Increasing the amounts of renewable energy in the mix of energy sources is an important goal to assist in reducing GHG emissions. Renewable portfolio standards and feed-in tariffs are two schemes that are useful to consider for regulating the use of renewable energy. This chapter will consider these as well.

Sources of U.S. Greenhouse Gases

In 1992 the United States signed and ratified the United Nations Framework Convention on Climate Change which required signatories to provide annual reporting of GHG emissions. For the U.S., that reporting is done by the U.S. EPA which follows guidelines set forth by the United Nations for reporting emissions. These guidelines change often to assure that the most recent techniques and knowledge are included in future reporting cycles. Each year, the EPA provides revised estimates of GHG emissions and sinks as prescribed by the Good Practice Guidance provided by the IPCC.[1] These guidelines are issued so that all reporting countries may be easily compared.

In 2006, the U.S. emitted 7,054.2 teragrams or million metric tons of CO_2 equivalent (Tg CO_2 Eq.) or GHGs into the atmosphere. As Figure 1 shows, the primary GHG emitted is CO_2, which comprises 84.8 percent of U.S. GHG emissions or 5,983.1 Tg CO_2 Eq. The combustion of fossil fuels is the main source of these emissions. Methane (CH_4) accounts for 7.9 percent of emissions (555.3 Tg CO_2 Eq.) and comes mainly from intestinal fermentation releases from domestic animal husbandry, decay of landfill wastes, and natural gas systems. Nitrous oxide (N_2O) accounts for 5.2 percent of releases (367.9 Tg CO_2 Eq.) and comes primarily from agricultural soil management (nitrogen-fixing crops and fertilizer) and fossil fuel use for transportation. The remaining 2.1 percent of emissions (147.8 Tg CO_2 Eq.) comes from a mix of the discharges from chemicals used to replace ozone depleting substance

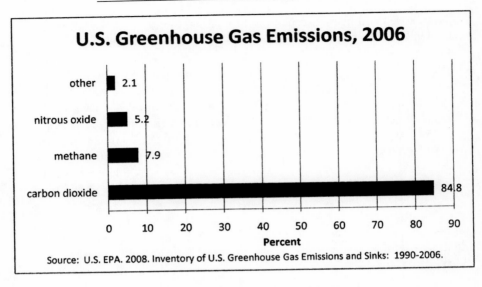

Figure 1: U.S. Greenhouse Gas Emissions, 2006.

(primarily HFC-23), from sulfur hexafluoride (SF_6) releases associated with electricity transmission, and from perfluorocompounds (PFC) emissions associated with semiconductor manufacturing and the production of aluminum.[2]

In analyzing GHG emissions, it is important to consider not just the percentage of overall emissions that they represent, but also their relative contribution to global warming associated with their specific characteristics. One such characteristic is how long the substance remains in the atmosphere. Another is to calculate the indirect effects of the substance through analysis of how it interacts with other substances to produce other greenhouse gases or how it alters the radiative balance of the earth. The IPCC developed the Global Warming Potential (GWP) weighted scale to allow comparisons across substances to determine their relative impact on global warming.[3] Using this scale, CO_2 from fossil fuel emissions accounted for 80 percent of U.S. GWP-weighted emissions in 2006, making it by far the most important gas to consider.[4] That said, the GWP of non–CO_2 emissions can be substantial. Methane, for instance, has a GWP of 21, meaning that methane is 21 times more effective than carbon dioxide in trapping heat in the atmosphere. The GWP of N_2O is 310. HFC-23 has a GWP of 11,700. The GWP of SF_6 scores 23,900 on the IPCC scale. In 2006, these non–CO_2 emissions accounted for 20 percent of U.S. GWP-weighted emissions.[5] Release of these, even in very small amounts, can have substantial impacts.

U.S. Producing and End-Use Consuming Sectors

For GHG emissions, we need to consider five consuming sectors: industrial, transportation, commercial, residential, and agriculture. Electricity generation emits a good deal of GHG emissions, but since electricity is consumed by end-use sectors it needs to be considered separately. As Figure 2 shows, industrial consumers accounted for about 29 percent of the GHG emissions in 2006 (2,029.2 Tg CO_2 Eq.). About 68 percent of these emissions were from the direct burning of fossil fuels (1,371.5 Tg CO_2 Eq.) while the rest of the emissions came from electricity use (657.7 Tg CO_2 Eq.). Transportation accounted for about 28 percent of U.S. GHG emissions in 2006 (1,974.5 Tg CO_2 Eq.) almost all of which resulted from the direct use of petroleum products including gasoline and oil. Only a small portion of emissions from the transportation sector came from electricity use (5.0 Tg CO_2 Eq.). Commercial end-users accounted for 17 percent of GHG emissions (1,204.4 Tg CO_2 Eq.) and electricity use accounted for 67 percent of those emissions (809.8 Tg CO_2 Eq.). Residential users produced about 17 percent (1,187.8 Tg

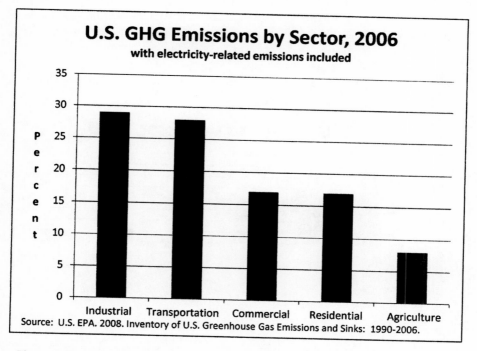

Figure 2: U.S. GHG Emissions by Sector, 2006 with electricity-related emissions included.

CO_2 Eq.) of the nation's GHG emissions in 2006. Of these emissions, more than 70 percent (843 Tg CO_2 Eq.) came from electricity use. Agriculture accounted for about 8 percent of U.S. GHGs in 2006 (595 Tg CO_2 Eq.). Of these emissions, only about 10 percent (62.2 Tg CO_2 Eq.) came from electricity use.[6]

Energy use is the key producer of GHG emission in the U.S.[7] In 2006, 6,076.9 Tg CO_2 Eq. of GHG emissions or 86 percent of total U.S. emissions can be traced to energy use. The U.S. consumed energy from the following sources: petroleum (39 percent), coal (22 percent), natural gas (22 percent), renewable (9 percent), and nuclear (8 percent). Of these, only renewable and nuclear energy do not produce GHG emissions. As Figure 3 shows, electricity generation in the U.S. in 2006, if considered separately, was responsible for the emission of 34 percent of U.S. GHG emissions in 2006 or 2,377.8 Tg Co_2 Eq.

The amount of GHG emissions released by the electric power industry is dependent on the fuel used to produce the electricity. Coal, which is used to provide for more than half of all the electricity produced in the U.S. in 2006, is a high producer of CO_2 emissions.[8] Table 1 shows the sources and amounts of U.S. emissions that account for about 95 percent of U.S. GHG emissions. Because the overwhelming source of GHG emissions in the U.S. is from fossil fuel use, the primary way to curb those emissions will have to include a shift away from fossil fuels.[9]

It is clear from Table 1 that the burning of coal and gas in stationary facil-

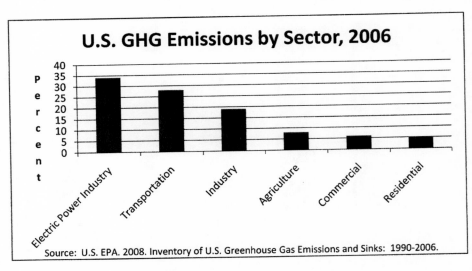

Figure 3: U.S. GHG Emissions by Sector, 2006

Major Sources and Types of U.S GHG Emissions, 2006.

Source and Type of Emissions	Tg CO2 Eq.	Percent of Total U.S. Emissions
CO2 Emissions from Stationary Combustion - Coal	2065.3	29%
CO2 Emissions from Mobile Combustion - Road and Other	1643.0	23%
CO2 Emission from Stationary Combustion - Gas	1121.9	16%
CO2 Emissions from Stationary Combustion - Oil	594.3	8%
Direct N20 Emissions from Agricultural Soil Management	214.7	3%
CO2 Emission from Mobile Combustion - Aviation	170.6	2%
CO2 Emissions from Non-Energy Use of Fuels	138.0	2%
CH4 Emissions from Enteric Fermentation	126.2	2%
CH4 Emissions from Landfills	125.7	2%
Emissions from Substitutes for Ozone Depleting Substances	110.4	2%
Fugitive CH4 Emissions from Natural Gas Systems	102.4	1%
Fugitive CH4 Emissions from Coal Mining	58.5	1%
Indirect N20 Emissions from Applied Nitrogen	50.3	1%
CO2 Emissions from Iron and Steel Production	49.1	1%
CO2 Emissions from Cement Manufacture	45.7	1%
CO2 Emissions from Mobile Combustion - Marine	42.4	1%
CH4 Emissions from Manure Management	41.4	1%
Total Emissions without LULUCF	7017.3	95%

Source: U.S. EPA. 2008. Inventory of U.S. Greenhouse Gas Emissions and Sinks: 1990-2006.

Table 1: Major Sources and Types of U.S. GHG Emissions, 2006

ities and vehicles used on the nation's road are the three largest single contributors to U.S. emissions.

U.S. Land Use, Land Use Change, and Forestry

Land use, changes in land use, and changes in forest land affect the emission and removal of greenhouse gases from the atmosphere. Methane, nitrous oxide, and carbon dioxide are the main gases to consider when looking at land use, land use change and forestry. Land use, land use changes, and forestry can add to GHG emissions in a variety of ways. The application of synthetic fertilizers to forests and crop lands increases N_2O emissions. Forest fires also result in emissions of carbon dioxide, methane, and N_2O. Deforestation or conversion of pasture land to crop land increases emissions. In 2006, emissions from forest fires, fertilization, and land changes constituted about 5 percent of all U.S. emissions.[10]

On the other hand, the uptake of carbon dioxide from the atmosphere, or carbon sequestration, results from a number of practices including urban tree planting and forest management that preserves the number of trees. All vegetation acts as a sink for carbon, as does harvested wood not burned. Changes in vegetation on farm lands also act to sequester carbon dioxide. These changes are produced mostly by converting seasonal crop vegetation to permanent pastures and hay production. Growth of urban and rural forests along with increased acreage planted with trees increases carbon sequestration. The use of conservation tillage practices on farm land and increased use of organic fertilizers (manure) in agriculture allows soils to sequester carbon. In 2006, in total the use of these practices resulted in carbon sequestration that offset U.S. emissions by 883.7 Tg CO_2 Eq. or 12.5 percent of total GHG emissions, thus lowering U.S. net emissions to 6,170.5 Tg Co_2 Eq.[11]

Trends in U.S. GHG Emissions

Since the inventory began in 1990, U.S. emissions of GHGs have increased by 14.7 percent. U.S. emissions of CO_2 have increased on average a little more than 1 percent annually from 1990 to 2006.[12] These increases are due primarily to growth in the domestic economy, increased consumption of electricity, and increased use of transportation. Changes in patterns of consumption can be traced to an increasing population as well as price fluctuations, the dominant technology in use, and seasonal climate changes (warm winters and cool summers). Methane emissions have declined about 8 percent since 1990 in large part because of improvements in landfill gas capture and improvements in natural gas systems. N_2O emissions have come down by about 4 percent since 1990 in large part due to improvements in automobile control technologies. HFCs are up significantly since 1990 in large part because of the phase outs of CFCs under the Montreal Protocol and the use of HFCs as replacement chemicals. PFCs and SF_6 emissions have declined. Land use, land use changes and forestry trends since 1990 reveal a pattern of increasing sequestrations of GHGs.[13]

When long term trends are considered by economic sectors (with their use of electricity included in the analysis), the industrial sector has in recent years reduced its GHG emissions a slight bit. The transportation sector has increased its share of emissions since 1990 and continues to show an upward slope. The commercial and residential sectors have increased their emissions slightly while agriculture remains fairly flat. Analysis of trends with electricity generation disaggregated reveals that both electricity generation and transportation show steady upward trends in their contribution to GHG emissions since 1990. Agriculture as well as the commercial and residential sectors show very little change over the 16 years when their electricity use is considered separately. Industry shows a slight decline in its contribution to GHG emissions.[14]

Tracking Emissions

Tracking emissions is the first step to understanding and solving the problem of global warming. The United States, as a participant in the 1992 United Nations Framework Convention on Climate Change, is required to track GHG emissions annually and to report these emissions to the United Nations. The EPA tracks emissions and removals (sequestrations) and develops an annual report of the U.S. greenhouse gas inventory. The report also supplies information on the activities that cause emissions and removals, as well as an explanation of the methods used to make the calculations. The inventory report is used not only by policy makers but also by scientists for tracking, policy assessment, and for inputs into atmospheric and economic models.[15] The EPA uses IPCC guidelines to produce its annual inventory report.

In 2006 the IPCC published accepted methods for inventory tracking which are used internationally. The standards specify which gases need to be measured, the format for reporting, and the sectors and subsectors to be tracked. These include energy; industrial processes and products; agriculture, forestry and other land uses (AFOLU), and waste. Each sector is made up of categories (e.g., transportation) and sub-categories (e.g., cars). The IPCC methodologies require countries to construct their inventories from the sub-category level and to provide total emission by summation. Calculations of emissions consist of multiplying activity data (the extent to which human activity takes place) by emission factors (coefficients that quantify the emissions or removals per activity). For example, in the energy sector, fuel consumption constitutes activity data while CO_2 or other GHG emitted per unit of fuel consumed constitutes the emissions factor. This calculation is the basis of all reporting and is termed tier 1. However, more complex methodologies may be used to deal with issues associated with lag times between consumption and emissions (such as the lag associated with the time it takes material to decompose in landfills) and for allowing the use of more complex modeling. These are termed tier 2 and tier 3 methods and while they are more complex they are generally considered more accurate. Tier 1 methods are designed to use readily available national data with default emissions factors. The use of a higher tier methods is encouraged for key categories, that is activities that the inventory analyst determines contribute heavily to a country's emissions or removals.[16]

Within the U.S. many states and regions have established separate inventories. As of 2008, 46 states had completed a GHG inventory. Idaho's is in process and only Arkansas, South Carolina, Nebraska, and North Dakota have no policy for such a calculation. Many states use the inventory to help them create a Climate Change Action Plan. As of 2008, 32 states had completed such a plan and 6 are in process. However, 13 states have no policy in place to develop an action plan.[17]

California is a leader amongst the states in the development of a registry. In 2001, anticipating that carbon would eventually be regulated; California created the California Climate Action Registry (CCAR). It was begun as a private nonprofit organization formed by the state of California and serves as a voluntary registry for GHG reporting by corporations, universities, cities and counties, government agencies and environmental organizations.[18] Many companies voluntarily joined the registry with the hope that they would eventually get credit for early efforts they took to reduce their GHG emissions. When The Global Warming Solutions Act (AB32) took effect on January 1, 2007, all companies were required to register their emissions with the California Air Resources Board's (CARB) Mandatory Reporting program.[19]

The Climate Registry (TCR) is a sister organization of the CCAR that grew out of CCAR's initial efforts. Like CCAR, TCR is a voluntary reporting registry but it serves all of North America rather than just California. Both CCAR and TCR cover all 6 Kyoto gases (CO_2, CH_4, N_2O, PFCs, SF_6) and use U.S. EPA and IPCC emission factors for calculations.[20] TCR serves both businesses and governments. As of 2008, 40 U.S. states, 6 Mexican states, and 9 Canadian provinces were members.

Annex B countries that are parties to the Kyoto Protocol are required to have national greenhouse gas inventories that are used to determine compliance with reduction requirements. These data also provide a basis for understanding how well the various mechanisms of the Kyoto Protocol are working, especially emissions trading.[21]

Voluntary Regulation of Greenhouse Gases

The world first began its attempts to regulate GHG emission in the 1990s. The first of these efforts came with the United Nations Framework Convention on Climate Change which instituted a system of voluntary emissions reductions by member states. The failure of these states to lower their emissions under the voluntary regime resulted in the mandatory reductions implemented by the Kyoto Protocol. Since the U.S. did not ratify the Kyoto Protocol, no mandatory reductions were part of U.S. policy through the end of the Bush administration. Following the failure of the Senate to ratify Kyoto, the Clinton administration promised to stabilize GHG emissions by 2000 by reliance on a series of voluntary measures. This was ineffectual. The Bush administration's official policy was one of support for voluntary reductions only citing cost and potential harm to the U.S. economy as key reasons.[22] The Obama administration has called for an economy-wide cap-and-trade system for the U.S. but Congress must approach such a program before it would go into operation.

The corporate fight against mandatory regulation of GHG emissions in the U.S. was spearheaded by the Global Climate Coalition, an industry lobbying group organized by ExxonMobil. The Coalition tried to avoid regulation by aggressively working to discredit the scientific evidence behind climate change. Many leading U.S. companies were part of the coalition including General Motors, Chrysler, The Dow Chemical Company, Duke Energy Corporation, DuPont, Ford Motor Company, Southern Company, Shell Oil, BP America, and the U.S. Chamber of Commerce. The Global Climate Coalition was active until 2002 when it disbanded and many companies began to call for stable national regulation. The shift occurred for several reasons. Some companies were beginning to experience negative public relations as they became identified with anti-environmental positions. International companies already had to deal with the implementation of the Kyoto Protocol. The states were beginning to put together their own and regional GHG reduction plans and many companies preferred one national plan rather than many state and regional regulations. Uncertainty makes planning very difficult so many of the companies decided to quit fighting to achieve some certainty. Many of these companies began to realize that regulations would be forthcoming and they wanted to position themselves so that they could have some influence over the type of regulations adopted.[23]

Efforts by companies and environmental groups to push for mandatory national GHG regulations resulted in the creation of the United States Climate Action Partnership (USCAP) in 2006. The founding members of USCAP included Alcoa, BP America, Caterpillar, Duke Energy, DuPont, and General Electric. They joined Environmental Defense, Natural Resources Defense Council, Pew Center on Global Climate Change and the World Resources Institute—four major environmental organizations. Their goal is to push Congress to "enact legislation requiring significant reductions of greenhouse gas emissions" and to "guide the formulation of a regulated economy-wide, market-driven approach to climate protection."[24] Since its inception, USCAP has grown to include a number of additional companies including AIG, Chrysler, ConocoPhillips, Deere & Company, The Dow Chemical Company, Exelon, Ford, General Motors, Johnson & Johnson, PepsiCo, Shell, Siemens, and Xerox. Additional environmental partners include National Wildlife Federation and The Nature Conservancy. USCAP advocates a national cap-and-trade system with allowances given freely to participants. They seek a system with credits for early actions taken as well as flexible mechanisms including offsets for projects that promote removals (sinks).[25]

Voluntary programs to reduce GHG emissions include nonprofit organizations such as TerraPass, an offset web site that allows individual or business members to purchase offsets. TerraPass uses the money to invest in projects that reduce GHG emissions. TerraPass uses an independent third party auditor to verify its activities. Its projects include farm methane management, landfill gas capture, and wind power. The site allows individuals and businesses to calculate their carbon footprint and then to purchase offsets in the same amount.[26] There are a number of offset vendors, many of which specialize in offsetting air travel.

In 2002 a voluntary carbon market opened in the United Kingdom. The UK Emissions Trading Scheme (ETS) ran through 2006. Its primary objective was to develop expertise before the establishment of mandatory markets associated with the Kyoto Protocol. It was not a full cap-and-trade system in which members have strict emissions limits; rather it was a hybrid system that included some members under a cap-and-trade system and others under a credit-based system in which members had relative reduction targets that allowed for company growth and even increases in GHG emissions. The UK ETS was generally not perceived to be an effective system for emissions reductions in part because its voluntary status resulted in the exclusion of high GHG producers from participation.[27]

In 2003, the Chicago Climate Exchange (CCX) opened for voluntary trading of carbon emissions by American businesses. The CCX is the only carbon market in North America. It was the world's first integrated GHG emissions registry, reduction and trading system. CCX members include American Electric Power, DuPont, Ford, IBM, Bayer, Tampa Electric, Green Mountain Power, University of Minnesota, Tufts University, World Resources Institute, and Rocky Mountain Institute. CCX includes as members cities including Portland, Oregon; Oakland, California; and Chicago, Illinois; and the state of New Mexico.[28] The CCX has about 130 members who enter into legally binding agreements to cut their emissions by a certain amount within a specified time frame. If they are successful in meeting their goals, they receive credits they can sell or bank. If they fail to meet the goals, they have to purchase credits on the exchange.[29]

Criticism of voluntary regulatory measures centers on the fact that participation is not mandatory and thus few organizations, businesses, and individuals take part. Voluntary regulation produces far fewer results than does mandatory regulation that compels participation and imposes penalties for lack of compliance.

Mandatory Regulation of Greenhouse Gases

The Kyoto Protocol established a cap-and-trade system as the administrative mechanism to support its mandatory GHG reductions. The Protocol replaced the system of voluntary GHG reductions established under the UNFCCC because the latter simply did not produce results. As a result of the Kyoto Protocol, carbon trading was implemented among Annex B states. The trading system was modeled after the successful U.S. mandatory SO_2 trading system that was initiated as part of the Acid Rain Program of the Clean Air Act of 1990.

Cap-and-trade systems establish an overall cap, or the maximum allowed emissions, and issue allowances to those who operate under the system. Each allowance represents authorization to emit. If polluters wish to emit more than their allocated amount, they must purchase additional allowances on the carbon trading market. These additional allowances are made available by other potential polluters who manage to reduce their emission bellow their authorized amount and can therefore offer them for sale. The central idea is that over years the cap is lowered, thus reducing overall emissions, while polluters are free to meet their established goals in the most cost effective way.

The largest mandatory GHG emissions trading market in the world is the European Union Emissions Trading Scheme (EU ETS). About 85 percent of trading volume of the EU ETS is operated by the European Climate Exchange (ECX), a subsidiary of the Chicago Climate Exchange. Over 50 leading businesses are members. Members of the ECX include banks such as Barclays, Goldman Sacks, Morgan Stanley, Merrill Lynch and Deutsche Bank as well as energy companies including Shell, BP, and Sempra Energy Europe.[30] The ECX provides a European platform for carbon emissions trading with standardized contracts and uniform procedures to enable transparent and verifiable transactions.[31] By 2007 the world's carbon markets were trading US$64 billion worth of carbon allocations. In that year the EU ETS itself traded US$50 billion.[32] Carbon markets are a fast growing commodity. Estimates are that global carbon markets will grow to US$3 trillion over the next two decades.

While phase I of the Kyoto Protocol was effective in establishing a functioning market, there is a question regarding its impact on emissions reductions. One of the major criticisms of the cap-and-trade system under the Kyoto Protocol is that too many allowances (the cap) were issued resulting in the price collapse of the market in 2006 when it became known that supply of allowances exceeded demand.[33] Allegations of fraud and double-counting also raise questions about the accuracy of using offsets to meet emissions goals. These complaints have resulted in new international standards to increase transparency.[34]

The first U.S. based mandatory cap-and-trade system is associated with the Regional Greenhouse Gas Initiative. In 2003 New York proposed and got commitments from 9 states in the northeast for RGGI with a mandatory cap-and-trade system for carbon. In 2006, the CCX established the New York Climate Exchange (NYCX) and the Northeast Climate Exchange (NECX) to develop financial instruments for the cap-and-trade portions of RGGI.[35] RGGI launched on January 1, 2009.

Other efforts seem likely to use cap-and-trade schema. Like RGGI, the Western states along with British Columbia and Manitoba in partnership with the Western Climate Initiative are pursuing a cap-and-trade scheme. WCI includes California, Oregon, Washington, New Mexico, Arizona, Utah, Montana, British Columbia and Manitoba. WCI calls for the establishment of a cap-and-trade system by the end of 2009.[36] California's AB 32, passed in 2007, commits the state to the first economy-wide emissions reductions, likely to be implemented using a cap-and-trade approach.[37] The commitment of the Obama administration to a national cap-and-trade system will likely build on the carbon markets already in development for use by states and regions.

Carbon Tax

Part of the allure of a cap-and-trade scheme is that it is market-based. Beginning in the 1980s, the United States began to look to the market as a source of innovation for regulation. The deregulatory impulse that began in that decade was founded on a belief that markets could be used more effectively than traditional command and control regulation. Markets were seen as the source of innovation, efficiency, and effectiveness while traditional government regulatory action was looked on as failing on most if not all of those criteria. Traditional command and control approaches imposing fixed limits on emissions and designating emissions reduction or abatement technologies were rejected.

Efforts emerged to use the market, whenever possible, to implement government policy. Using market-mechanisms was first implemented as part of the acid rain program under the Clean Air Act. This proved successful and so the idea of expanding the use of cap-and-trade schemes to other pollutants became popular. At the urging of the U.S., the Kyoto Protocol adopted cap-and-trade as its primary mechanism for emissions reductions. Despite the fact that U.S. pulled out of the agreement, international carbon markets were established. Domestic carbon markets were also established to manage both voluntary and mandatory state and regional GHG emissions reduction efforts.

Not all analysts think that such markets are the best way to regulate emissions. A carbon tax is an alternative to both traditional command and control regulation and cap-and-trade schemes. Carbon taxes work by raising the cost and price of products that produce GHG emissions, thus discouraging their use. Carbon taxes would likely be implemented as internationally "harmonized" by multinational agreements.[38]

There are several issues with the carbon tax approach. A tax would not assure a certain reduction of GHG emissions as would a cap. However, a tax has the added benefit of producing a predictable revenue stream that could be used for abatement efforts. Or, if a nation decided that the carbon tax should be revenue neutral, revenues could be returned to the taxpayers through reductions in other taxes (such as payroll taxes in the United States). Alternatively, revenues could be returned to energy producers earmarked as R&D funds for new research on renewables. The fact that a carbon tax would produce a predictable revenue flow to government might also be a potential problem. If policy makers viewed the tax as a new source of revenue to be used to finance other government obligations rather than as a means to abate pollution then the tax would not achieve its purpose. A carbon tax has the benefit of being transparent and will not result in the development of a cadre of carbon traders, as a cap-and-trade system by necessity will.

Any policy mechanism used to reduce GHG emissions will share three critical characteristics. First, a carbon tax shares the same pitfall as the Kyoto Protocol's cap-and-trade system in the need to ensure that developing nations participate in efforts to lower their emissions. A carbon tax, to be effective in the long run, would have to include all nations but it might be phased in at certain GDP per capita levels to allow developing countries time to join the regime over time. Whether the administration is done by a tax or a cap-and-trade regime, the key reality is that there must be global participation to solve this global problem. Second, regardless of whether a cap-and-trade or tax regime is used, the price of fossil fuel will increase. The question of how to manage who pays the most of those increases and who will be hurt the most is a question of social justice that will have to be addressed regardless of the mechanism. Third, whether GHG reductions are achieved by a tax or by trading emissions, enforcement needs to be considered and compliance needs to be attained.

Several U.S. cities and counties have experimented with a carbon tax. Boulder, Colorado became the first municipality to implement a carbon tax beginning in 2006. The tax charges citizens $1.33 extra per month on their electric bills, while businesses pay $3.80 additional. The funds are used to put in place energy programs that will reduce overall energy use.[39] The San Francisco Bay area voted in 2008 to charge businesses in 9 Bay area counties a carbon tax of 4.4 cents per ton of emissions. The tax is not high enough to alter behavior but the revenue generated will fund energy use reduction programs.[40]

Rex Tillerson, CEO of the world's largest oil company, ExxonMobil, in a sweeping change of position announced in January of 2009 support for a carbon tax. This dramatic shift in position was owed to the increasing pressure that ExxonMobil is feeling regarding its long-held stand against regulation of GHG emissions. Some of that criticism came from the Rockefeller family at the 2008 annual shareholder's meeting. Tillerson's support for the tax, as opposed to a cap-and-trade approach, stems from his belief that a tax would be a more efficient way of reflecting the cost of carbon in all decisions, including investment decisions made by firms as well as product choices made by consumers.[41]

Renewable Portfolio Standards and Feed-in Tariffs

Efforts to promote the use of renewable energy are a form of regulation linked to GHG emissions reductions. Renewable portfolio standards are legal requirements that electricity generators use a mandatory percent of renewable energy sources to produce their electricity. RPS come in a variety of forms but most attempt to create a friendly albeit competitive market for energy produced from renewables, a dependable source of purchasers, and a trading market based on Renewable Energy Certificates which are used by generators to show compliance with PRS laws or policies. The key to any RPS is that it creates an on-going demand for renewable energy thus encouraging independent supplies to enter the market. As late as 2009, the U.S. did not have a national RPS; however, many states have established their own RPS laws or policy goals to promote the use of renewable energy. The Obama administration called for a national standard immediately after inauguration.

Renewable Portfolio Standards came into use when the U.S. moved to deregulation of the electric industry in the late 1970s. Electricity generation in the United States, since its beginnings with Thomas Edison's 1882 New York City plant, had been characterized by large centralized power plants. These huge utilities, serving large geographic regions, possessed monopoly ownership of production equipment, transmission lines, and control over retail delivery. Accordingly, they were highly regulated. The structure of the electricity generators came under study during the wider policy debates that emerged in the 1970s and 1980s regarding the value of deregulation for the transportation and communications sectors. The idea behind the deregulatory movement was that the introduction of competition would decrease prices for consumers. Electric deregulation also brought the opportunity for states to address the issue of energy dependence by reexamining the mix of fuels used for electricity generation.

The national restructuring of the electricity industry began in 1978 with the passage of the Public Utilities Regulatory Policies Act (PURPA). Passed in the years of the OPEC oil price shocks, PURPA required utilities to compare the costs of adding new capacity (termed "avoided cost") with the cost of purchasing electricity from independent power producers using renewable energy and to select the least expensive option. States were given the authority to set the avoided cost level and to determine the point at which mandatory renewable energy purchases would be required. The 1992 Energy Policy Act expanded PURPA to include a wider range of electricity generators, effectively creating a deregulated wholesale market for electricity across the United States. This law allowed independent power producers from any geographical region to sell electricity to industry or utilities in other regions of the country. Transmission lines were opened to facilitate such a market.[42] The restructuring of the wholesale market for electricity was accompanied, to a certain extent, by restructuring of the retail market as well. The decision of whether to allow consumers a choice in their purchase of electricity is one of the ways states restructured their retail markets. Several states put in place programs that required retailers to disclose the energy mix used to produce electricity and to permit customers to select a renewable energy option. Some states also moved toward restructuring their retail markets by introducing competition between providers.[43]

A number of states took advantage of the window opened by deregulation to address the issue of increasing the amount of renewable energy in their overall electricity generating energy portfolio. A variety of different policy mechanisms were tried. For example, in 1998 California put in place the use of production incentives to encourage the use of renewable energy. A series of subsidies paying a fixed rate per kilowatt hour (kWh) of electricity produced from renewables were offered. Pennsylvania, in 2000, put in place a program adapted from the California model but tailored it to supporting wind power alone.[44] Minnesota, in 2002, provided $9 million to support the development of commercial biomass and wind power.[45] California, Pennsylvania, and Massachusetts each initiated buy-down programs for solar panels—that is, providing customers rebates or tax credits for a percentage of the cost for the purchase and installation of solar panels. The California program merely returned a percentage of the capital cost for installed capacity. Pennsylvania and Massachusetts returned a higher percentage of capital cost based upon the performance efficiency of the solar cells installed.[46] Several states experimented with putting a renewable portfolio standard in place at the time of retail restructuring (Connecticut, Maine, Massachusetts, Nevada, New Jersey, Pennsylvania and Texas) and others considered it (Arizona, Iowa, Vermont and Wisconsin).[47] These programs were very popular and spread to many states. By 2007, 22 U.S. states had RPS laws or policies.[48]

RPS designs vary. Either retail suppliers or generators of electric power may be required to purchase renewable energy. RPS are generally implemented using a system of tradable Renewable Energy Certificates to track renewable energy purchases and to assure compliance. Using tradable RECs can make an RPS flexible and reduce the administrative overhead necessary for enforcement. With tradable RECs, the retailer or generator of electricity must obtain credits equal to their RPS obligation. This obligation can be determined by requiring a fixed percentage of total Megawatts (MW) produced or sold to be from renewables.[49]

To meet these requirements, retail suppliers or generators can either construct and operate their own facilities using renewables, purchase RECs packaged with renewable power from independent renewable energy providers, or purchase RECs from a private credit market (without purchasing the energy itself). The RECs set up several desirable features. By providing compliance flexibility, they reduce the overall cost of the RPS. Also, the use of tradable RECs ensures that the cheapest sources of renewables will be developed first, thus lowering the cost of renewable energy overall. With the use of RECs retailers or generators do not have to develop their own sources of renewables if they do not want to because they can purchase credits to fulfill their obligations on the open market.[50]

An alternative approach is the feed-in tariff (FIT) which has been used successfully in Europe and is under some use in several U.S. states. FITs require electric utilities to provide long-term fixed price contracts to renewable energy generators. Most FITs also require the utilities to provide the interconnections necessary so that all renewable energy generators can "feed in" to the grid. FITs have been successful in Europe where they have driven explosive growth in renewable energy. FITs have spread worldwide. As of 2007, 18 European Union countries, Brazil, Indonesia, Norway, Israel, South Korea, Nicaragua, Sri Lanka, Switzerland, and Turkey had FITs in place. The oldest of these FITs was established in Germany in the 1990s and under it renewable energy generators were given contracts for fixed payments for the renewable energy they produced for 20 years. FITs in Germany, Spain, and Denmark have resulted in the installation of 53 percent of the world's total wind energy capacity between 1990 and 2005.[51]

Germany's FIT has been central to the creation of a new industry in about 15 years. By 2006, Germany employed 214,000 people in the renewable energy sector and Spain over 100,000. Estimates are that if the U.S. was to put in place a similar FIT, an industry could be created employing over 350,000. As more and more countries adopt policies that require the introduction of renewables into their energy supply sources, these job opportunities will continue to grow. In addition, the demand for new technologies, will drive costs down and create a set of related jobs in management, sales, installation, service, advice, and technical support. [52]

Germany's FIT has also created the world's largest solar energy market. Germany's government has stated that because of the FIT Germany will be getting 27 percent of its energy from renewables by 2020, and consequently avoiding the release of 59 million tons of GHGs. The EU studied the effects of FITs versus RPS with tradable RECs and in 2005 released a report showing that FITs were generally more effective and efficient in large part because the stable prices produced with a FIT created investor confidence and lowered the cost of capital used to finance renewable projects. FITs are being introduced in the U.S. typically as a special condition under a RPS. Several states use FITs to promote adoption of a specific technology under their general RPS rules. Several states (California, Texas, New York, and Connecticut) are using the FITs long-term fixed price tariffs to contract for the development of utility-scale renewable energy generators. [53]

The Obama administration has set a national goal for the expanded use of renewables. The pledge is for 10 percent of U.S. electricity to come from renewable sources by 2012, and 25 percent by 2025. What policy mechanisms will be used to meet these goals is not yet apparent but both a national RPS and a FIT are likely under consideration.

Conclusion

The partial regulation of GHG emissions in the U.S. by 2009 was due to a mix of voluntary and mandatory regulations along with the adoption of renewable energy promotion strategies in the states and regions. When the Obama administration took office, no national mandatory regulations for GHG emissions existed although several regional agreements among the states had begun to phase in such regulations. During the years of the Bush administration, the U.S. had withdrawn from the Kyoto Protocol, which had been negotiated under the Clinton administration, and relied only on voluntary reductions of emissions. That policy did not produce any reduction in U.S. emissions.

By the end of the Bush administration, combustion of coal, primarily to generate electricity, accounted for 29 percent of U.S. emissions. The other major sources of emissions included another 23 percent from road-based transportation, 16 percent from stationary combustion of gas, and 8 percent from stationary combustion of oil. These 4 sources accounted for 76 percent of U.S. GHG emissions. If other uses of fossil fuels are included in the total, such as marine use and aviation, the total comes to more than 80 percent. Compliance with the Framework Convention on Climate Change requires tracking and annual reporting of emissions according to IPCC guidelines.

By the end of the Bush administration, some organizations crucial to tracking and administering emissions had emerged. A rudimentary U.S. carbon market, first in the form of the Chicago Climate Exchange and later including the Northeast and New York Climate Exchanges, had emerged to support emissions trading under a cap-and-trade emissions reduction scheme. Until trading under RGGI went into effect in 2009, such transactions were voluntary. Other voluntary markets, like TerraPass, were created to allow individuals and businesses to track and offset their emissions. To support the cap-and-trade scheme under the Kyoto Protocol, an international carbon market developed. The European Union Emissions Trading Scheme and the European Climate Exchange, a subsidiary of the Chicago Climate Exchange, became the largest carbon markets. While the carbon markets emerged, debate continued as to their effectiveness in comparison to a carbon tax.

The Obama administration took office with a commitment to change U.S. energy and environmental policy. The Obama administration came out in favor of a mandatory cap-and-trade scheme to reduce U.S. GHG emissions, to build a clean energy future, to support greater reliance on renewable energy, and to make the U.S. a leader on climate change.[54] Each of these goals is a profound reversal of the policies undertaken during the Bush administration. What these commitments mean for the partially built emissions reduction system that emerged without federal leadership under the Bush administration remains to be seen.

7

Technological Solutions

Global warming poses a great threat to life on Earth. We must find ways to reduce emissions so that atmospheric levels of greenhouse gases can be stabilized. At the same time, global warming is already under way. Every nation on the planet is already feeling its impacts so in addition to reducing GHG emissions that will have devastating impacts in the future, we must simultaneously adapt to a changing planet. Technology has a huge role to play in both.

A large number of technologies have applications that may help provide a global warming solution. Some of these technologies are off-the-shelf, that is, are fully developed and ready for deployment. Some are already in use but their use needs to be expanded. Other technologies need further research and development or research, development, and demonstration (RD&D) before they can be expected to be adopted by public and private sector organizations and thus diffused through society.

For the United States, the technologies that may play a substantial role in mitigating GHG emissions are those that can be applied to the greatest sources of U.S. emissions—CO_2 emissions from stationary combustion of coal; CO_2 emissions from cars, trucks, and other mobile sources; CO_2 emissions from stationary combustion of gas; and CO_2 emissions from stationary combustion of oil. Together these accounted for 76 percent of U.S. GHG emissions in 2006. Technologies that can be applied to the electric power industry and transportation are especially crucial because 34 percent and 28 percent of U.S. emissions, respectively, come from these sectors.[1] Clearly, energy technologies are particularly important in this mix.

Non-fossil fuel sources of energy include wind, solar, biomass, hydroelectric, wave, and geothermal. After a brief overview of energy use in general, the technologies associated with the use of energy from each of these sources are discussed in this chapter. In addition to these sources, the chapter will explore the use of storage technologies in general and batteries in particular. These are important because many sources of non-fossil fuel energy are intermittent as well as because hybrid and electric cars rely on batteries. The potential increased use of batteries as an energy source raises important questions about how the batteries are charged. If the charge comes from renewable energy, then use of batteries will be clean. If, however, the charge comes from coal, GHG emissions will be part of battery use. Such considerations are obviously important. In addition with batteries, the eventual disposal must be a factor. Each of these technologies is currently in use but R&D continues on each of them. Improvements may come making them better technologies in the fight against climate change. The chapter discusses the continuing R&D for each technology.

Since it is unlikely that we will at any time in the near future end the use of coal for the production of electricity, it is important to consider technologies that will allow for its continued use through long-term carbon sequestration. The chapter will discuss the R&D for carbon capture and storage (CCS) technologies and the prospects for clean-coal. A great deal of hope is attached to the use of hydrogen as a source of energy. Before hydrogen can be used as a fuel it first has to be generated in sufficient quantity. As with batteries, the source of the generation may or may not be sustainable or free from GHG emissions. Renewed interest in nuclear energy as a viable energy source has been spawned by the climate crisis. The chapter discusses the controversy sounding the use of nuclear power as part of the energy portfolio. The chapter concludes with a discussion of geoengineering as a potential technical solution for global warming.

Renewable Energy Use

Modern societies run on energy. Households, businesses, government and the civil sector depend on reliable affordable energy. Energy is needed for heating, air conditioning, transportation, refrigeration, manufacturing, industrial processes, agricultural production, communications, and to run electronic equipment. Dependable and reasonably priced sources of energy are essential to the smooth operation of modern economies and societies.

Developed nations primarily rely on fossil fuels for their energy needs, and have since the Industrial Revolution. Coal, oil, and natural gas fuel factories, provide for transport, and supply household needs. There is a direct relationship between fossil fuel use and development, especially in the early stages of development, so energy use among developing nations increases as they develop. Fossil fuel use has many drawbacks not the least of which is its contribution to global climate change. Fossil fuels are also limited in quantity and will eventually be exhausted. For the United States and other nations without sufficient domestic supplies of the needed types of fossil fuels, the use of these fuels traps countries in a spiral of imports of fossil fuels and exports of cash resulting in both a massive transfer of wealth and a security threat. The security threat becomes greater when exporting countries are not friendly to importing countries.

Energy can also be derived from sources that are sustainable. Often these sources are common geological features such as sunshine, blowing wind, moving water, or geothermal heat released from the Earth. Sources of sustainable energy can be grown when agricultural production is used for energy crops. This biomass can be replanted year after year to provide a virtually limitless source of energy. Waste can be converted into fuel when agricultural and forest wastes or landfill gas is burned.

All fuels need technology and a developed infrastructure to function. The technology and infrastructure that supports the use of fossil fuels is well developed. It includes pipelines, tankers (ocean and road), refineries, railroads, power plants, and transmission lines. The technology and infrastructure needed to support the use of sustainable energy has not yet been fully developed. Shifting to a society that relies primarily on sustainable sources of energy makes logical sense for environmental, security, and long-term viability reasons but making the transition is not easy. The fossil fuel economy and infrastructure are well entrenched. Diffusion of new technologies and processes takes time and often requires assistance to get over the barriers of initial adoption. This is where public policy plays a crucial role. While energy is and will remain a private sector industry, the public sector does play a role in helping sustainable energy gain a foothold in the economy.

It is also important to point out that conservation and energy efficiency have a large and important role to play in the movement toward a sustainable energy society. Green building designs that drastically reduce the need for heating and air conditioning, advanced designs for transport including vehicles designed to run partially or totally on ethanol or electric power that vastly increase mileage, as well as energy efficient appliances and lighting are all of enormous value. The more conservation and energy efficiency are brought into play, the easier it will be to provide for remaining energy needs using renewables.

The current use of renewable sources of energy in the U.S. is small. Consumption of all forms of energy in the U.S. in 2003 was 98.22 quadrillion BTUs (Quads)[2]. Of this about 40 percent was consumption of energy from petroleum products, 23 percent natural gas, 23 percent coal, 8 percent nuclear power, and 6 percent renewable energy.[3] Of that 6 percent, 1 percent was from solar, 46 percent was from biomass, 5 percent was from geothermal, 46 percent was from hydroelectric, 2 percent was from wind, and 1 percent was from solar.[4] In 2003, of the 3,883 billion kilowatthours (kWh) of electricity generated in the United States, about 71 percent came from fossil fuels, 20 percent from nuclear power, 7 percent from hydroelectric plants, and the remaining 2 percent from non-hydro renewables. Of that 2 percent, 71 percent was derived from biomass, 16 percent from geothermal, 13 percent from wind, and less than 1 percent from solar and photovoltaic sources.[5]

By 2007, not much had changed. In that year, 101.61 Quads of energy were consumed in the U.S. The increased use reflects both the growth of the economy over those years and the growth in population. Fossil fuels comprised 85 percent of the energy consumed. Petroleum consumption was 39 percent of total consumption, coal 22 percent, and natural gas 23 percent. Nuclear had remained steady at 8 percent. Renewable energy had grown by 1 percent to 7 percent of the total energy consumed in the U.S. in 2007.[6] Table 1 shows U.S. energy consumptions by energy source between 2002 and 2007.

One of the main barriers to renewable energy is its costs. In 2007, the

U.S. Energy Consumption by Energy Source, 2003-2007
(Quadrillion Btu)

Energy Source	2003	2004	2005	2006	2007
Total	98.209	100.351	100.503	99.861	101.605
Fossil Fuels	84.078	85.830	85.816	84.662	86.253
Coal	22.321	22.466	22.795	22.452	22.786
Coal Coke Net Imports	0.051	0.138	0.044	0.061	0.025
Natural Gas	22.897	22.931	22.583	22.191	23.625
Petroleum	38.809	40.294	40.393	39.958	39.818
Electricity Net Imports	0.022	0.039	0.084	0.063	0.106
Nuclear	7.959	8.222	8.160	8.214	8.415
Renewable	6.150	6.261	6.444	6.922	6.830
Biomass	2.817	3.023	3.154	3.374	3.615
Biofuels	0.414	0.513	0.595	0.795	1.018
Waste	0.401	0.389	0.403	0.407	0.431
Wood Derived Fuels	2.002	2.121	2.156	2.172	2.165
Geothermal	0.331	0.341	0.343	0.343	0.353
Hydroelectric Conventional	2.825	2.690	2.703	2.869	2.463
Solar/PV	0.064	0.065	0.066	0.072	0.080
Wind	0.115	0.142	0.178	0.264	0.319

Source: Energy Information Administration (EIA), May 2008

Table 1: U.S. Energy Consumption by Energy Source, 2003-2007

average cost of residential electricity in the U.S. was 10.64 cents per kilowatt hour. Prices vary by state with a low of 6.35 cents per kilowatt hour in Idaho to a high of 24.13 cents per kilowatt hour in Hawaii. That high represents and extreme as the highest price in the lower 48 states was 18.67 cents per kilowatt hour in Connecticut.[7] It is against this cost that renewables must compete if they are to make significant market penetration.

While current forms of renewables remain a small source of power used in the world and the United States, they will become an increasing part of the energy story as time moves on. New sources of renewable energy will be invented and this will increase their use. Also, better ways to make use of existing sources and increased reliance on them will increase their overall contribution to the world's energy supply. The advantages of renewables are too great to overlook and in a carbon-constrained world their development and extended use will be necessary.

Wind Energy

The widespread development of wind power in the U.S. began after the energy crisis of 1973 with the development of demonstration projects by the Department of Energy (DOE) and NASA.[8] Wind-generated electricity has been the fastest growing alternative energy source in the last few decades. By the end of 2006, total world wind energy capacity was over 74,000 MW representing a capital investment of over $100 billion. Annual growth in worldwide wind capacity is about 25 percent. Total U.S. capacity by the end of 2006 was 11,600 MW or nearly 16 percent of the world's total capacity.[9] That said, wind energy produced slightly more than 0.3 percent of all the energy consumed in the U.S. in 2007.[10]

Wind energy currently is typically generated by large industrial wind mills that feed their generation into the electricity grid, however, the U.S. has many examples of nonintegrated smaller wind mills being used historically for purposes such as pumping well water. Wind power is non-polluting in operation, emitting no greenhouse or other gases. It has been criticized for the noise the turbines produce, the unattractive visual display the turbines make, and for the fact that the turbines kill a fair share of birds. On the whole, wind power has a low impact on the environment — far lower than fossil fuel or nuclear power — and it is sustainable. The cost of the wind itself is free so the costs of operation are associated only with turbine production, maintenance, and transmission.[11]

The U.S. has a very large potential for wind power. Wind energy capacity is rated on a scale of 1 to 6 where 3 is marginal, 4 is considered good, 5 is very good, and 6 is excellent. A rating of 3 indicates that wind speeds average 12 mph at 33 feet of elevation while a rating of 5 indicates average wind speeds of 14 mph at the same altitude. The top ranked wind states in the U.S. are North Dakota, Texas, Kansas, South Dakota, Montana, and Nebraska. Each has the potential to generate more electricity than is produced by the U.S. nuclear industry, however, potential is not production. Large-scale wind energy development costs are between 4 and 6 cents per kilowatt hour, depending on the site, making wind energy a viable economic alternative to other forms of power production.[12]

Wind has problems associated with its use. First, wind is intermittent which means that storage technologies and reserve capacities are required if wind is to be relied on as a sole source. But these problems can be overcome. A simple example is using wind power to pump water into high reservoirs of existing hydroelectric operations and then allowing that water to flow and produce electricity when the wind is not blowing. Intermittency can create problems for grid planning if it is fed directly into the grid. Forecasting of wind is not that accurate, which creates an additional set of problem for grid operators. Fluctuations in wind speed can create stability problems for the grid and increase the cost of grid management, especially as the percent of electricity on the grid coming from wind sources increases. Second, the windiest places are typically located far from population centers where electricity is consumed. This creates a problem of transmission. The states with high wind energy producing capability are located in the Midwest and Rocky Mountains but most of the U.S. population is located on the two coasts.[13] This same problem exists even within states. For instance, Texas is a high wind energy producer and a high population state but within the state the wind capacity is located in the west while the population is concentrated in the east.[14]

The development of offshore wind holds potential for taking greater advantage of higher and steady wind speeds. Off shore wind is under development in Europe and the United States although it has proved controversial in both locations due to concerns for esthetics as well as sea life. European countries have developed considerable offshore wind expertise. These facilities have the advantage of being closer to populations.[15] Smaller scale wind turbines are being developed for use primarily for off-grid applications. Urban wind turbines are also under development. These could link to rooftop solar cells and be tied to the grid. Such systems could use net metering to sell excess electricity produced back to the grid operators.[16]

Solar Energy

Solar power can be used in a variety of ways. Photovoltaic cells (PV) directly convert sunlight to electricity. Concentrating Solar Power (CSP) uses a series of mirrors to collect and reflect the solar energy, converting it into heat that can produce electricity thorough a steam turbine or heat engine that drives a generator.[17] Low temperature solar collectors use the sun to provide solar thermal energy for solar hot water, solar space heating, and solar pool heaters.[18]

A primary use of solar power is in the form of photovoltaic generation which directly converts sunlight into electricity. PV cells are a well known technology having received a great deal of advertisement after NASA adopted the technology for the space program. The price for solar cells has dropped considerably since then; however, PV cells remain relatively expensive. PV cells do offer a cost effective alternative to off-grid and small power applications but the extent of their penetration into the wider market depends of improved cell efficiency and lower costs. Efficiency continues to increase and cost keeps on decreasing as the market for PV cells grows. PVs are commonly used in telecommunications equipment, small consumer equipment, water pumps, gate openers, battery charging, vaccine refrigeration, and solar lighting. PV systems also provide power for utility scale power plants.[19]

Concentrating Solar Power provides either utility scale electricity generation or smaller on site generation. CSP plants make power by initially using mirrors to focus sunlight to heat a suitable fluid, which, when it reaches high temperatures, is used to drive a turbine or power an engine that drives an electricity generator.[20] Smaller CSP units can be located on the site where the electricity is needed and can produce up to 25 kilowatts of power. Larger units are capable of producing many megawatts and typically feed their production into the electricity grid. These larger units can be integrated with storage devices that allow for the uninterrupted supply of electricity during cloudy periods or at night. These can be combined with natural gas generators so that the fossil fuel source can be called upon when needed to provide reliable electricity supply.[21]

Low temperature solar collectors use both passive systems requiring no moving parts and active systems with some moving parts, to transfer the heat of the sun to water or a space to partially or totally offset the need to use other sources of power. The efficiency and reliability of solar heating systems have increased dramatically in the last decades, but R&D continues with the aim of designing even more cost-effective solar heating systems.[22]

Solar energy produced a trivial amount, less than .07 percent, of all the energy consumed in the U.S. in 2007.[23] The potential for solar power, though, is great. It has been estimated that even at 20 percent efficiency and with use on one percent of the land area of the U.S., PV systems could generate about eight times the current U.S. electricity generation, or about three times the total wind energy potential of the U.S. Despite this potential, solar power remains expensive, although prices are dropping. New developments in technology, such as the application of thin films solar, could result in significant cost reductions.[24] In 2009, the average cost of solar power in the U.S. was about 30 cents per kilowatt hour or about 2 to 5 times the cost of residential electricity across the country.[25]

Even as the cost of conventional PV comes down, conventional PV still depends on sunshine to generate electricity. Nanoantenna PV is a new class of PV that is being developed. Nanoantenna PV uses nanoscale gold antennas to convert infrared radiation emitted by any heat source to electricity. These nanoantenna PV could work not only during the day drawing on sunlight but also at night drawing on heat from the Earth or buildings. The potential is that this technology might be more efficient than traditional solar cells.[26]

Biomass

Biomass, the use of plants and animals for energy, has been used since prehistory. Today, innovative technologies tailored for the use of biomass allow for its use in applications ranging from heating homes to fueling cars and running electrical equipment.[27] Biomass comes from a variety of sources including agriculture, forests, brackish water ponds, and urban areas. Agricultural biomass includes harvest residues, process wastes, and energy crops such as corn. Forest biomass includes logging residues, mill residues, and woody energy crops. Urban biomass includes municipal solid waste, sewage, landfill gas, and used cooking oils. Saline water technologies can also make use of brackish water. This salty water grows algae industriously and these algae can be harvested to extract biodiesel feed stocks, a form of biomass that can be used to produce energy.[28] In 2007, the U.S. generated about 3.5 percent of its energy from biomass.[29]

A widely used application of bioenergy is ethanol which has drawn considerable interest since the energy crisis of the 1970s but progress toward more extensive in the U.S. was spotty. Some countries have had enormous success with bioenergy. Brazil uses sugarcane to produce ethanol and powers about 40 percent of its motor fleet using it. With rising costs of oil after 2005, ethanol production once again became popular. Under the Bush administration, ethanol production from corn was encouraged and by the end of 2006 ethanol production in the U.S. increased to nearly five billion gallons a year with the stated goal of increasing production to 35 billion gallons by 2017.[30] To achieve these goals, EPA announced new standards in 2007 that required refiners to use at least 7.5 billion gallons of ethanol in gasoline by 2012. The new standards had been authorized by the Energy Policy Act of 2005 which sought, among other things, to boost ethanol use.[31]

Ethanol derived from corn, however, has some untoward consequences. For instance, in 2008 as more of the world turned to producing greater amounts of the fuel from food crops, food prices climbed worldwide creating a situation of food insecurity in many nations. The United Nations warned that despite the benefits of biofuels, there are dangers including forests being cut to create new farm land and raising food prices.[32] Within the United States, climbing corn prices resulted in more land planted with corn in 2007 than since World War II.[33] The increased acreage planted resulted in a glut in refining capacity.[34] The situation eventually resulted in the bubble collapsing. In addition, there is some concern that ethanol produces more ground-level ozone than gasoline and could result in serious health effects.[35]

Ethanol and biodiesel derived from cellulosic feedstocks, such as corn stalks or other plant material could expand the amount of ethanol produced; however, the production costs about double those for using corn kernels. R&D needs to be done to reduce those costs to make cellulosic ethanol viable. For ethanol to be fully integrated into the transportation sector, two other shifts must occur. First, the number of cars that can run on fuel that is primarily composed of ethanol (E85 or higher) or higher blends of biodiesel needs to be increased. In 2006 only 4.5 million flexible fuel vehicles with this capacity were on U.S. highways. Second, the infrastructure for delivering ethanol and biodiesel to gas stations where it can be sold to consumers needs to be improved. In 2007 only about 1 percent of fueling stations in the U.S. offered E85 or higher blends of biodiesel as an option.[36]

Biofuels can also be produced from algae but more R&D needs to be done to convert algae to fuel on a commercial scale.[37] Several demonstration projects have shown that algae grow very quickly in the CO_2- rich environments of exhaust from fossil fuel power plants. Several demonstration projects have been undertaken in Massachusetts, Arizona, and Louisiana. This technology might have excellent impacts if commercialized as it would permit algae to capture and reduce some of the daytime emissions of fossil fuel power plants and cement manufacturing operations. The carbon captured in the algae is released when the algae are burned, but gasoline would not be burned and so its emissions would be offset. Algae have also been successfully grown in brackish and salt water.[38] Bioengineering is currently trying to develop bacteria, algae, and other microbes that can produce biofuels without the disruptive impact on food supplies that biofuels created from food sources possess.[39]

Wave and Tidal Energy

Since the oceans cover so much of the surface of the Earth, there is an interest in finding practical ways to exploit the energy in them. Electricity can be generated from the motion of waves or tides. Wave generators typically float on the surface of the water and the movement of the water can be tapped to drive a generator. The electricity is delivered to land via an underwater cable. Wave power is less intermittent than wind or solar. Wave energy might be a useful source of energy for some coastal regions. This technology, though, is still under R&D and has not yet been demonstrated in any large-scale project.[40] Tidal energy has been used to generate electricity by using the flow of water in tides to turn turbines. Tides are predictable and can be captured with precisions, however, tides only flow twice a day and so alternative sources of power need to be online when the tides are not moving.

Three types of wave energy technology are used. The first type uses pitching devices, buoys or floats to generate electricity using the rise and fall of ocean swells to drive hydraulic pumps. This fist type is the most commonly used. The second variety uses an oscillating water column device to generate electricity from the rise and fall of water within the column. Air is driven out of the column's top and this air dives a turbine. The third type uses a tapered channel or overtopping device that concentrates the wave and drives it into a reservoir. Electricity is generated when the water in the reservoir is released to drive a hydropower turbine. The world's first commercial wave power plant, generating 2.25 MW but expected to expand to 22.5 MW, is located off the shore of Portugal. Tidal power technologies typically involve building a tidal dam or tidal barrage across a narrow channel or bay. The water flows drive a turbine. The La Rannce power plant in France is the world's first and largest tidal barrage producing 260 MW of power. Tidal barrages have environmental impacts, including obstructing fish. Recent R&D on tidal energy has focused primarily on the development of underwater tidal turbines which are very similar to wind turbines. These tidal turbine farms are located offshore in strong currents and the electricity generated is delivered to land via an underground cable. A pilot tidal turbine farm was installed in New York's East River in 2006 by Verdant Power. The company hopes to expand the facility in the future to commercial scale. Wave and tidal power are emissions-free. There is some concern associated with marine life but the impact is expected to be small. They have an advantage over wind turbines as they have little visual impact.[41]

Geothermal Energy

Geothermal energy comes from the heat at the Earth's magma interior. In some places the heat transfers to rock and water close to the Earth's surface and this source can be drawn upon for its energy. While most of the Earth's geothermal resources are in the Pacific Rim, in the U.S. the base of geothermal resources are in the West. California, Alaska, and Hawaii hold the overwhelming majority of these resources for the U.S.[42]

Many technologies have been developed to make use of geothermal energy which can be drawn from steam or water reservoirs below the Earth's surface. These sources can be tapped by drilling into them. These resources can be used on both large and small scales. For instance, a utility can use the hot water and steam from reservoirs that are relative close to the surface of the earth to drive electric generators. The heat produced from geothermal sources can be directly used in buildings to provide heating and cooling in residential homes and public buildings. Some geothermal resources are miles beneath the earth's surface in the hot rock and magma. More R&D needs to be done to determine how these resources can be utilized.[43]

In 2007, the U.S. generated 0.3 percent of its overall energy from geothermal sources.[44] The largest geothermal production site in the world is in California, about 70 miles north of San Francisco. The Geysers, as the operation is named, consists of more than 20 separate power plants that produce more than 750 MW of electricity from steam wells that they tap. Since geothermal energy requires no fuel, it is emissions-free.[45]

Storage Technologies

Because wind and solar energy are likely to play an increasing role in renewable energy generation, having a viable storage technology is vital. Batteries are also essential to the continued development of hybrid and electric vehicles. There are several types of batteries including lead-acid, nickel-cadmium, sodium-sulfur, lithium-ion, zinc-air, and nickel-metal-hydride (NiMH). Each has difference costs and characteristics. Lead-acid batteries are reliable and low cost but they are also heavy which makes them problematic for certain applications. Nickel-cadmium batteries are a well established technology but they are expensive. Sodium-sulfur batteries provide good storage and can operate in high temperatures. Lithium-ion batteries are inexpensive but need more R&D. Zinc-air batteries are expensive and have a low life cycle. Nickel-metal-hydride batteries are popular and lightweight.[46] These NiMH batteries are currently used in hybrid cars.

R&D to find a battery that is inexpensive, lightweight, and capable of thousands of recharges has been underway for many years but breakthroughs are still awaited. The most promising technology for new breakthroughs is the lithium-ion battery. These new batteries will be similar to batteries used in cell phones and laptop computers but will not use carbon, which is a safety concern and the cause of several recalls of batteries used in laptops. Lithium-ion batteries using lithium-titanium oxide or lithium-iron oxide electrodes have characteristics that make them likely candidates for use in all-electric cars and for plug-in hybrids. They have a high storage capacity, can be charged and discharged 10,000 to 15,000 times without loss of performance, are safe, and can be recharged quickly. They are still too expensive but costs are coming down.[47]

The idea of using vehicles with storage capacity to exchange power with the grid when there is a need for greater grid power is one that has been considered since the 1990s. Passenger vehicles are parked about 95 percent of the time, so allowing vehicle-to-grid (V2G) transfers could allow utilities great flexibility. Utilities could contract with government or corporate fleets, for instance, to allow the utility to draw on the stored power in these vehicles when needed. Only a small fraction of the cars on the highways, perhaps 3 to 5 percent, would have to be under contract for a V2G system to work reliably. A V2G system could store electricity during off-peak hours and supply it during peak hours. A V2G system could also provide backup for wind power to compensate for intermittency. Many technical details of such a potential system have yet to be worked out but it seems likely that a global positioning system (GPS) or other technology could be used to locate vehicles available at any one time for V2G transfer, thus making such a system feasible.[48]

Ultracapacitors have the potential to provide a portable source of electrical storage. They are superior to chemical batteries in many ways. Capacitors store electricity as electrostatic force. Electrons can move in and out of a capacitor much faster than they could from a chemical battery, therefore the charging time is much faster. Also, batteries eventually degrade and need to be replaced when they can no longer take a charge but capacitors can be recharged virtually unlimitedly. While capacitors are not new, R&D on nanolaminate and polymer technology offers great potential for the development of a new generation of capacitors. These new capacitors will have the ability to store large amounts of energy in small, light, and durable packages making them far superior to chemical batteries.[49]

Carbon Capture and Storage

The idea behind carbon capture and storage (CCS) or sequestration is to reduce the amount of CO_2 at the source of its emission, particularly at power plants using coal to generate electricity. When coal is used to generate electricity, two pounds of CO_2 is emitted for every kilowatt generated. A 1000 MW coal power plant emits over 20,000 metric tons of CO_2 each day[50] or about 6 million tons per year.[51] The idea behind CCS is to capture the CO_2 before it is released into the atmosphere and permanently storing it so that it is never released. This can be done by absorbing the CO_2 from the total gas power plant emission and then storing it by injecting the CO_2 into underground storage such as old oil or gas wells or injecting it under the sea for storage under sediments. The CO_2 might also be redirected toward natural sinks like forests, vegetation, and soils where it could be directly used by the ecosystem.[52] Using saline reservoirs where the CO_2 could form a carbonate is a promising storage alternative that has been investigated by the state of Utah which has many saline reservoirs. The geological storage of CO_2 uses injection technology developed by the oil and gas industry for enhanced oil recovery but more R&D needs to be done to determine how long the CO_2 would remain isolation in geological storage and what leakage rates might occur.[53] Development of commercially viable CCS is important because so many coal power plants are in operation and will likely continue in operation into the near future.

Conventional coal power plants are carbon intense but a newer power plant technology called integrated gasification combined cycle (IGCC) might provide a solution. IGCC plants use heat and pressure to burn off the impurities in the coal and convert it into a gas which is then burned to turn a turbine. IGCC plants are more efficient than conventional coal plants, use far less water, and produce less ash and solid waste. It is much less expensive to capture CO_2 from an IGCC plant than from a conventional plant. The combination of IGCC with CCS might create a way for the continued burning of coal into the future without posing a threat to the climate.[54]

Beginning in 2003, the Department of Energy sponsored a multiyear R&D program to develop the world's first zero-emissions power plant using IGCC with CCS. Called FutureGen, the plan called for the integration of advanced coal gasification technology along with a hydrogen research initiative and carbon sequestration. The goal was initially stated as validating the technical feasibility and economic viability of IGCC with CCS by operating a 275 MW prototype plant that would produce both electricity and hydrogen with zero emissions. FutureGen was set up as a public-private partnership between DOE and an alliance of coal producers, electricity utilities, international participants, and state governments. Among the industrial partners were American Electrical Power, Southern Company, CONSOL Energy, Rio Tinto Energy America, Peabody Energy, PPL Corporation, BHP Billiton, Foundation Coal Corporation, China Huaneng Group, and Anglo American. FutureGen was to be a $1 billion cost-shared project.[55] By 2006, the Future-Gen Alliance had selected 12 competing sites in seven states as potential locations for the plant. These were narrowed down to 4 sites later that year.[56] The effort foundered primarily due to high cost and was restructured in 2008. The new effort seeks to partner with industry to build multiple IGCC commercial scale plants. The DOE will provide funding not for the plants but rather for the addition of CCS technology to plants that will be operational by 2015. The restructured FutureGen program abandoned the goal of producing hydrogen.[57]

Private sector efforts to capture CO_2 are also underway. One technique, developed by Alstom, aims at capturing carbon from conventional power plants by using chilled ammonia to absorb the gas. Demonstration projects are underway by American Electric Power, a major utility, at their Mountaineer plant in West Virginia. The demonstration project will use the chilled ammonia process to capture the CO_2 and then compress it into liquid form and inject it 9,000 feet below the surface.[58] This demonstration project is not commercial scale. If successful, a commercial scale demonstration project will follow.

CCS has some considerable problems associated with it. Carbon sequestration is expected to raise the price of electricity by 20 to 25 percent. Using the CO_2 for enhanced oil recovery could lower the cost, but that would not be possible in all regions of the country. The potential of sites to serve as geological repositories varies across the country. Texas, Wyoming, Illinois, and West Virginia are well suited but Georgia, North Carolina, South Carolina, Massachusetts, Vermont, and New Hampshire are not. Widespread implementation of geological sequestration of CO_2 would be a huge engineering project. Hundreds of underground sites would have to be surveyed, drilled, and maintained. The sheer quantity of CO_2 emissions coming from the nations power plants would necessitate a vast network of underground storage reservoirs.[59]

Hydrogen-Based Energy

Hydrogen, like electricity, is a clean energy carrier but its impact on the environment depends on how it is produced. If it is produced using renewable energy or nuclear power, its use will not emit greenhouse gases into the atmosphere. If it is produced using fossil fuels, then GHG emissions will occur. A great deal of R&D is underway on hydrogen fuel cells for transportation with the hope of making them commercially viable by 2020. Vehicles using fuel cells would be zero emissions vehicles and assuming the hydrogen was produced from clean energy sources, no GHG emissions would occur.[60]

While hydrogen is currently commercially produced using natural gas, production of it using renewable energy sources is still in the R&D stage. A potential idea is to use landfill gas to produce hydrogen; however, it would not produce large quantities. To generate the quantities of hydrogen that would be necessary to make it a viable fuel, other means would have to be used. Methods of producing hydrogen using solar power would likely involve using some type of feedstock, such as biomass, which is processed to produce hydrogen.[61] The Department of Energy runs a Hydrogen, Fuel Cells, and Infrastructure Technologies program which is engaged in R&D and working with industrial partners to speed the introduction of these technologies.[62]

Nuclear Energy

In 2007, nuclear power generated slightly more than 8 percent of all the energy used in the U.S. [63] and 19.4 percent of the electricity. The U.S. has 104 operating nuclear power plants, near a quarter of the world's 440 nuclear reactors. Worldwide, nuclear power accounts for 16 percent of the world's electricity. Thirty one countries have nuclear reactors.[64] Nuclear power became relatively unpopular in the United States after the 1979 Three Mile Island accident and in many European nations after the 1986 Chernobyl disaster. The Three Mile Island accident occurred in Harrisburg, Pennsylvania, and while no one was hurt, thousands of people were evacuated and for several days as the threat of a release of radioactive material was feared. The Chernobyl accident in a power plant near Kiev in what was then the Soviet Union was a much more severe event. An explosion and fire destroyed the plant and there was a massive release of radioactive substances into the environment. The Soviet government initially denied anything had happened, thus failing to warn people to stay indoors and away from the radioactivity. Eventually the release was picked up on European monitors and more than 100,000 people were evacuated. Land across Europe was affected as the radiation made its way across borders.[65]

Nuclear power is controversial not only because of these disasters that have soured many on the technology but also because of the nuclear waste produced by the reactors. Nuclear power, once thought of as power too cheap to meter, became very expensive. The last 20 nuclear reactors built in the U.S. cost ten times as much as a natural gas plant. The industry in the United States declined after the Three Mile Island accident. The European nuclear industry has a mixed record. Some countries, like France, are very favorable to the industry while others, like Germany, have put policies in place to eliminate nuclear plants. China, India, and Japan plan to increase their reliance on nuclear technology.[66] China plans to add 30 more reactors to their inventory by 2020 and India's goal is to generate 25 percent of its electricity from nuclear power by 2050. The International Atomic Energy Agency estimates that by 2025 another 60 nuclear plants will be built worldwide.[67]

The global climate crisis has spurred new interest in nuclear power as a way to deliver the increasing amounts of electricity demanded without increasing GHG emissions. As a consequence, nuclear power is on the rise in many parts of the world and is under reconsideration in nations where it had begun to decline after Three Mile Island and Chernobyl. Prominent environmentalists have come out in favor of nuclear power, including Hugh Montefiore of Friends of the Earth and Patrick Moore, cofounder of Greenpeace. Their support for nuclear energy has alienated them from many in the environmental community but it has also caused thoughtful contemplation by other environmental activists and countries.[68] Advocates for increased nuclear power use also argue that the waste must be recycled through reprocessing to reduce the quantity of waste and need to dispose of it. They suggest that nuclear power is the only viable option to deliver the growing demand for electricity worldwide.[69] Advocates also claim that newer reactor designs are safe and produce much less waste than older reactors.

Changed attitudes toward nuclear power are emerging. Sweden, for instance, had banned building new nuclear power plants but reversed that 30 year old ban in 2009. It now plans to replace its 10 operating reactors with new ones. Public support in Sweden has shifted as nuclear power has been seen as a weapon in the fight against climate change. British prime minister Gordon Brown wants to build a new generation of reactors across the UK. Germany is also considering its commitment to eliminate nuclear power from its portfolio.[70] Within the United States, applications for licenses for nuclear plants increased for the first time since Three Mile Island. The Nuclear Regulatory Commission anticipates applications for 25 new nuclear power plants.[71]

Geoengineering

Mention should be made of the variety of alternative approaches to reversing global warming that fall under the rubric of geoengineering. There are two general types of geoengineering: albedo management and carbon management. Albedo management reduces heat in the short-term by blocking or reflecting a small portion of the sunlight hitting the Earth. Carbon management uses a variety of techniques to sequester large amounts of atmospheric carbon. Albedo management includes cloud brightening, stratospheric particle injection to mimic the effects of a large volcanic eruption, and putting mirrors in space to reflect a portion of solar radiation back into space before it reaches the Earth. Carbon management techniques include biochar burial, trees and plants engineered to absorb more CO2, and air capture which uses a chemical process to capture CO_2 from the atmosphere.[72]

Developing techniques to cool the Earth is controversial in large part because some think it may take attention away from reducing GHG emissions or adaptation. Geoengineering is also thought of as being risky because of the unknowns associated with a planetary engineering project that may produce untoward or even devastating consequences. Practical problems arise in terms of world governance: Who should decide what action should be taken and in what time frame? If negative consequences occur, who is liable for them? Others, however, suggest that humans are already geoengineering the planet through their GHG emissions.[73]

Conclusion

Renewable energy comes from ordinary sources including sunshine, wind, the movement of water, the heat of the earth, and the growth of plants and animals. These sources of energy were used almost exclusively prior to the Industrial Revolution when the shift to fossil fuel use occurred. Coal, oil, and natural gas continue today to provide most of the energy used in the developed and developing world.

Fossil fuel use, however, poses problems. While there is controversy regarding when fossil fuel depletion will occur, there is agreement that these fuels will eventually be exhausted. There is a critical need to reduce greenhouse gases emissions associated with global climate change and to stabilize the atmospheric concentration of greenhouse gases at levels that will avert the most dire consequences of global warming. For both of these reasons, the search for alternative fuel sources is essential.

The development of a number of new technologies and their application to renewable and conventional sources of power are critical to solve the climate change problem. Key to these is the wind power. Wind-generated electricity has been the fastest growing alternative energy source in the last 20 years but wind energy produced slightly more than 0.3 percent of all the energy consumed in the U.S. in 2007. Wind energy is typically generated by large industrial wind mills that feed their generation into the electricity grid, however, smaller distributed applications of wind power are in development. Wind power is non-polluting in operation, emitting no greenhouse or other polluting gases. The U.S. has a very large potential for wind power. Large-scale wind energy development costs are between 4 and 6 cents per kilowatt hour, depending on the site, making wind energy a viable economic alternative to other forms of power production. Wind has problems associated with its use the most important of which is that wind is intermittent. This necessitates the development of storage technologies and reserve capacities if wind is to be reliable. An additional problem is that wind power is typically produced far from population centers where electricity is consumed and this creates a problem of transmission. Offshore wind and smaller scale off-grid and urban turbines have great potential

Solar power, either through PV cells or CSP, is an emerging alternative energy source for commercial scale production. Low temperature solar collectors are also effective for distributed solar hot water, solar space heating, and solar pool heaters. While promising, solar energy produces inconsequential amounts of all the energy consumed in the U.S. Improvements in efficiency and reductions in cost will have to occur before solar becomes a viable alternative energy source.

Innovative technologies tailored for the use of biomass allow for its use in applications ranging from heating homes to fueling cars and running electrical equipment. The U.S. generates more than 3 percent of its energy from biomass with ethanol being the most widely used application of bioenergy. Ethanol production and use has been on the increase in the last decade, favored both by energy legislation and administrative directive. Ethanol derived from corn, however, has some unanticipated and negative consequences. Production of fuel from food crops caused food prices to climb worldwide in the late 2000s, resulting in food insecurity in many nations. The United Nations also cautions about ethanol's impact on deforestation as more land is planted with corn. Within the United States, climbing corn prices resulted in a sharp shift to corn over other crops. The increased acreage planted was accompanied by a quick increase in refining capacity which turned out to be an oversupply and resulted in a market downturn. The key to using ethanol and biodiesel wisely is to produce it from cellulosic feedstocks rather than food crops. Although this increases the price of production, R&D may bring those prices down. For ethanol to be fully integrated into the economy, the number of cars that can run E85 or higher blends of biodiesel must be increased and the infrastructure for delivering ethanol and biodiesel to gas stations must be improved. R&D on promising other sources of biofuels, like algae, must continue.

Electricity generation from waves or tides appears to be a promising source of renewable energy. While several commercial power plants are in operation worldwide, more R&D needs to done if any reasonable amount of energy is to be supplied from waves and tides. Recent R&D has focused primarily on the development of underwater tidal turbines which could be grouped in tidal turbine farms and located offshore. Demonstration projects are underway.

Geothermal energy provides some hope of clean alternative energy. While the U.S. does not have many sources of geothermal power, some near surface applications have been commercially developed at utility scale. More R&D needs to be done to determine how hot rock and magma resources can be utilized. Less than one half of one percent of U.S. energy comes from geothermal applications.

The continued development of batteries may provide a solution to intermittent wind power generation and to the continued development of hybrid and electric vehicles. R&D to find a battery that is inexpensive, lightweight, and capable of thousands of recharges has been underway for many years but breakthroughs are still needed. When such batteries come into common use, they may become part of a vehicle-to-grid application. A V2G system could store electricity during off-peak hours and supply it during peak hours or provide backup for wind power to compensate for intermittency.

If coal is to remain a fuel source then carbon capture and storage must be developed. Carbon sequestration has some large negatives associated with it. It is costly. Sites suitable to act as long-term repositories have to be found. Widespread implementation of geological sequestration would be a very large engineering and infrastructure project as many underground sites would have to be surveyed, drilled, and maintained. CCS may be dependent on eliminating conventional coal power plants and replacing them with integrated gasification combined cycle plants that enable much less expensive CCS. Development of demonstration plants to combine IGCC with CCS and the production of hydrogen has proven illusive. The restructuring of FutureGen to eliminate hydrogen production and to reduce the programs cost have set this potential innovation back. Private sector efforts to capture CO_2 are underway and demonstration projects of commercial scale may be forthcoming.

Hydrogen is a clean energy carrier but its impact on the environment depends on how it is produced. If it is produced using renewable energy or nuclear power, its use will not emit GHG into the atmosphere but if it is produced using fossil fuels, then emissions will occur. A great deal of R&D is underway on hydrogen fuel cells for transportation applications. Breakthroughs are needed.

Nuclear power is controversial. While nuclear reactors generate nearly 20 percent of the electricity used in the U.S., nuclear power also generates waste and poses a safety threat. Nuclear power became relatively unpopular in the United States after the Three Mile Island accident. The Chernobyl disaster underscored the safety concerns posed by nuclear power. Nuclear power is also expensive. While nuclear power declined in the U.S. and in parts of European after these accidents, some countries remain favorably disposed to nuclear power. Worldwide, the nuclear industry is expected to grow. Concern over global warming has provoked renewed interest in and reconsideration of nuclear power. Advocates argue that nuclear power is the only viable off-the-shelf technology available to deliver the growing demand for electricity worldwide without contributing to global warming.

Geoengineering approaches, while still theoretical, are being carefully considered. Both albedo management and carbon management schemes are under consideration. While geoengineering is not yet a reality, some consider it dangerous and it will likely result in unintended consequences. That said, the ability to intervene using engineering projects to cool the Earth may be a viable solution if such solutions are feasible and economical.

As this chapter has shown, a wide array of technologies are being considered, improved, and deployed in the fight against climate change. No one technology is the single solution. Continued R&D is essential if solutions are to be found to combat climate change while still supplying the world's increasing demand for energy.

8

Energy Efficiency, Conservation, Demand Side Management, and Other Solutions

Using the best available technologies to supply energy is important but it is only half of the equation. Equally important is controlling the demand for energy through new technologies, energy efficiency, and conservation. Improvement in energy efficiency is the easiest and most cost effective way to reduce the demand for energy in residential and commercial buildings, in industry and in transportation. Residential users consume energy mainly for space heating, air conditioning, and hot water. Conservation and efficiency efforts in these applications will yield great savings. Lighting accounts for much of the energy used in the commercial sector as does space heating and cooling. Improvements in these systems can have enormous impacts. Industry uses energy in many of the same ways that the residential or commercial sectors do, that is, to heat, cool, and light spaces, however industry also uses energy for industrial processes. These processes must be improved to achieve maximum efficiency and conservation. Industry has generally been eager to adopt energy efficient technologies and processes as they become available and this practice has both saved industry money and reduced their consumption. This chapter describes many available opportunities for energy savings in the residential, commercial and industrial sectors.

One of the most promising areas for improvement in energy efficiency and conservation is in transportation. Improvements in fuel efficiency in cars, motorcycles, and light trucks will provide enormous savings and cut GHG emissions substantially. Introduction of more electric cars, hybrids, and plug-in hybrids are an important component that will improve the fuel efficiency of the transportation sector. The largest and most immediate gains, however, will come from overall higher fuel efficiencies of all vehicles. Increasing the overall average gas mileage of the total U.S. fleet is necessary. This chapter discusses energy efficiency and conservation in the transportation sector.

One of the key ways to increase energy efficiency while at the same time providing for far greater use of renewable energy is through the development of the "smart grid." The smart grid will revolutionize the U.S. electric grid which was originally created in the early 20th century. Back then there was little attention paid to efficiency, reliability, distributed sources of generation, and security. The U.S. electric grid still relies on now obsolete technologies, such as mechanical switches, and suffers from the inability to provide grid managers with real-time performance data. Because grid managers lack essential information, they are not able to effectively manage the grid. The grid suffers from many problems as a result. Feeding in many sources of distributed energy into the grid is a problem. Failures in any one grid locality can cause cascading blackouts in multiple locations. The current grid is also a security threat because of its centralized structure and lack of ability to "fix" itself when problems emerge. A smart grid will address concerns about energy efficiency, environmental impacts on climate change, reliability, affordability, national security, and global competitiveness. Progress toward building the smart grid will occur in two stages. First, readily available technology will be deployed to create a grid that will function more efficiently. In time the smart grid will fully emerge. The smart grid will be a fully integrated intelligent network using two-way digital communication. The components and development of a smart grid are discussed in this chapter.

Reduce, reuse, and recycle behaviors also have a role to play. One of these is the recovery and reuse of landfill gas. Landfills account for more than twenty percent of the human-related methane releases, and methane is a potent greenhouse gas. Capturing and burning landfill gas reduces emissions. Landfill gas to energy projects may provide significant energy while displacing the amount of fossil fuel that would otherwise have been used. Recycling reduces energy use because with few exceptions it takes less energy to recycle a material than to make a product from virgin materials. The energy saving recouped from recycling is a very good way to fight climate change. This chapter discusses the implementation of these strategies.

Other approaches are useful for addressing climate change. Land use and changes in land use have a large impact on GHG emissions. Using the natural carbon cycle to reduce the amount of CO_2 in the atmosphere is an important part of addressing climate change. The most basic approach is by increasing plant growth. Plants absorb CO_2 from the atmosphere and it remains stored for long periods. Forest management, reforestation, and elimination of deforestation are important ways to reduce greenhouse gas concentrations in the atmosphere as are the use of reduced tillage and use of better crop management techniques in agriculture. Changes in land use can be very effective in reducing carbon emissions and providing for the creation of a greater number of sinks. This chapter discusses the role of land use, land use changes, and forestry in climate change.

Finally, individual actions can affect global warming. Lifestyle choices can increase or reduce a person's carbon footprint. While actions by any one individual may not have a global impact, the combined actions of many can. It is not only individuals that can participate in lifestyle changes. Businesses, offices, schools, government facilities can all act to encourage behavioral shifts that will result in lower carbon emissions. This chapter concludes with a discussion of the myriad ways personal lifestyle choices may reduce greenhouse gas emissions.

Energy Efficiency and Conservation

Not enough emphasis has been placed on the importance of scaling up the level of energy efficiency obtained from buildings, equipment, vehicles, and products for reducing GHG emissions. Improvements in energy efficiency can vastly reduce the demand for energy in the residential, commercial, and industrial sectors as well as in transportation. Many steps can be taken in the short-term at modest cost to reduce energy consumption. Many of the necessary products that need to be used to promote energy efficiency are readily available off-the-shelf technologies and processes. Improvement in energy productivity is the most cost effective way to reduce global GHG emissions. These improvements are also the most rapidly available solutions to reduce energy consumption and GHG emissions.[1]

It is perhaps important to note that much of the energy produced by power plants for use by end consumers is lost at the power plant itself when it is discharged as waste heat. Improvements need to be made to address this loss. While not easy or inexpensive, this waste heat can be recovered and put to use in a variety of ways. These include hot water for industrial use (cogeneration), aquaculture with increased fish growth due to warm water cultivation, greenhouse heating, desalination of seawater, and air preheating. For example, the Long Island Lighting Company for several years ran a commercial oyster cultivation business as a sideline to use their waste heat. Several plants in Florida have used waste heat to run commercial shrimp farms. The warm waters heated by the waste heat of TVA's Gallatin steam plant have been used to grow catfish. Aside from aquaculture, the use of waste heat for heating buildings or hot water systems is difficult because of the relatively low temperature of the waste heat. Cooling water at most power plants exits the plant at temperatures between 80 and 100 degrees Fahrenheit so transporting the water any distance is not economical. When waste heat is used to heat buildings, those structures need to be in near proximity to the plant. On a smaller and non-power plant scale, a measure of waste heat is lost from buildings through ventilation, steam, or hot water that can be recovered. Exhaust gases can be used to preheat air that might enter the structure as cold air from the outside before it goes to a boiler or furnace for full heating. In residences, a good deal of heat is lost in hot water that goes down the drain. Some of the energy in the water from sinks, showers, and laundry (grey water) can be used to preheat cooler urban or well water before it enters a residential water heater.[2]

Of the energy that is actually delivered to end consumers, energy efficiency efforts can greatly reduce energy use.[3] The production, distribution, and consumption of electricity are particularly important to understand since so much of modern American society is powered by electricity. But it is also important to consider the fact that the electricity sector is intimately tied to other key utilities including water, telecommunications, and natural gas.[4]

Demand for energy for residential uses is primarily for space heating, air conditioning, and hot water. Much of the heat used in space heating is lost through poor structural design or through inefficient heating systems. This is also true for water heaters which typically use electricity or gas to heat water to relatively low temperatures when energy sources such as solar could do the job much more efficiently. Demand for energy in the commercial sector is primarily for space heating and, like in the residential sector; the demand is higher than it needs to be due to poor structural design and inefficient heating systems. For the commercial sector, lighting is also an important factor, accounting for about one fourth of the total energy used. Offices, schools, and stores have a large lighting demand. Lights are a double edged sword. Lights heat the air which drives up the need for air conditioning in warm weather but they reduce the need for space heating in the colder months.[5] The predominant climate dictates the extent to which lighting is a drag on energy use.

The U.S. Green Building Council runs the Leadership in Energy and Environmental Design (LEED) rating system which is a third party certification system of structures rating them on energy efficiency operation and good design. LEED is a standard that is widely accepted as the benchmark for green buildings. The U.S. Green Building Council provides a great deal of information for building designers and owners regarding how to improve a structure's energy performance.[6] Building performance can also be improved through DOE's Buildings Technologies Program, housed in the Office of Energy Efficiency and Renewable Energy. This program works with the building industry and manufacturers to conduct research on technologies and practices to improve energy efficiency of structures.[7]

Most residential and commercial buildings can be improved through readily available technologies and products such as good insulation and efficient lighting, appliances, heating and cooling systems. Passive solar structural designs that enable the building to receive and retain heat from the sun in the winter but be shaded from that heat in the summer are also important. For most U.S. building this may be achieved simply by having an adequate number of south facing windows that are shaded in the summer. Solar water heating can reduce the overall need for energy as can natural lighting systems such as solar tube lights.

Replacing incandescent bulbs with compact fluorescent bulbs increases the efficiency of lighting systems by three to four times and compact fluorescent bulbs last longer, making them economical in the long-term. Light-emitting diode (LED) lighting systems are twice as efficient as compact fluorescents. When these new lights are coupled with motion detectors and photoelectric switches, electricity demand for lighting, especially in the commercial sector, can be greatly reduced.[8] Consider the savings if just supermarkets had automatic sensors to power lights in their refrigeration units so that they would turn off when no customers were present in the aisle. Nationwide, the savings just in lighting could be enormous if energy efficient bulbs and systems were used. The Department of Energy and Environmental Protection Agency have determined that if every household in the U.S. replaced just one incandescent light bulb with a compact fluorescent bulb, the savings would be enough to light more than 3 million homes for one year or the equivalent to the power of one nuclear power plant.[9]

Installation of programmable thermostats is one of the easiest ways to improve efficiency in heating, ventilating, and air conditioning of residential and commercial buildings. By reducing heating and cooling when the building is not occupied, programmable thermostats have great potential to save energy. Insulation and new heating equipment for existing buildings can reduce energy consumption up to 85 percent when comprehensive renovation measures are used. For new buildings, high-grade insulation combined with high-efficiency windows, ventilation, and heat recovery systems allow new homes to have near zero energy consumption.[10]

Standby power consumption in electrical devices like TVs, DVDs, and computers is also an issue. Many electrical devices cannot be turned off without completely unplugging them. While plugged in they use power even if they are not in use to maintain clocks, retain settings, and allow for rapid start features. While any single device draws a trivial amount of power in standby mode, together the consumption adds up. It is estimated that at least

10 percent of the electricity consumed by U.S. households is for standby power.[11] Nationwide, the cost is estimated to be $4 billion a year that could be avoided by plugging electronic devices into a power strip that is switched off when the device is not in use.[12]

The Department of Energy and Environmental Protection Agency jointly provide the Energy Star Program which identifies energy efficient products. Founded in 1992, the program is showing results. It is projected that in 2007 alone Energy Star promotions helped save consumers of those products $16 billion in electric bills and reduced GHG emissions by the equivalent of removing 27 million cars from the highways. Households can save up to one third of their electricity use by purchasing appliances displaying the Energy Star logo. This logo is awarded to products that meet DOE energy efficiency standards. Businesses can save almost half of what they would spend on electricity if they paid better attention to energy efficient products, machines, and appliances. The Energy Star program offers a partnership to businesses so that they can work with EPA and DOE to manage their energy performance and track savings. EPA provides partners with a performance rating system for their buildings to further reduce energy use.[13]

Industry uses energy in ways that differ from the use in the residential or commercial sectors. Industry uses energy to heat materials being worked on, to produce steam for manufacturing processes, for driving machines and motors, distillation, and for reduction of ores to metals. Petroleum and natural gases are used as feedstocks for production of products. Industry also must provide lighting, heating, and air conditioning for its facilities. In addition to using all the technologies and products available to the residential and commercial sectors to reduce their energy use, industry must also improve their industrial processes to maximize savings. Much of the improvement in production processes results from the application of new technologies and innovation.[14] Industry can benefit from substantial savings in energy bills by quick adoption of new energy efficient products and processes. Industry has shown a clear willingness to do so.

One such effort is the alliance of industrialists and environmentalists to ban the incandescent light bulb. In 2007 the Alliance to Save Energy pledged to push for higher efficiency standards at the federal, state and local level. The plan is to demand the replacement of the incandescent light bulb by compact fluorescents, LEDs, and other technologies that may emerge.[15] When it comes to adoption of energy efficient products and processes, technology firms are on the leading edge. Technology firms are voluntarily moving to cut industrial use of electricity. By lessening the amount of electricity used by servers and data centers, these high tech firms hope to greatly reduce their energy use. In 2007 an alliance was born between Advanced Micro Devices, Hewlett-

Packard, IBM, Sun Microsystems, Dell, Microsoft and a few other companies. They established a nonprofit called the Green Grid to reduce the amount of electricity used by servers and data centers which make up a central component of high technology firms.[16]

These efforts, while commendable, could be greater. Part of the problem rests with the Department of Energy which is many years behind schedule in issuing mandatory energy efficiency minimum requirements for a host of residential, commercial, and industrial buildings and products. The delay in DOE's issuance of these standards is costing billions in missed energy savings.[17] For several decades the Congress passed a series of laws demanding stricter efficiency standards on 30 categories of products, as varied as residential air conditioners to industrial boilers. Nevertheless, the DOE never issued the regulations required by the legislation, even after being ordered by the courts to do so as part of the resolution of a 2005 law suit by 14 states against the DOE. Under the Bush administration DOE never complied with the court order and Bush left office without DOE finalizing 15 standards. The Obama administration ordered the Energy Department to immediately draft the long overdue standards in 2009.[18]

Great opportunities for improvement in energy efficiency and conservation exist in the transportation sector. In 2006, highway vehicles used 80 percent of the energy used in the transportation sector, with cars, trucks, and motorcycles accounting for 61 percent of the energy use and heavy trucks and buses for the rest. Non highway transportation includes air, water, pipeline and rail. Together these modes of transportation used 20 percent of the energy used by the transportation sector with air accounting for 9 percent, water for 5 percent, pipeline for 3 percent and rail for 2 percent.[19] Given these statistics, clearly the most likely place to find the widest savings is cars, motorcycles, and light trucks. Electric cars, hybrids, and plug-in hybrids will go a long way to improving some of these inefficiencies.

Hybrid's provide high fuel economy and drastically lower emissions. Hybrids combine an internal combustion engine that runs on gasoline with a battery and electric motor which assists the internal combustion engine or takes over completely for the gasoline engine. Hybrids use regenerative braking recharge the battery. Many hybrid vehicles have an automatic idle that shuts the gasoline engine off while the vehicle is stopped. By using the electric motor to supplement the gasoline engine, hybrids obtain better fuel efficiency and emit much less pollution than conventional vehicles.[20]

Hybrids can be further enhanced by making them "plug-ins." With some modifications, hybrids can be plugged into a wall socket to recharge an additional battery which allows them to run totally on that battery until it is fully discharged. After the first electric battery is spent, the vehicle shifts to standard hybrid operation. In addition, hybrids can be made to run as flexible fuel vehicles so that they can operate on ethanol or other renewable fuels.[21]

Electric vehicles run entirely on batteries. How beneficial they are to the environment depends on what source of power is used to charge the batteries. The same is true of plug-in hybrids. If they are charged using renewable sources of energy then they provide excellent reductions in GHG emissions as well as the other tailpipe emissions that cause serious deterioration of urban air quality. There are a limited number of full-sized electric vehicles available commercially and more R&D needs to be done to produce these vehicles cheaply and in mass quantity.[22] The main problem with electric vehicle is the limited range of operation before the battery is discharged. While automakers have introduced electric vehicles in the past, none has captured much of a market share.

New technologies must be accompanied by overall higher fuel efficiencies of all vehicles by imposing higher mandatory CAFE standards. For years the Big Three automakers in the U.S. fought against higher CAFE standards and they were supported by the Bush administration in their efforts.[23] In 2007 CAFE standards were raised by Congress from 27.5 miles per gallon on cars and 22.2 miles per gallon for light trucks, including minivans, SUVs and pickups to a fleet-wide standard of 35 miles per gallon.[24] A more stringent standard would do much to improve energy efficiency and conservation.

Simple behavioral changes can also improve energy savings in transportation. The Department of Energy suggests that aggressive driving wastes gas. Speeding, rapid acceleration, and hard breaking can lower highway gas mileage by as much as one third and city mileage by 5 percent. Use of vehicle air conditioning also increases fuel use. Proper inflation of tires and keeping them correctly aligned can improve gas mileage by more than 3 percent. While the savings to an individual person may seem small, if the entire population were to make these behavioral changes, the savings would be significant. Unfortunately, the widespread desire for technological fixes as opposed to adopting behavioral changes, typically means that the real savings that could be gained from them are overlooked if not publically scorned.[25]

Changes to vehicles, even those that burn conventional gasoline, hold promise for greater energy efficiency. Use of lighter weight materials like plastic or composites reduces overall vehicle weight and increases fuel efficiency. Iron and steel components can be replaced by aluminum. The traditional internal combustion engine is very inefficient leaving great room for improvement. Computers can be used to turn off cylinders at cruising speeds, thus saving fuel. Shifts to alterative engines, especially engines that can be fueled by clean diesel, offers promise. These engines are more efficient and emit one fourth the carbon dioxide as gasoline engines.[26]

The Smart Grid

The development of a smart grid in the U.S. will be an important step forward to controlling GHG emissions for several reasons. First, a smart grid will be more efficient and will therefore waste less energy while at the same time reducing the demand for peak electricity. Second, a smart grid will allow for full use of renewable energy from distributed sources—something the traditional American electric grid cannot do very readily. Finally, a smart grid will allow consumers to monitor and control their electricity use, enabling them to use power more efficiently and cheaply.

The U.S. electric grid is based on century-old technology. It consists primarily of centralized power plants run by utilities that make power available to consumers by routing it through numerous substations, transformers, and transmission lines. Once the electricity has reached a substation, the utility typically cannot monitor it anymore. If electricity goes out in a location, the utility will not know without outage calls from consumers and then they have to try to figure out just where the problem has occurred and then dispatch repair teams to fix the problem.[27] The U.S. grid consists of about 9,200 electric generating units with more than 1 million MW of capacity connected by more than 300,000 miles of transmission lines. At the recommendation of the Federal Energy Regulatory Commission (FERC), the grid is run by Independent System Operators (ISO) or Regional Transmission Organizations (RTO) which are nonprofit organizations that are responsible for coordinating supply with demand. An ISO can be in charge of the grid for one or more states.[28] Failures in any one locality can cause cascading failure in multiple locations, as the Northeast blackout of 2003 showed.

The Federal Smart Grid Task Force was established by the Energy Independence and Security Act of 2007 to act as the coordinator of smart grid activities across the federal government. Drawing on experts from the Energy Department, EPA, FERC, the National Institute of Standards and Technology, and the Department of Homeland Security, the Task Force provides information and standards for smart grid technologies.[29] Development of a smart grid is essential to meeting the goals of the U.S. Climate Change Technology Program Strategic Plan which calls for reduction of GHG emissions.[30]

Efforts to develop the smart grid were undertaken because the old grid was developed long before modern concerns were issues in design. Current concerns include energy efficiency, environmental impacts including climate change, reliability, affordability, national security, and global competitiveness. The inefficiency of the grid is a problem. If the grid were just 5 percent more efficient, the reductions in GHG emissions would be the equivalent of taking 53 million cars off the road. The grid is stressed beyond its capacity. Three of the last five major blackouts have occurred in the last decade. Blackouts and brownouts are due to the slow response times of mechanical switches that are still in common use on the grid, the lack of real-time analytical capacity to sense problems and inability to repair or isolate outages, and lack of information available to grid operators. Blackouts have high economic costs—every time the power goes out firms cannot do business. Security analysts also argue that the central nature of the grid makes it a target for terrorists. For all these reasons, a new smart grid must be developed.[31]

Progress toward the smart grid will occur in stages. In stage one, readily available technology will be added to the grid to create a "smarter" grid that will function more efficiently. As progress continues, within a decade or perhaps sooner, the smart grid will fully emerge, transforming the old grid into a fully integrated intelligent network. The smart grid will have the capacity to use two-way digital communication. An Advanced Metering Infrastructure (AMI) will be deployed that will enable consumers to use electricity more economically and more efficiently. Electricity will be priced in real-time on the smart grid and consumers will be notified of prices via smart home controllers or devices. Consumers will be able to program preferences for electricity use into their controllers or devices, thus reducing demand when prices are high.[32] Smart grid technologies to help consumers monitor and control their electricity demand include smart thermostats and smart meters.[33] Researchers discovered many years ago that moving electric meters from hidden locations to highly visible ones resulted in a significant reduction of household energy use. When consumers can see what they are consuming, they reduce consumption. More feedback leads to better control and empowerment of consumers.[34] Google, the large Internet search engine company, has a prototype web application that takes information from smart meters and displays household energy consumption by appliance. Google anticipates that web applications such as this will enable consumers to cut demand by as much as 15 percent.[35]

The smart grid will have technology to enable better supply side management as well. Visualization technology will be built into the smart grid, enabling grid operators to better oversee their activities. Grid operators will be able to integrate real-time weather and usage information which will lead to better management. If blackouts occur, information about them will be transmitted instantaneously so the events will be self isolating. Phasor Measurement Units (PMU) will sample voltage and current many times each second, providing greatly enhanced information to grid managers. Improvements in visibility made possible by PMU will allow the grid to manage distributed generation so that more sources of renewable energy can be brought on line. As more and more renewable generation devices, like solar panels, are widely distributed across the consumer community, the efficiency of the grid will increase because the distance between generation and use will decrease. The smart grid will be a computerized distributed energy network with a two-way flow of electricity and information.[36]

The full development of a smart grid will revolutionize the entire power generation and delivery system in the U.S. It will provide producers and consumers with more information and control that will reduce demand a nd improve delivery. There will be a reduction in the need to construct new power plants as supply is used more effectively. As a result, GHG emissions will be greatly reduced not only because of the increased use of renewable energy but also because of improved efficiency of the grid itself. The generation of electricity in the U.S. accounts for 40 percent of CO_2 emissions. Smart grid deployment is a critical tool in fighting global warming.[37]

Landfill Gas Recovery

About 64 percent of all U.S. municipal solid waste (MSW) is disposed in approximately 1,800 MSW landfills. Landfills account for 23 percent of the human-related methane releases. Landfills also release other pollutants that contribute to ozone formation and hazardous air pollutants. Landfill gas is about half methane and half CO_2 and water vapor. Burning landfill gas reduces emissions of methane and the other harmful pollutants. More than 400 MSW landfills in the United States recover and burn landfill gas to generate heat or electricity while other sites just recover the gas and flare it as required by law. Both prevent GHG emissions but using the landfill gas to generate heat or electricity also displaces the coal or other fossil fuel that would otherwise be used to generate the heat or electricity.[38]

It is estimated that nearly 600 landfills have the potential to develop landfill gas to energy (LFGTE) projects in the U.S. in the future, almost doubling the amount of energy produced. LFGTE projects already in operation currently provide energy for more than 1 million homes. LFGTE projects typically produce gas for 20 years. Use of this alternative source of fuel both prevents GHG emissions and displaces fossil fuel use.[39] Landfill gas is collected by drilling wells into the landfill and installing collection pipes in the wells. Once collected it can be mixed with natural gas to fuel conventional turbines or used alone to fuel small or combined cycle turbines. Landfill gas can also be used in fuel cells that use chemical reactions to generate electricity.[40]

Recycling

Recycling reduces energy use because it almost always takes less energy to recycle a material than to make a product from virgin materials. For example, recycling aluminum scrap to make new aluminum cans takes 95 percent less energy than producing new cans from virgin ore. Paper can be recycled to make new paper, saving trees and water. For each ton of paper made from recycled material, 17 trees are saved and half the water is used. Glass can be recycled to make new glass, and so on. By using materials more than once, landfill space is not needed and natural resources are conserved.[41] Recycling can also be used to convert one product use into another such as using wastepaper to make boxes.

Recycling became popular in the 1970s in large part because of lack of landfill space but has suffered from a volatile economic situation. Shortage of markets for recycled goods has made recycling a boom and bust industry. Among the most recovered products are lead-acid batteries (93 percent), major steel appliances (90 percent), corrugated boxes (71 percent), newspapers (82 percent), steel cans (60 percent), and aluminum cans (44 percent). Other products have lower recycling rates including containers and packaging where about one-third were recycled, followed by paper, plastics, rubber, leather and textiles with recycle rates of about 26 percent.[42] Since energy saving from recycling is a very good way to fight climate change, more effort should be put into creating strong markets for recycled materials.

Land Use, Land Use Changes, and Forestry

An approach to reducing GHG emissions involves using the natural carbon cycle to reduce the amount of CO_2 in the atmosphere. The most fundamental approach is photosynthesis and plant growth which absorbs CO_2 from the atmosphere and deposits it in the organic compounds that make up plant material and the organic components of soil. A great deal of the carbon taken up by plants is rapidly recycled back into the atmosphere when it is eaten or burned or through decomposition, however some carbon remains stored for long periods especially in wood and organic soil materials. There are a variety of potential ways to keep the carbon sequestered in plant materials. For instance, reduced tillage or use of better crop management techniques can keep carbon in agricultural soils. Management changes in forestry can increase forest growth rates and produce larger trees. Changes in land use are important. The conversion of marginal croplands to grass or trees can be effective in reducing carbon emissions. Other agricultural practices affect greenhouse gases. Methane, produced by ruminant livestock and manure decomposition, can be reduced by grazing management, altered livestock feeding practices, and by better manure management. [43]

Recent studies show that trees in the tropics are getting bigger and thus are able to soak up more carbon dioxide. Almost twenty percent of fossil fuel emissions are absorbed by forests in Africa and Asia and by the Amazon. Compared to the 1960s, each hectare of African forest by 2009 was trapping an additional 0.6 ton of carbon a year. Over the world's total tropical forests, this extra carbon sink amounts to 4.8 billion tons of CO_2 per year. These recent studies have challenged the prior concept that mature forests were carbon neutral, with new trees merely absorbed the amount of carbon put off by dying trees. The new studies suggest that increased CO_2 in the atmosphere is responsible for the increased growth of forests and therefore also responsible for the forests' ability to become a larger sink.[44] Such studies point to the obvious importance of policies that protect established forests and reforestation efforts.

Lifestyle Choices

Individual actions can impact the environment in general and global warming in particular. Many individuals make personal lifestyle choices to reduce their carbon footprint. These include such actions as reducing waste by choosing reusable products, buying products with minimal packaging to reduce waste, and recycling. Other common actions individuals can take are to use less heat and air conditioning by setting the thermostat higher in summer and lower in winter, adding insulation, and weatherizing their houses. Switching to compact fluorescents or LEDs will save energy and reduce emissions. Many people decide to drive less. They switch to mass transit or bike and walk. Others focus on simple car improvements to increase gas efficiency like making sure tires are adequately inflated. Using consumer power to buy energy efficient products is another personal strategy that many adopt. Key choices are buying fuel efficient cars and energy efficient appliances. Using less hot water can reduce GHG emissions so many people decide to set the water heater's temperature lower, buy low-flow shower heads, and wash clothes in cold water. Many set the energy saving switch on the dishwasher and let the dishes air dry. Turing off lights and other electronic devices when they are not needed saves electricity and reduces emissions. Installing power strips that can be turned off to cut standby power use saves energy. People can plant trees and other vegetation that will act as carbon sinks. Individuals can get home energy audits from utility companies to identify areas in their homes that are not energy efficient. Utilities often offer rebate programs to help pay for some of the cost of energy efficiency improvements. Many people think it is essential to encourage others to conserve.[45]

Many individuals have adopted a simpler lifestyle, choosing to consume less and therefore pollute less. They purchase only what they really need and are conscious of how their selections affect the environment. For instance, buying food shipped to local markets from far distant places wastes energy and is something that some people will not do. Also, people reduce or eliminate their meat consumption to reduce the negative impacts animal husbandry has on global warming.

Habitat adaptation is being considered by both individuals and communities. One aspect of this adaptation is reducing the size of the average home which increased from 1,500 square feet in the 1970s to over 2,200 square feet in 2000. Larger homes consume more energy and "McMansions" consume considerably more. Many communities are encouraging the development of higher-density, urban communities with smaller, affordable, homes.[46]

Individuals can choose to reduce the impact of their carbon emissions by voluntarily measuring their carbon footprint, reducing what they can, and purchasing offsets to address the emissions they cannot reduce. Many environmental organizations have offset programs that use voluntary contributions of money to support carbon reduction efforts underway. For instance, the Nature Conservancy,[47] The Climate Trust,[48] and Carbonfund.org[49] are just three prominent voluntary offset programs that allow individuals to offset the portion of their carbon footprint that they cannot reduce.

The workplace may have a strong role to play in individual lifestyle choices. For instance, a new trend in energy savings is coming from employers that permit workers to shift to a four day work week. Such changes reduce transportation emissions and may result in lower utility costs if organizations actually shut down one day a week. Some state governments have experimented with four day work weeks without reducing services by relying more heavily on online service delivery.[50] The expansion of telecommuting options has the potential to yield large environmental and energy benefits. Telecommuting adds over $300 billion to the economy through greater productivity while reducing the number of cars on the highway and the emissions they create. The benefits from telecommuting have been well known for many years and yet widespread adoption remains depressed. Organizational managers frequently resist losing control of workers and are thus reluctant to allow them to work at out-of-sight locations.[51]

Conclusion

As this chapter has shown, energy efficiency, conservation, and demand side management each have a large role to play in reducing GHG emissions. Individual actions matter. The small choices by many add up to real savings by the whole. Personal lifestyle choices to reduce carbon emissions include driving less, driving an energy efficient vehicle, reducing waste, recycling, using less heat and air conditioning, and living and working in low impact structures. Personal choices include using consumer power to buy energy efficient products and commodities, adopting a simpler lifestyle, and consuming less. Individuals can reduce the impact of their carbon emissions by voluntarily measuring their carbon footprint, reducing the emissions they can, and purchasing offsets to address the emissions they cannot reduce through the many organizations that have programs in place to enable these actions. Individuals and organizations can take other measures to limit their negative impacts on the climate system including altered work schedules, recycling and reuse of otherwise foolishly discarded materials, and tapping into new sources of energy such as landfill gas.

Working with the natural carbon cycle to reduce the amount of CO_2 in the atmosphere is an important strategy. Good forestry and agricultural management practices can reduce emissions. Management changes in forestry can increase forest growth rates and produce larger trees. Returning marginal croplands to grass or trees will reduce carbon emissions. Recent studies point to the importance of policies that protect established forests and promote reforestation efforts.

One of the most important changes will be the development of a smart grid with the capacity to use two-way digital communications and smart metering devices. Consumers will be able to program preferences for electricity use into their smart meters, reducing demand when prices are high. Visualization technology built into the smart grid will empower grid operators to integrate real-time weather and usage information for better management. Most importantly, improvements in visibility will allow the grid to manage the distributed generation of power as more sources of renewable energy feed into the grid. As more power is generated locally, the efficiency of the grid will increase. This will have the added benefit of reducing the need for additional generation capacity to meet peak demand that so often relies on dirty coal generation. Wide-spread blackouts will be eliminated as the smart grid isolates problems in the real-time and reroutes supply to meet demand. The development of a smart grid will modernize and transform the entire power generation and delivery system in the U.S. The smart grid will vastly reduce GHG emissions through the increased use of renewable energy and improved efficiency.

The greatest benefits will come from improvements in energy efficiency that will reduce the demand for energy in the residential housing, offices, hospitals, stores, schools, and industrial facilities. Energy efficiency and conservation efforts in the transportation sector will also have large pay-offs.

Improvements in space heating, air conditioning, and hot water for residential homes and commercial buildings will reduce GHG emissions. Improvement in lighting for offices, schools, and stores will have a beneficial outcome. Improving the energy performance of the built environment through good design and improved technologies is important. Most buildings can be improved through readily available technologies and products including high-quality insulation, efficient lighting, appliances, heating and cooling systems. Reducing standby power consumption further reduces consumption and makes dwellings more efficient. Industrial facilities can benefit from each of these conservation and efficiency efforts in addition to improving their energy use in industrial processes. If government standards for energy efficiency across a broad spectrum of products were updated and heightened, great savings could occur. Finally, there are large improvements in energy efficiency and conservation to be achieved in the transportation sector. Improvement in CAFE standards that result in fleet-wide efficiency improvements would reduce fuel consumption and GHG emissions. Greater adoption and use of hybrid vehicles, electric vehicles, and plug-in hybrids will yield substantial improvements in energy efficiency and conservation in the transportation sector. As this chapter has shown, the combined efforts for more energy efficiency, conservation, and effective demand side management can be an potent tool in the fight against climate change.

Appendix
Web Resources

Alliance for Climate Protection sponsors the *We Can Solve It Campaign.* The Alliance for Climate Protection is a nonprofit, nonpartisan organization formed by former Vice President and Nobel laureate Al Gore. The mission of the Alliance is to build political will to solve the climate crisis. The We web site can be found at http://www.wecansolveit.org/.

American Association for the Advancement of Science (AAAS) provides Global Climate Change Resources. The web page provides links to many scientific sources and provides resources for teachers and reporters. The site includes a carbon footprint calculator and reports on what can be done to fight climate change. AAAS's web site can be found at http://www.aaas.org/news/press_room/climate_change/.

American Meteorological Society provides information on how the weather is changing and positions that the organization has in effect and under consideration regarding these changes. The American Meteorological Society web site can be found at http://www.ametsoc.org/policy/2007climatechange.html.

Arizona Climate Action Initiative provides information on how the state is approaching the climate crisis. The site contains reports released by the Arizona government that detail what impacts climate change will have on the state along with links to the state's climate change action plan. The Arizona Climate Action Initiative web site can be found at http://www.azclimatechange.gov/.

Audubon Global Warming Campaign seeks to fight climate change primarily through education and political action. The web site contains information on how global warming will affect many species and how to contact political leadership via petitions on global warming. The Audubon Global Warming Campaign web site can be found at http://www.audubon.org/globalwarming/.

California Air Resources Board maintains a web site that provides full information on the implementation of California's Global Warming Solutions Act of 2006 and other efforts to deal with global warming. The site includes details of the carbon trading mechanism that is required under the law, mandatory committees, and reporting requirements. The California Air Resources Board web site can be found at http://www.arb.ca.gov/cc/cc.htm.

California Climate Change Portal provides access to the central clearinghouse of information regarding California's actions on climate change. The site includes background information on California's efforts to combat climate change and details of California's Global Warming Solutions Act of 2006. Access to California's greenhouse gas inventory is provided. The California Climate Change Portal can be found at http://www.climate change.ca.gov/.

The Carbon Trust was set up by the UK government in 2001 as an independent business organization. Its mission is to assist firms lower their carbon footprint and thus increase the pace of movement toward a reduced carbon world. The Carbon Trust provides a variety of services including providing carbon labels that measure the carbon footprint of a variety of services and products, certifying organizations that are committed to making carbon reductions, and helping to develop new low-carbon technologies. The Carbon Trust's web site can be found at http://www.carbontrust.com/EN/Ho me.aspx

Catholic Coalition on Climate Change provides current church teaching on the climate crisis. The site provides access to proclamations of the U.S. Conference of Catholic Bishops as well as Coalition activities. The Catholic Coalition on Climate Change web site can be found at http://www.catholicsandclimatechange.org/.

Centers for Disease Control and Prevention provides information on climate change and public health. The CDC provides information on the health effects of increased temperature, increased extreme weather events, and other indirect exposures and health effects. The Centers for Disease Control and Prevention web site on climate change and health can be found at http://www.cdc.gov/ClimateChange/.

Chicago Climate Exchange is the first voluntary carbon market in the United States. The exchange provides a site that allows online registration, carbon trading, offset registration, and information about trading volume and price. Links are provided to the European Exchanges. The Chicago Climate Exchange web page can be found at http://www.chicagoclimatex.com/.

Congressional Budget Office maintains a site for climate change which focuses on budget issues associated with the climate threat. The CBO site provides interesting information on the design of a cap-and-trade system along with a great deal of material dealing with the economics of climate change policy. The Congressional Budget Office's web site can be found at http://www.cbo.gov/publications/collections/collections.cfm?col lect=9.

Connecticut Climate Change Action Plan site provides documents and links to state decisions on climate change, its state action plan, and potential solutions. The Connecticut Climate Change Action Plan web site can be found at http://www.ctclimatechange. com/StateActionPlan.html.

Conservation Law Foundation is a nonprofit organization with a mission of helping New England reduce its carbon footprint. Staff attorneys work to affect global warming policies through court actions and by influencing government officials. They focus on transportation and the power production sector. The key areas of their focus include climate protection, energy efficiency, clean energy and air pollution. The Conservation Law Foundation's web site can be found at http://www.clf.org.

Council on Foreign Relations provides an interactive Crisis Guide that shows the anticipated effects of climate change globally by region. They provide access to information that discusses various options for dealing with global warming. The Council on Foreign Relations web site can be found at http://www.cfr.org/publication/17088/crisis_guide.html.

Department of Ecology, State of Washington provides a web site with details of actions being taken by the state to address the issue of climate change. The Western Climate Initiative is explored as are cap-and-trade issues, climate registries, and the green economy. Reports from the University of Washington's Climate Impact research groups are provided. The Department of Ecology, State of Washington web site can be found at http://www.ecy.wa.gov/climatechange/index.htm.

Earthjustice provides information on global warming and addresses specifically coal, energy, efficiency, national rulemaking and standards, state and regional work, wildlife, and the Arctic. The Earthjustice web site can be found at http://www.earthjustice.org/our_work/issues/global-warming/index.html.

Energy Information Administration provides information on the link between energy use and the emission of greenhouse gases. The site provides many useful graphics which detail the association. Energy Information Administration's web site can be found at: http://www.eia.doe.gov/bookshelf/brochures/greenhouse/Chapter1.htm.

Environmental Defense Fund's Fight Global Warming Campaign provides information on the dangers, science, and myths about climate change. They provide a carbon footprint calculator. Environmental Defense Fund's web site can be found at http://www.fightglobalwarming.com/.

Environmental Justice and Climate Change Initiative is a coalition of environmental justice, climate justice, religious, and advocacy groups with the mission of educating policy makers and the public regarding climate justice issues. EJCC partners with the Alliance for Climate Protection and the We campaign. EJCC's web site can be found at http://www.ejcc.org/.

Evangelical Environmental Network provides a web site with a wide number of resources available to show activities related to Creation Care and Climate Change. The Evangelical Environmental Network web site can be found at http://www.creationcare.org/.

Federal Resources for Educational Excellence is an outstanding site that provides links to 43 resources for teaching about climate change. These resources have been complied by many government science programs like the NSF, NASA, and NOAA. Resources provided by universities and nonprofit organizations are also listed. This is a one-stop-shop with links to some of the best resources available for teaching about climate change. The Federal Resources for Educational Excellence web site can be found at http://free.ed.gov/subjects.cfm?subject_id=155&toplvl=47&res_feature_request=1.

Florida Climate Change is a site created by the Chief Financial Officer of Florida in collaboration with Florida's Commissioner of Agriculture and Consumer Services to alert Floridians to the danger to their state from global warming. The site includes interactive maps of land lost to sea-level rise and a discussion regarding financial losses likely as a result of climate change. Florida Climate Change web site can be found at http://www.floridaclimatechange.com/.

Global Climate Change Research Explorer is an outstanding site sponsored by the National Science Foundation. It provides what they refer to as an "Exploratorium" which allows site visitors to explore the Earth's biosphere (the whole area of the Earth's surface, atmosphere and the sea that is inhabited by living creatures), atmosphere, cryosphere (frozen parts of the Earth including polar ice caps, glaciers, sea ice, and permafrost), hydrosphere (the portions of the Earth's surface that is water, including seas and water in the atmosphere), and the global affects of global warming. The site integrates data from many fields including physics, chemistry, biology, geology, meteorology, oceanography, and sociology. The site provides information on how scientists gather data, test theories, and draw conclusions about global warming. The Global Climate Change Research Explorer web site can be found at http://www.exploratorium. edu/climate/.

Global Environmental Facility is an international partnership of 178 countries, non-profit organizations, companies, and international organizations. The GEF funds environmental project worldwide. The mitigation and adaptation projects currently being sponsored by the GEF are detailed. The Global Environmental Facility web site can be found at http://www.gefweb.org/interior.aspx?id=232.

Illinois Climate Change Advisory Group is responsible for creating a long-term strategy for Illinois to respond to the climate change threat. The site provides links to state-based environmental issues associated with climate change and documents policy efforts underway or already taken. The Illinois Climate Change Advisory Group web site can be found at http://www.epa.state.il.us/air/climatechange/.

Interfaith Center on Corporate Responsibility provides a primer on climate change and what industries most contribute to it including the oil and gas industry, electric power, automotive, and appliance manufacturing. The site provides information on how it is working with these industries to improve their corporate performance. The web site can be found at http://www.iccr.org/issues/globalwarm/index.php.

Intergovernmental Panel on Climate Change, an organization that shared the 2007 Nobel Prize with Al Gore, provides a site from which visitors can read or download all of the major publications and reports of the IPCC. The site also provides organizational background information on the IPCC and a schedule of meetings and meeting documentation. The IPCC's web site can be found at http://www.ipcc.ch/.

International Energy Agency provides information on the energy dimension of climate change. The site provides access to information on emissions trading and the Clean Development Mechanism of the Kyoto Protocol. The site provides access to publications dealing with energy issues and climate change. The site provides access to a data base of member countries policies toward energy and climate. The International Energy Agency's web site can be found at http://www.iea.org/Textbase/subjectqueries/keyresu lt.asp?KEYWORD_ID=4106.

Iowa Climate Change Advisory Council provides information on Iowa's inventory of greenhouse gas emissions, and the interim and final action plan. The Iowa Climate Change Advisory Council's website can be found at http://www.iaclimatechange.us/.

Kyoto Protocol is an international agreement to reduce greenhouse gas emissions. The web page provides considerable detail about the agreement, the clean development mechanism, joint implementation, and emissions trading. The site also provides information on inventory registry, compliance, and monitoring. The site can be found at http://unfccc.int/kyoto_protocol/items/2830.php.

League of Women Voters Global Climate Change Advisory provides information on why the League has concluded that climate change is the worst environmental problem that confronts the world and why the League supports immediate action. The site contains information on political action taken by the League to encourage clean energy and action on climate change. The League's web site can be found at http://www.lwv.org/AM/Template.cfm?Section=Global_Climate_Change.

Maryland Commission on Climate Change provides information regarding the impacts of climate change on the state. The commission provides access to the state climate action plan as well as links to the RGGI agreement of which Maryland is a party. The Maryland Commission on Climate Change's web page can be found at http://www.mde.state.md.us/Air/climatechange/index.asp.

Midwest Governor's Greenhouse Gas Accord hosts a site that provides information on the agreement and its progress. Links are given for the other regional agreements as well as registries. The Midwest Governor's Greenhouse Gas Accord web site can be found at http://www.midwesternaccord.org/.

Minnesota Climate Change Advisory Group provides advice to the state regarding climate change implications. This group works with government, nonprofits, and the business community to create ways that Minnesota can implement energy savings through the Next Generation Energy Initiative. The Minnesota's Climate Change Advisory Group's web site can be found at http://www.mnclimatechange.us/.

Missouri Department of Natural Resources provides a web site dealing with climate change and state actions. The web page provides basic information for the state and greenhouse trends and projections. The Missouri Department of Natural Resources web site can be found at http://www.dnr.mo.gov/energy/cc/cc.htm.

Montana Climate Change Advisory Committee is responsible for formulating a policy for the state on climate change. The site provides access to Montana's Climate Change Action Plan as well as links to many documents. The Montana Climate Change Advisory Committee's web site can be found at http://www.mtclimatechange.us/CCAC.cfm.

NASA's Global Warming World Book provides excellent and extensive factual information on global warming including satellite imagery, videos, and interactive features, and 3D images. NASA's Global Warming World Book web site can be found at http://www.nasa.gov/worldbook/global_warming_worldbook.html.

NASA's Jet Propulsion Laboratory provides an excellent site with current information on sea ice, sea level, carbon dioxide, global temperature and the ozone hole. The site includes a number of interactive visuals that allow the visitor to see changes in ice, sea level, carbon dioxide, and global temperatures over recent history. This is an excellent site for graphically understanding the impacts of global warming. The evidence of anthropogenic causes is clearly provided as effects, solutions, and remaining uncertainties. NASA's Jet Propulsion Laboratory's web site can be found at http://climate.jpl.nasa.gov/.

The National Academies Climate Change web site provides information associated with all the Academies studies and publications on climate change. The site provides fundamental scientific information about climate change as well as sophisticated policy advice. The National Academies web site can be found at http://dels.nas.edu/climatechange/.

National Wildlife Federation provides information on how to deal with climate change's impacts on wildlife. Links are provided to the Climate Action Center. The web site can be found at http://www.nwf.org/globalwarming/.

Natural Resources Defense Council provides extensive information on all aspects of global warming at it applies to air, land, water, oceans, wildlife, health, environmental justice, U.S. law and policy, nuclear technologies, smart growth, and recycling. The Natural Resources Defense Council's web site can be found at http://www.nrdc.org/glob alwarming/Default.asp.

The Nature Conservancy, a nonprofit environmental organization, hosts a site on climate change that provides detailed information on how individuals and organizations can offset their carbon emissions. The site includes a carbon calculator and the site accepts monetary donations to offset carbon emissions. The funds received go to fund projects The Nature Conservancy has in place that reduce greenhouse gas emissions worldwide. The site provides broad information on conservation strategies to combat climate change. The Nature Conservancy's web site can be found at http://www.natu re.org/initiatives/climatechange/.

New Jersey Global Warming spotlights efforts in New Jersey to fight climate change. The site provides a carbon footprint calculator, links to the state's strategic plans regarding climate change, and greenhouse gas reporting requirements in the state. The New Jersey Global Warming web site can be found at http://www.nj.gov/globalwarming/.

New Mexico Climate Change Advisory Group provides information on the New Mexico Climate Change Action Plan and strategies being developed in New Mexico to deal with the likely consequences of global warming. The New Mexico Climate Change Advisory Group web site can be found at http://www.nmclimatechange.us/.

NOAA's Satellite and Information Service provides information on global climate change reporting as well as data on imaging and climatology. The National Climate Data Center (NCDC) maintains the world's largest archive of weather data. The site provides access to NCDC data as well as numerous publications. Data is provided for U.S. temperature, precipitation and drought; U.S. and global extremes; snow data; hurricane data; and other climate monitoring. NOAA's web site on climate change can be found at http://www.ncdc.noaa.gov/oa/climate/climateextremes.html.

Oregon, Climate Change in reports on efforts in Oregon to address climate change. The site provides information on observed climate changes and strategies to confront them. The site provides information of the WCI and Oregon's role in it as well as on the Climate Registry. Climate Change in Oregon's web site can be found at http://www.orego n.gov/ENERGY/GBLWRM/climhme.shtml.

Pennsylvania Climate Change Roadmap provides information on how Pennsylvania plans to deal with the impacts of climate change. Links to the full report are provided. The Pennsylvania Climate Change Roadmap web site can be found at http://www.pecpa. org/roadmap.

Pew Center on Global Climate Change provides information on global warming basics, the science of climate change, the impacts of climate change, technological solutions, and the economics of climate change. The site includes information on a number of the Center's initiatives including: policy briefs, U.S. climate legislation, the post–Kyoto international framework, the Pew coal initiative, corporate strategies, and state or regional climate action programs. The Pew Center on Global Climate Change web site can be found at http://www.pewclimate.org/.

Regional Greenhouse Gas Initiative (RGGI) provides information on the ten-state partnership that makes up RGGI and its efforts. The site contains information on emissions tracking, carbon auctions, and allowable offsets. The RGGI web site can be found at http://www.rggi.org/home.

Sierra Club Clean Energy Campaign provides useful information on how repowering the U.S. with green energy will result in job creation and the only significant way to stem climate change. The site contains information on residential construction and the Smart Grid. The Sierra Club's web site can be found at http://www.sierraclub.org/energy/.

Terrapass provides a web site that allows visitors to measure their carbon footprint and to purchase offsets to cover their emissions. The site provides services to individuals as well as businesses. Also provided are the programs descriptions of how Terrapass invests the offset money and how it is reducing greenhouse gas emissions. The Terrapass web site can be found at http://www.terrapass.com/.

Transportation and Climate Clearinghouse is a central portal for all issues associated with transportation and climate change created and maintained by the U.S. Department of Transportation. The site provides information on greenhouse gas inventories, analytic methods and tools for measuring greenhouse gas emissions from transportation, and potential impacts of climate change on the transportation infrastructure. The site also contains information on how knowledge of climate change can be used for transportation decision making. DOT's web site can be found at http://climate.dot.gov/.

United Nations Development Program energy and environment efforts include climate change. The UNDP programs seek to align development efforts with climate mitigation and adaption efforts that do not slow development efforts. The site provides information on Clean Development Mechanism projects, the Millennium Development Goals and carbon constraints, interactions between UNDP and the Global Environmental Facility, and the Reduced Emissions from Deforestation and Degradation in Developing Countries program. United Nations Development Program web site can be found at http://www.undp.org/climatechange.

United Nations Environmental Program provides excellent information on climate change. The site includes information to define and describe climate change; what can be done to combat climate change; UNEP actions on climate change; UNEP's efforts at mitigation, adaptation, communication, and science. The site provides access to questions and answers with UN experts on climate change. The UNEP's web site can be found at http://www.unep.org/themes/climatechange/.

United Nations Framework Convention on Climate Change is an extensive site that provides essential background and detail of the international agreements associated with climate change. The site also provides information on national reports, greenhouse gas data, the methods and science used, parties to the agreements, observer nations, and the United Nations Secretariat charged with overseeing the international climate change treaty negotiation and assessment process. The UNFCCC's web site can be found at http://unfccc.int/2860.php.

USAID provides information about integrating climate change with development and its climate change program. USAID funds development efforts that reduce greenhouse gas emissions, support reforestation, conservation, and biodiversity. The USAID web site can be found at http://www.usaid.gov/our_work/environment/climate/.

U.S. Climate Change Science Program integrates research done by thirteen federal agencies on climate change. The site contains access to reports of the program and of the U.S. Global Change Research Program. The U.S. Climate Change Science Program web site can be found at http://www.climatescience.gov/.

U.S. Climate Change Technology Program is a multi agency planning and coordinating group with a mission of speeding the development and deployment of technologies that can reduce, avoid, or capture greenhouse gas emissions. The site provides access to the strategic plan of the CCTP as well as a technical review of the U.S. Climate Program's R&D portfolio. The U.S. Climate Change Technology Program web site can be found at http://www.climatetechnology.gov/.

USDA's Office of Global Climate Change is the central organization within the Department of Agriculture that provides analysis on the impacts of climate change on agriculture and forestry. The site provides links to reports and greenhouse gas inventories with particular attention to methane. USDA's Office of Global Climate Change web site can be found at http://www.usda.gov/oce/global_change/.

U.S. Department of Energy provides information on voluntary registries in the U.S., activities of the Committee on Climate Change Science and Technology Integration, and activities of the Climate Change Technology Program. DOE's web site can be found at http://www.energy.gov/environment/climatechange.htm.

U.S. Department of State provides information on on-going federal government diplomatic efforts to deal with the issue of climate change. Specific information is provided for the Asia-Pacific Partnership on Clean Development and Climate, Major Economies Process on Energy Security and Climate Change, and Bilateral and Regional Climate Change Partnerships.The State Department's web site can be found at http://www.state.gov/g/oes/climate/.

U.S. Environmental Protection Agency provides an extensive amount of information about climate change. The information on the site includes basic information about global warming, frequently asked questions, the science of climate change, greenhouse gas emissions, health and environmental effects, EPA regulatory efforts, U.S. climate change policy, climate change economics, and what you can do to reduce your carbon footprint. The site contains a carbon calculator so that visitors can measure their own carbon footprint. The EPA's web site can be found at http://www.epa.gov/climatechange.

U.S. Forest Service Climate Change Resource Center provides information and tools for resource managers that nzeed to make decisions for projects and planning for lands in the West. The site details the changes that climate change has already brought to the West and provides decision support models and simulations to assist decision making. The U.S. Forest Service Climate Change Resource Center web site can be found at http://www.fs.fed.us/ccrc/.

U.S. Geological Survey provides information on climate change science research and on a number of dynamic systems that are affected by climate change. Information is provided for Atlantic estuaries, Alaska, Antarctic coastal change, the Everglades, glacier studies, lake systems, and other issues. The USGS web page can be found at http:// geochange.er.usgs.gov/.

U.S. National Assessment of Climate Change provides a full assessment of the impacts of climate change for the United States with special reports on agriculture, water, health, forests, coastal areas and marine resources. The site includes links to other important U.S. assessments and working groups. The U.S. National Assessment of Climate Change web site can be found at http://www.usgcrp.gov/usgcrp/nacc/.

Vermont Governor's Commission on Climate Change provides access to actions the state is taking vis-à-vis climate change. Documents are posted. The Vermont Governor's Commission on Climate Change web site can be found at http://www.vtclimatechange.us/.

West Coast Governor's Global Warming Initiative provides information on the agreement between California, Oregon, and Washington to reduce global warming pollution. Links are provided to a number of reports and studies that focus on the impacts of global warming to the West. The West Coast Governor's Global Warming Initiative web site can be found at http://www.ef.org/westcoastclimate/.

Western Climate Initiative provides information on the regional agreement and its progress. The site contains information on the partners, economic analysis, public involvement, meetings and events and status reports. The Western Climate Initiative web site can be found at http://www.westernclimateinitiative.org/.

Woods Hole Oceanographic Institution's Abrupt Climate Change research program looks at the dangers of rapid shifts in climate due to the buildup of greenhouse gases in the atmosphere. The site provides information about global warming and the oceans, ocean monitoring systems, and polar research. Woods Hole Oceanographic Institution's Abrupt Climate Change web site can be found at http://www.whoi.edu/page.do?pid=12455.

World Bank provides detailed information on how global warming is affecting the developing world and what is being done to stop it. The site includes information on climate investment funds, vulnerability and adaptation, mitigation, and programs under development. The site contains information on the different regions of the world and how they are and will be impacted by global warming. The World Bank web site can be found at http://web.worldbank.org/WBSITE/EXTERNAL/TOPICS/ENVIRONMENT/EXTC C/0,,menuPK:407870~pagePK:149018~piPK:149093~theSitePK:407864,00.html.

World Health Organization provides a site that emphasizes climate change and human health. Information is provided about temperature–related illness and death, air pollution-related effects, water- and food-borne related diseases, insect and rodent related diseases, effects of food and water shortages, and mental, nutritional, infectious impacts. The World Health Organization web site can be found at http://www.who.int/global change/climate/en/.

World Wildlife Fund's site on climate change provides information on news associated with global warming, as well as frequently asked questions, and facts about global warming. The site includes a variety of audio video materials as well as photos. The WWF's web site can be found at http://www.panda.org/wwf_news/.

Chapter Notes

Chapter 1

1. Spencer Weart, *The Discovery of Global Warming*, updated online edition, http://www.aip.org/hsitory/climate (accessed May 15, 2007). See also Spencer Weart, *The Discovery of Global Warming* (Cambridge: Harvard University Press, 2003).

2. Gladwin Hill, "Warming Arctic Climate Melting Glaciers Faster, Raising Ocean Level, Scientist Says," *New York Times*, May 30, 1947, p. 23.

3. Jacqueline Berke and Vivian Wilson," Our Climate Changes," *Washington Post*, November 17, 1947, p. 11.

4. H. Le Treut, R. Somerville, U. Cubasch, Y. Ding, C. Mauritzen, A. Mokssit, T. Peterson, and M. Prather, "Historical Overview of Climate Change," in *Climate Change 2007: The Physical Science Basis*, Contribution of Working Group I to the Fourth Assessment Report of the Intergovernmental Panel on Climate Change, S. Solomon, D. Qin, M. Manning, Z. Chen, M. Marquis, K.B. Averyt, M. Tignor and H.L. Miller, eds. (Cambridge: Cambridge University Press, 2007).

5. Weart.

6. Jacqueline Vaughn, *Environmental Politics: Domestic and Global Dimensions* (Belmont, CA: Thomson Wadsworth, 2007).

7. Sam Pope Brewer, "Study Says Man Alters Climate," *New York Times*, September 23, 1971, p. 22.

8. Walter Sullivan, "Scientists Ask Why World Climate is Changing: Major Cooling May Be Ahead," *New York Times*, May 21, 1975, p. 92. See also James P. Sterba, "Climatologists Forecast Stormy Economic Future," *New York Times*, July 12, 1976, p. 40.

9. Walter Sullivan, "Scientists Warn of Expected Rise of Carbon Dioxide Content in Air," *New York Times*, October 12, 1976, p. 18. See also Weart.

10. Robert C. Cowen, "Burning Too Much Coal Could Change Climate," *Christian Science Monitor*, April 22, 1977, p.1.

11. Walter Sullivan, "Climate Peril May Force Limits on Coal and Oil, Carter Aide Says," *New York Times*, June 3, 1977, p. 55.

12. Walter Sullivan, "Climate Specialists, in Poll, Foresee No Catastrophic Weather Changes in Rest of Century," *New York Times*, February 18, 1978, p. 9.

13. Weart.

14. Le Treut et al.

15. Walter Sullivan, "Increased Burning of Fuels Could Alter Climate," *New York Times*, November 20, 1979, p. C1.

16. Walter Sullivan, "Study Finds Warming Trend That Could Raise Sea Levels," *New York Times*, August 22, 1981, p. 1.

17. Robert Reinhold, "Evidence is Found of Warming Trend," *New York Times*, October 19, 1981, p. A21.

18. Phillip J. Hilts, "The Federal Report: Global Warming Trend is Forecast by the EPA," *Washington Post*, October 19, 1983, p. A25.

19. Philip Shabecoff, "Haste on Global Warming Trend is Opposed," *New York Times*, October 21, 1983, p.A1.

20. James Gleick, "Rare Gases May Speed the Warming of the Earth," *New York Times*, April 30, 1985, p. C1.

21. Philip Shabecoff, "Sharp Cut in Burning of Fossil Fuels is Urged to Battle Shift in Climate," *New York Times*, June 24, 1988, p. A1.

22. Rajendra K. Pachauri, *16 Years of Scientific Assessment in Support of the Climate Convention*, Intergovernmental Panel on Climate Change, 2004, http://www.ipcc.ch/pdf/10th-anniversary/anniversary-brochure.pdf (accessed January 14, 2008).

23. Le Treut et al.

24. Pachauri.

25. Weart.

26. Le Treut et al.

27. "IPCC 2007: Summary for Policymakers," Working Group I, p. 3.

28. Ibid, p.5.

29. "IPCC 2007: Summary for Policymakers," Working Group I.

30. Le Treut et al.

31. U.S. Environmental Protection Agency, *Inventory of U.S. Greenhouse Gas Emissions and Sinks: 1990–2005* (Washington, D.C.: U.S. EPA, 2007).

32. Le Treut et al.

33. "IPCC 2007: Summary for Policymakers," Working Group I. See also U.S. EPA, *Inventory of U.S. Greenhouse Gas Emissions and Sinks: 1990–2005.*

34. "IPCC 2007: Summary for Policymakers," Working Group I.

35. Ibid.

36. U.S. EPA, *Inventory of U.S. Greenhouse Gas Emissions and Sinks.*

37. "IPCC 2007: Summary for Policymakers," Working Group I.

38. Ibid., p.7.

39. "IPCC 2007: Summary for Policymakers," Working Group I.

40. Ibid., p.13.

41. "IPCC 2007: Summary for Policymakers," in *Climate Change 2007: The Physical Science Basis*, Contribution of Working Group II to the Fourth Assessment Report of the Intergovernmental Panel on Climate Change, M.L. Parry, O.F. Canziani, J.P. Palutikof, P.J. van der Linden, and C.E. Hanson, eds. (Cambridge: Cambride University Press, 2007), p.8.

42. "IPCC 2007: Summary for Policymakers," Working Group II.

43. Ibid.

44. Ibid.

45. Paul John Beggs and Hilary Jane Bambrick, "Is the Global Rise of Asthma an Early Impact of Anthropogenic Climate Change?" *Environmental Health Perspectives* 113(8): 915–919. See also Paul John Beggs, "Impacts of Climate Change on Aeroallergens: Past and Future," *Clinical and Experimental Allergy* 34: 1507–1513.

46. Lewis Smith, "Climate Change 'Will Lead to Warfare over Food and Water,'" *Timesonline*, http://www.timesonline.co.uk/tol/news/environment/article3241362.ece (accessed January 24, 2008).

47. "IPCC 2007: Summary for Policymakers," Working Group II.

48. Ibid., p. 12.

49. "IPCC 2007: Summary for Policymakers," Working Group II.

50. Carlos Corvalan, "Climate Change and Human Health," *Bulletin of the World Health Organization* 85(11): 830–832.

51. "IPCC 2007: Summary for Policymakers," Working Group II.

52. Jennifer Fisher Wilson, "Facing an Uncertain Climate," *Annals of Internal Medicine* 146(2): 153–155.

53. Yafeng Shi, Yongping Shen, Ersi Kang, Dongliang Li, Yongjian Ding, Gouwei Zhang, and Ruji Hu, "Recent and Future Climate Change in Northwest China," *Climatic Change* 80 (2007): 379–393.

54. "IPCC 2007: Summary for Policymakers," Working Group II.

55. Ibid.

56. Elisabeth Rosenthal, "As Earth Warms Up, Tropical Virus Moves to Italy," *New York Times*, December 23, 2007, http://www.nytimes.com/2007/12/23/workd/europe/23virus.html (accessed January 13, 2008).

57. "IPCC 2007: Summary for Policymakers," Working Group II.

58. Marc Kaufman, "Decline in Snowpack is Blamed on Warming," *Washington Post*, February 1, 2008, p. A01.

59. Richard A. Kerr, "Global Warming Is Changing the World," *Science* 316 (2007): 188–190.

60. "IPCC 2007: Summary for Policymakers," Working Group II.

61. Maggie Fox, "Tropical Dengue Fever May Threaten U.S.," *Reuters*, January 8, 2008, http://www.reuters.com/articlePrint?articledId=USN0847856420080108 (accessed January 13, 2008).

62. Eliza Barclay, "Is Climate Change Affecting Dengue in the Americas?" *The Lancet* 371: 973–974.

63. "IPCC 2007: Summary for Policymakers," Working Group II.

64. Larry Hinzman, Neil Bettez, W. Robert Bolton, F. Stuart Chapin, Mark Dyurgerov, Chris Fastie, Brad Griffith, Robert Hollister, Allen Hope, Henry Huntington, Anne Jensen, Gensuo Jia, Torre Jorgenson, Douglas Kane, David Klein, Gary Kofinas, Amanda Lynch, Andrea Lloyd, A. David McGuire, Frederick Nelson, Walther Oechel, Thomas Osterkamp, Charles Racine, Vladimir Romanovsky, Robert Stone, Douglas Stow, Matthew Sturm, Craig Tweedie, George Vourlitis, Marilyn Walker, Donald Walker, Patrick Webber, Jeffrey Welker, Kevin Winker, and Kenji Yoshikawa, "Evidence and Implications of Recent Climate Change in Northern Alaska and Other Artic Regions," *Climatic Change* 72: 251–298.

65. Le Treut et al.

66. "IPCC 2007: Summary for Policymakers," Working Group II.

67. "IPCC 2005: Guidance Notes for Lead Authors of the IPCC Fourth Assessment Report on Addressing Uncertainties," Inter-

governmental Panel on Climate Change, July 2005.

68. Richard A. Kerr, "A Worrying Trend of Less Ice, Higher Seas," *Science* 311: 1698–1701.

69. Hinzman et al.

70. Roger Pielke, Jr., Tom Wigley and Christopher Green, "Dangerous Assumptions," *Nature* 452: 531–532.

71. "IPCC 2007: Summary for Policymakers," in *Climate Change 2007: Mitigation*, Contribution of Working Group III to the Fourth Assessment Report of the Intergovernmental Panel on Climate Change, B. Metz, O.R. Davidson, P.R. Bosch, R. Dave, L.A. Meyer, eds. (Cambridge: Cambridge University Press, 2007).

72. Corvalan.

73. Nicholas Stern, *The Stern Review on the Economics of Climate Change*, HM Treasury Cabinet Office, 2006, http://www.hm-treasury.gov.uk/media/999/76/closed_short_executive_summary.pdf (accessed April 2, 2007).

74. Kenneth J. Arrow, "Global Climate Change: A Challenge to Policy," *Economists' Voice*, 2007, www.bepress.com/ev (accessed June 30, 2007).

75. Stephen Leahy, "Climate Change-US: Delay Now, Pay Dearly Later," *Interpress Service News Agency*, October 23, 2007, http://www.ipsnews.net/print.asp?idnews=39674 (accessed October 23, 2007).

76. Government Accountability Office, *Climate Change: Financial Risks to Federal and Private Insurers in Coming Decades Are Potentially Significant*, Report to the Committee on Homeland Security and Governmental Affairs, U.S. Senate, GAO-07-285, 2007.

77. Stern.

78. Ibid.

79. Laura MacInnis, "Millions of Jobs at Risk from Climate Change: U.N.," *Reuters*, November 12, 2007, http://www.reuters.com/articlePrint?articleId=USL127232522007112 (accessed November 15, 2007).

80. Ari Levy, "Google Plans to Develop Cheaper Solar, Wind Power," *Bloomberg.com*, 2007, http://www.bloomberg.com/apps/news?pid=20670001&refer=home&sid=ar7BFZU9PVJE (accessed December 1, 2007).

81. Matt Richtel, "Start-up Fervor Shifts to Energy in silicon Valley," *New York Times*, March 14, 2007, http://www.nytimes.com/2007/03/14/technology/14valley.html (accessed March 15, 2007).

82. Jonathan Lash and Fred Wellington, "Competitive Advantage on a Warming Planet, *Harvard Business Review* 85(3): 94–102.

83. Laurens M. Bouwer, Ryan P. Crompton, Ebergard Faust, and Peter Hoppe, "Confronting Disaster Losses," *Science* 318: 753.

84. Andrew Dlugolecki, "Climate Change and the Insurance Sector," *The Geneva Papers* 33: 71–90.

85. Paul Reynolds, "Security Council Takes on Global Warming," *BBC News*, April 16, 2007, http://news.bbc.co.uk/go/pr/fr/-/2/hi/americas/6559211.stm (accessed April 17, 2007).

86. Andrew Klug, *Global Warming: A National Security Issue?* Naval War College, Newport, RI, 2006.

87. Military Advisory Board, *National Security and the Threat of Climate Change*, SecurityAndClimate.cna.org, 2007.

88. Ibid.

89. Ibid.

90. Andrew C. Revkin and Timothy Williams, "Global Warming Called Security Threat," *New York Times*, April 15, 2007, http://www.nytimes.com/2007/04/15/us/15warm.html (accessed April 16, 2007).

Chapter 2

1. Thomas D. Peterson and Adam Z. Rose, "Reducing Conflicts Between Climate Policy And Energy Policy in the U.S.: The Important Role of the States." *Energy Policy* 34 (2006): 619–631.

2. Vaughn.

3. Weart.

4. Vaughn.

5. Samuel P. Hays, *A History of Environmental Politics Since 1945* (Pittsburg: University of Pittsburg Press, 2000).

6. Weart.

7. John M. Broder, "At Climate Meeting Bush Does Not Specify Goals," *New York Times*, September 29, 2007, http://www.nytimes.com/2007/09/29/washington/29climate.html (accessed December 29, 2007).

8. Thomas Fuller and Elisabeth Rosenthal, "Bitter Divisions Exposed At Climate Talks," *New York Times*, December 14, 2007, http://www.nytimes.com/2007/12/14/world/14climate.html (accessed December 13, 2007).

9. Thomas Fuller and Andrew C. Revkin, "Climate Plan Looks Beyond Bush's Tenure," *New York Times*, December 16, 2007, http://www.nytimes.com/2007/12/16/world/16climate.html (accessed December 17, 2007).

10. Sondra Bogdonoff and Jonathan Rubin, "The Regional Greenhouse Gas Initiative: Taking Action in Maine," *Environment* 49: 9–16.

11. Peterson and Rose.

12. Jonathan H. Adler, "Can California Catch a Waiver?" *National Review*, May 24, 2007, http://article.nationalreview.com/?q=YWVlOGEzZjk3NWE5MmI2Yzk1MWZjZmUyNjNkYmJkZjA (accessed January 3, 2008).

13. Kirsten H. Engel, "Mitigating Global Climate Change In The United States: A Regional Approach," *N.Y.U. Environmental Law Journal* 14: 54–85. See also Barry G. Rabe, *Statehouse and Greenhouse: The Emerging Politics of American Climate Change Policy* (Washington, D.C.: Brookings Institution Press, 2004).

14. Bogdonoff and Rubin.

15. Union of Concerned Scientists, *AB 32: Global Warming Solutions Act*, 2006, http://www.law.stanford.edu/program/centers/enrlp/pdf/AB-32-fact-sheet.pdf (accessed December 27, 2007).

16. James A. Holtkamp, "Dealing With Climate Change In The United States: The Non-Federal Response," *Journal of Land, Resources, & Environmental Law* 27: 79–86.

17. Ryan M. Colker, "States Take Initiative," *ASHRAE Journal*, August 2007, p. 64.

18. Holtkamp.

19. Colker, p. 64.

20. Holtkamp.

21. Colker, p. 64.

22. U.S. Conference of Mayors, *U.S. Conference of Mayors Climate Protection Agreement*, 2005, http://usmayors.org/climateprotection/agreement.htm (accessed December 28, 2007).

23. Cool Cities, *Cool Cities: Solving Global Warming a City at a Time*, 2005, http://coolcities.us/ (accessed December 28, 2007).

24. Dianne Rahm, ed., *Sustainable Energy and the States: Essays on Politics, Markets, and Leadership* (Jefferson, North Carolina: McFarland, 2006).

25. Henrik Selin and Stacy D. Vandeveer, "Canadian-U.S. Environmental Cooperation: Climate Change Networks and Regional Action," *American Review of Canadian Studies* 35(2): 353–378.

26. Hays.

27. Selin and Vandeveer.

28. Pew Center on Climate Change, *What's Being Done in the States*, 2007, http://www.pewclimate.org/what_s_being_done/in_the_states (accessed November 6, 2007).

29. RGGI, *Participating States*, Regional Greenhouse Gas Initiative, 2007, http://www.rggi.org/states.htm (accessed December 29, 2007).

30. Emma Marris, "Western States Launch Carbon Scheme," *Nature* 446: 114.

31. RGGI, *Post-Model Rule Action Plan*, Regional Greenhouse Gas Initiative, 2006, http://www.rggi.org/modelrule.htm (accessed December 26, 2007).

32. Bogdonoff and Rubin.

33. Engel. See also Rabe.

34. John Byrne, Kristen Hughes, Wilson Rickerson, and Lado Kurdgelashvili, "American Policy Conflict in the Greenhouse: Divergent Trends in Federal, Regional, State, and Local Green Energy and Climate Change Policy," *Energy Policy* 35: 4555–4573.

35. Pew Center on Climate Change.

36. Western Governors' Association, *2005–06 Strategic Agenda*, 2005, http://www.westgov.org/wga_strtegic_agenda.htm (accessed September 23, 2007).

37. Doug Larson, executive director, Western Interstate Energy Board, personal interview, February 26, 2008.

38. Platts Electric Utility Week, "Western Renewable Tracking System to Help Utilities Meet State Requirements," *Platts Electric Utility Week*, July 9, 2007.

39. Pew Center on Climate Change.

40. Marris. See also Pew Center on Climate Change.

41. Engel. See also Great Plains Institute, *Powering the Plains*, 2007, http://www.gpisd.net/resource.html?Id=61 (accessed November 6, 2007).

42. Brad Crabtree, program director, Great Plains Institute, personal interview, March 7, 2008.

43. Midwest Governors' Association, Midwestern Energy Security & Climate Stewardship Summit, *Midwestern Greenhouse Gas Accord*, 2007.

44. Ibid.

45. Crabtree.

46. Engel.

47. Ibid.

48. Yvonne Gross, "Kyoto, Congress, or Bust: The Constitutional Invalidity of State CO_2 Cap-and-Trade Programs," *Thomas Jefferson Law Review* 28: 205–236.

49. Adler.

50. Holtkamp.

51. John J. Fialka, "States Want Higher Emissions Bar," *Wall Street Journal*, April 4, 2007, p. A6.

52. Linda Greenhouse, "Justices Rule Against Bush Administration On Emissions," *New York Times*, April 2, 2007, http://www.nytimes.com/2007/04/02/washington/02cnd-scotus.html (accessed April 2, 2007).

53. *Massachusetts v. Environmental Protection Agency 549 U.S. 1438* (2007).

54. Platts Coal Outlook, "House Panel To Review Deseret Power For Compliance With CAA," *Platts Coal Outlook* 31(39): 13.

55. Ethan Howland, "EPA Air Permit For Utah Coal-Fired Unit Raises Specter Of Environmental Appeal," *Platts Electric Utility Week*, September 10, 2007, 9.

56. Bob Egelko, "California's Emission-Control Law Upheld On 1st Test In U.S. Court," *San Francisco Chronicle*, December 13, 2007, http://www.sfgate.com/cgi-bin/article.cgi?file

=/c/a/2007/12/13/MN9QTSTAB.DTL (accessed December 14, 2007).

57. John M. Broder and Micheline Maynard, "Denial Of State Emission Plan Was Foreshadowed," *New York Times*, December 21, 2007, http://www.nytimes.com/2007/12/21/washington/21emissions.html (accessed December 28, 2007).

58. Margot Roosevelt, "California Sues Government for Rejecting Bid to Curb Emissions," *Los Angeles Times*, January 3, 2008, http://www.latimes.com/business/la-me-epa3jan03,1,6968553.story?ctrack=3&cset=true.

59. U.S. EPA, *Inventory of U.S. Greenhouse Gas Emissions and Sinks: 1990–2005*.

60. See EPA calculations at http://epa.gov/climatechange/emissions/state_energyCO2inv.html.

61. See United Nations Framework Convention on Climate Change statistics at http://unfccc.int/ghg_emissions_data/ghg_data_from_unfccc/time_series_annexi/items/3814.php.

62. See EPA calculations at http://epa.gov/climatechange/emissions/state_energyCO2inv.html.

63. See United Nations Framework Convention on Climate Change statistics at http://unfccc.int/ghg_emissions_data/ghg_data_from_unfccc/time_series_annexi/items/3814.php.

64. James Brooks, director, Bureau of Air Quality, Maine EPA, personal interview, February 26, 2008. See also Stephen Majkut, chief, Office of Air Resources Board, Rhode Island, personal interview, February 18, 2008, and Karl Michael, program manager, Energy Analysis Program, New York State Energy Research and Development Authority, personal interview, February 14, 2008.

65. Don Cleverdon, technical advisor to the District of Columbia Public Service Commission, personal interview, February 21, 2008.

66. Chris Nelson, senior air pollution control engineer, Connecticut, personal interview, February 21, 2008.

67. Joanne Morin, New Hampshire climate and energy manager, personal interview, February 22, 2008.

68. Diane Franks, program manager, Maryland Air Quality Planning Program, personal interview, February 15, 2008. See also Dick Valentinetti, director, Division of Air Quality Control, Vermont Agency of Natural Resources, personal interview, February 26, 2008.

69. Bill Lamkin, environmental engineer, Massachusetts Department of Environmental Protection, personal interview, February 14, 2008.

70. Janice Adair, special assistant to the director, Washington State Department of Ecology, personal interview, February 14, 2008.

71. Patrick Cummins, project manager, Western Governors' Association, personal interview, February 5, 2008. See also Jane Gray, executive director, Climate and Green Initiatives, Manatoba Province, personal interview, February 7, 2008.

72. Kurk Maurer, deputy director, Office of Policy, Planning and Operations, Arizona Department of Environmental Quality, personal interview, February 5, 2008.

73. Janice Adair, special assistant to the director, Washington State Department of Ecology, personal interview, February 14, 2008.

74. Rich Halvey, energy program director, Western Governors' Association, personal interview, February 22, 2008.

75. Sarah Cottrell, energy and environmental policy advisor for Governor Bill Richardson, personal interview, February 19, 2008.

76. Jane Gray, executive director, Climate and Green Initiatives, Manatoba Province, personal interview, February 7, 2008.

77. Sarah Wash, program associate, Biomass Program, Powering the Plains, personal interview, February 29, 2008.

78. Brendan Jordan, program manager, Great Plains Institute, personal interview, February 26, 2008. See also Rolf Nordstrom, executive director, Great Plains Institute, personal interview, February 28, 2008, and Mike Gregerson, program consultant, Powering the Plains, personal interview, February 29, 2008.

79. Kate Sheppard, "Diplomatic Sanity: Clinton Taps Todd Stern as her Climate Envoy," *Grist Environmental News and Commentary*, January 26, 2009, http://gristmill.grist.org/story/2009/1/26/11253/6739?source=daily (accessed January 27, 2009).

80. Barack H. Obama, *Inaugural Address*, January 20, 2009, http://www.whitehouse.gov/blog/inaugural-address/ (accessed January 21, 2009).

81. Barack H. Obama, *The Agenda: Energy and the Environment*, http://www.whitehouse.gov/agenda/energy_and_environment/ (accessed January 20, 2009).

82. Ibid.

83. John M. Broder, "Obama Directs Regulators to Tighten Auto Standards," *New York Times*, January 26, 2009, http://www.nytimes.com/2009/01/27/us/poliitics/27calif.html (accessed January 27, 2009).

84. Barack H. Obama, *Remarks by the President on Jobs, Energy Independence, and Climate Change*, East Room of the White House, January 26, 2009, http://www.whitehouse.gov/blog_post/Fromperiltoprogress/ (accessed January 28, 2009).

85. Lisa P. Jackson, *Memo to EPA Employ-*

ees, January 23, 2009, http://www.epa.gov/administrator/memotoemployees.html (accessed January 27, 2009).

86. Ibid.

87. John M. Broder, "Obama Directs Regulators to Tighten Auto Standards," *New York Times,* January 27, 2009, http://www.nytimes.com/2009/01/27/us/poliitics/27calif.html (accessed January 26, 2009).

88. Barack H. Obama, *Remarks by the President on Jobs, Energy Independence, and Climate Change,* East Room of the White House, January 26, 2009, http://www.whitehouse.gov/blog_post/Fromperiltoprogress/ (accessed January 28, 2009).

89. Ibid.

90. Ibid.

91. John M. Broder, "A Smaller, Faster Stimulus Plan, but Still with a Lot of Money," *New York Times,* February 14, 2009, http://www.nytimes.com/2009/02/14/us/politics/14stim-intro.ready.html (accessed February 15, 2009).

92. Marianne Lavelle, "The Climate Change Lobby," Center for Public Integrity, 2009, http://www.publicintegrity.org/investigations/climate_change/articles/entry/1171/ (accessed February 26, 2009).

93. David Adam, "Scientists Plan Emergency Summit on Climate Change," February 9, 2009, *Guardian.co.uk.* http://www.guardian.co.uk/environment/2009.feb/09/scientists-summit-climate-change (accessed February 10, 2009).

94. Lavelle, "The Climate Change Lobby."

95. Office of Management and Budget, *Budget of the United States, 2010,* http://www.whitehouse.gov/omb/assets/fy2010_new_era/A_New_Era_of_Responsibility2.pdf (accessed March 2, 2009).

96. Barack H. Obama, *Remarks by the President on Jobs, Energy Independence, and Climate Change* East Room of the White House, January 26, 2009, http://www.whitehouse.gov/blog_post/Fromperiltoprogress/ (accessed January 28, 2009).

Chapter 3

1. Lisa Nelson, "The Role of the United Nations: From Stockholm to Johannesburg," in *Handbook of Globalization and the Environment,* Khi V. Thai, Dianne Rahm, and Jerrell D. Coggburn, eds. (Boca Raton, London, and New York: CRC Press), pp. 155–176.

2. *Declaration of the United Nations Conference on the Human Environment,* 1972, http://www.unep.org/Documents.Multilingual/Default.asp?DocumentID=97&ArticleID=1503 (accessed May 15, 2007).

3. Ibid.

4. Nelson.

5. *Rio Declaration on Environment and Development,* 1992, http://www.unep.org/Documents.Multilingual/Default.asp?DocumentID=78&ArticleID=1163 (accessed May 15, 2007).

6. Ibid.

7. United Nations Division for Sustainable Development, *Agenda 21,* 2004, UN Department of Economic and Social Affairs, Division for Sustainable Development, http://www.un.org/esa/sustdev/documents/agenda21/index.htm (accessed May 15, 2008).

8. *United Nations Framework Convention on Climate Change,* 1992, http://unfccc.int/resource/docs/convkp/conveng.pdf (accessed May 15).

9. Ibid.

10. *The Kyoto Protocol to the United Nations Framework Convention on Climate Change,* 1997, http://unfccc.int/kyoto_protocol/items/2830.php (accessed May 15, 2008).

11. *Rio Declaration on Environment and Development,* 1992, http://www.unep.org/Documents.Multilingual/Default.asp?DocumentID=78&ArticleID=1163 (accessed May 15, 2007).

12. *United Nations Framework Convention on Climate Change,* 1992, http://unfccc.int/resource/docs/convkp/conveng.pdf (accessed May 15).

13. David Howard Davis, "European Global Warming Policy," in *Handbook of Globalization and the Environment,* Thai, Rahm, and Coggburn, eds., pp. 43–60.

14. Keith Bradsher, "Ford Announces Its Withdrawal from Global Climate Coalition," *New York Times,* December 7, 1999, http://query.nytimes.com/gst/fullpage.html?res=9900EOD9103ef934A96F9582 (accessed November 8, 2007).

15. Union of Concerned Scientists, *Global Warming: Responding to Global Warming Skeptics — Prominent Skeptics Organizations,* 2007, http://www.ucsusa.org/global_warming/science/skeptic-organizations.html (accessed November 9, 2007).

16. Union of Concerned Scientists, *Smoke, Mirrors and Hot Air: How ExxonMobil Uses Big Tobacco's Tactics to Manufacture Uncertainty on Climate Science* (Cambridge, Massachusetts: Union of Concerned Scientists, 2007).

17. Weart.

18. Davis, "European Global Warming Policy," in Thai, Rahm, and Coggburn, eds., pp. 43–60.

19. United Nations Framework Convention on Climate Change, "Emissions Trading," n.d., http://unfccc.int/kyoto_protocol/mechanis

ms/emissions_trading/items/2731.php (accessed May 19, 2008).

20. United Nations Framework Convention on Climate Change, "LULUCF Under the Kyoto Protocol," n.d., http://unfccc.int/metho ds_and_science/lulucf/items/4129.php (accessed May 19, 2008).

21. United Nations Framework Convention on Climate Change, "The Kyoto Protocol," 1997, http://unfccc.int/kyoto_protocol/items/2830.php (accesses May 15, 2008).

22. Ibid.

23. United Nations Framework Convention on Climate Change, "Mechanisms Under the Kyoto Protocol: Emsissions Trading, Clean Development Mechanism and Joint Development," n.d., http://unfccc.int/kyoto_protocol/mechanisms/items/1673.php (accessed May 19, 2008).

24. United Nations Framework Convention on Climate Change, "Registry Systems Under the Kyoto Protocol," n.d., http://unfccc.int/ky oto_protocol/registry_systems/items/2723.php (accessed May 19, 2008).

25. United Nations Framework Convention on Climate Change, "An Introduction to the Kyoto Protocol Compliance Mechanism," n.d., http://unfccc.int/kyoto_protocol/compliance/i ntroduction/items/3024.php (accessed May 19, 2008).

26. European Environmental Agency, *Greenhouse Gas Emission Trends and Projections in Europe 2007*, 2007, http://reports.eea.europa. eu/eea_report_2007_5/en (accessed May 22, 2008).

27. Martin Mittelstaedt, "Greenhouse-gas Emissions Decrease for Second Year," *Globe and Mail*, May 16, 2008, http://www.theglobeandm ail.com/servlet/story/RTGAM.20080516.wemi ssions17/BNStory/National/?page=rss&id=RT GAM.20080516.wemissions17 (accessed May 19, 2008).

28. Davis, "European Global Warming Policy," in Thai, Rahm, and Coggburn, eds., pp. 43–60.

29. Edwin Woerdman, "Hot Air Trading Under the Kyoto Protocol: An Environmental Problem or Not?" *European Environmental Law Review*, March 2005: 71–77.

30. Michael Szabo, " Russia May Hold on to Emission Rights," *PlanetArk World Environmental News*, May 15, 2008, http://www.planet ark.org/avantgo/dailynewsstory.cfm?newsi d=48299 (accessed May 19, 2008).

31. Davis, "European Global Warming Policy," in Thai, Rahm, and Coggburn, eds., pp. 43–60.

32. World Wildlife Fund, *Clean Energy Investment in Developing Countries Must Do Better*, 2007, http://www.panda.org/about_wwf/

what_we_do/climate_change/news/index.cfm? uNewsID=118260 (accessed May 22, 2008).

33. Steffen Kallbekken, *Crime and Punishment in the Kyoto Protocol*, Center for International Climate and Environmental Research, Oslo, 2004, http://www.cicero.uio.no/fulltext/ index_e.aspx?id=3029 (accessed January 22, 2008).

34. Chetan Chauhan, "India to Take Firm Stand on Global Warming," *Hindustan Times*, May 22, 2007, http://www.hindustantimes.c om/StoryPage/Print.aspx?ID=6649f9ac-3bel-4 4bb-81de-3a16295c3bb4 (accessed May 19, 2008).

35. Climate Change Research Center, *2007 Bali Climate Declaration by Scientists*, Climate Change Research Center, University of New South Wales, Sydney, Australia, 2007, http://w ww.climate.unsw.edu.au/bali/ (accessed December 8, 2007).

36. Harriette Cecilio, "World's Top Two Polluters U.S. and China Won't Commit to Mandatory Emissions Cuts," *All Headline News*, December 9, 2007, http://www.allheadli nenews.com/articles/7009403079 (accessed December 11, 2007).

37. Richard Black, "Big Steps Ahead on the Bali Roadmap," *BBC News*, 2007, http:// news.bbc.co.uk/1/hi/sci/tech/7136485.stm (accessed December 11, 2007).

38. Ibid.

39. E. Kuntsi-Reunanen and J. Luukkanen, "Greenhouse Gas Emission Reductions in the Post-Kyoto Period: Emission Intensity Changes Required under the 'Contraction and Convergence' Approach," *National Resources Forum* 30: 272–279.

40. Peter Spotts, "In Bali, New Incentive for developing Nations to Curb Emissions," *Christian Science Monitor*, December 14, 2007, http:// www.csmonitor.com/2007/1214/p01s03-wogi. htm (accessed December 14, 2007).

41. Richard Harris, "China Softens Stance on Emissions at Bali Meeting," Morning Edition, *National Public Radio*, December 13, 2007.

42. Jane Spencer and Tom Wright, "China, U.S. Spar at Climate Talks," *The Wall Street Journal Online*, December 6, 2007, http://onli ne.wsj.com/public/article_print/SB1196879224 42514687.html (accessed December 11, 2007).

43. Yvo de Boer and Toni Johnson, "Interview: Intelligent Financial Engineering Needed for Climate Deal," *New York Times*, May 19, 2008, http://www.nytimes.com/cfr/workd/slot 1_20080519.html?pagewanted=print (accessed May 23, 2008).

44. Alan Beattle, "Green Barricade: Trade Faces a New Test as Carbon Taxes Go Global," *Financial Times*, January 23, 2008, http://www. ft.com/cms/s/0/43640858-c9e1–11dc-b5dc-0

00077b07658.html?nclick_check=1 (accessed January 29, 2008).

45. Center for Sustainable Systems, *Greenhouse Gases Factsheets*, University of Michigan, 2007, http://css.snre.umich.edu/facts (accessed January 8, 2009).

Chapter 4

1. Barack H. Obama, *Inaugural Address*, January 20, 2009, http://www.whitehouse.gov/blog/inaugural-address/ (accessed January 21, 2009).

2. Earl Babbie, *The Practice of Social Research*, 11th ed. (Belmont, CA: Thomson Wadsworth, 2007).

3. H. Le Treut et al.

4. ExxonMobil, *Taking on the World's Toughest Energy Challenges*, ExxonMobil Summary Annual Report, 2007, http://www.exxonmobil.com/corporate/files/news_pub_sar_2007.pdf

5. Seth Shulman, et al. *Smoke, Mirrors & Hot Air: How ExxonMobil Uses Big Tobacco's Tactics to Manufacture Uncertainty on Climate Science* (Cambridge, MA: Union of Concerned Scientists, 2007).

6. Emily Robinson, "Exxon Exposed," *Catalyst* 6(1): 2–4.

7. Keith Bradsher, "Ford Announces Its Withdrawal From Global Climate Coalition," *New York Times*, December 1999, http://query.nytimes.com/gst/fullpage.html?res=9900E0D9103EF934A35751C1A96F958260 (accessed November 8, 2007).

8. Virginia Gerwin, "Climate Lobby Group Closes Down," *Nature* 414 (7): 567.

9. Shulman, et al.

10. Joe Walker, *Draft Global Climate Science Communications Action Plan*, American Petroleum Institute memo to Global Climate Science Team, 1998, http//:www.euronet.nl/users/e_wesker/ew@shell/API-prop.html (accessed September 19, 2008), p. 2.

11. Ibid., p. 3.

12. Ibid., p. 4.

13. Ibid., p. 5.

14. Ibid.

15. Ibid., p. 6.

16. Ibid.

17. Ibid., p. 3.

18. Edmund L. Andrews, "Testimony by Oil Executives is Challenged," *New York Times*, November 17, 2005, http://www.nytimes.com/2005/11/17/business/17oil.html?_r=1&scp=2&sq=cheney%20energy%20task%20force%20exxonmobil&st=cse&oref=slogin (accessed September 20, 2008).

19. Ken Brill, *Briefing Memorandum to Under Secretary Dobriansky*, United States Department of State, June 20, 2001.

20. Jennifer S. Lee, "Exxon Backs Groups that Question Global Warming," *New York Times*, May 28, 2003, http://query.nytimes.com/gst/fullpage.html?res=9802E1D91131F93BA15756C0A9659C8B63&scp=1&sq=exxon%20backs%20froups%20that%20question%20global%20warming&st=cse (accessed September 20, 2008).

21. Shulman, et al.

22. Lee.

23. Shulman, et al.

24. Lee.

25. Competitive Enterprise Institute, "About CEI," 2008, http://cei.org/about (accessed September 22, 2008).

26. Competitive Enterprise Institute, "Global Warming/Glaciers," 2008, http://cei.org/pages/co2.cfm (accessed September 21, 2008).

27. Competitive Enterprise Institute, "Global Warming FAQ," 2008, http://cei.org/sections/subsection.cfm?section=3 (accessed November 8, 2008).

28. George Marshall Institute, "News," 2008, http://www.marshall.org/subcategory.php?id=9 (accessed September 21, 2008).

29. Ibid.

30. Sourcewatch, "Oregon Institute of Science and Medicine," http://www.sourcewatch.org/index.php?title=Oregon_Institute_of_Science_and_Medicine, 2008 (accessed September 21, 2008). Also see Union of Concerned Scientists, *Global Warming Skeptics Organizations*, 2007, http://www.ucsusa.org/global_warming/science_and_impacts/global_warming_contrarians/global-warming-skeptic.html (accessed May 10, 2007).

31. Aaron M. McCright and Riley E. Dunlap, "Defeating Kyoto: The Conservative Movement's Impact on U.S. Climate Change Policy," *Social Problems* 50(3): 348–373.

32. Aaron M. McCright and Riley E. Dunlap, "Challenging Global Warming as a Social Problem: An Analysis of the Conservative Movement's Counter-Claims," *Social Problems* 47(4): 499–522.

33. Jimmy Carter, *Our Endangered Values: America's Moral Crisis* (New York: Simon & Schuster, 2005).

34. W. Henry Lambright, "Government and Science: A Troubled, Critical Relationship and What Can Be Done About It," *Public Administration Review* January/February 2008, pp. 5–18.

35. Frank Luntz, "The Environment: A Cleaner Safer, Healthier America," *The Luntz Research Companies — Strait Talk*, pp. 137–138.

36. Ibid., p. 138.

37. Lambright.

38. Andrew C. Revkin, "NASA's Goals Delete Mention of Home Planet," *New York Times*, July 22, 2006, http://www.nytimes.co m/2006/07/22/science/22nasa.html (accessed March 8, 2007).

39. Andrew C. Revkin, "Memos Tell Officials How to Discuss Climate," *New York Times*, March 8, 2007, http://www.nytimes. com/2007/03/08/washington/08polar.html (accessed March 8, 2007).

40. Andrew C. Revkin, "Climate Change Testimony was Edited by White House," *New York Times*, October 25, 2007, http://www.ny times.com/2007/10/25/science/earth/25clima te.html (accessed October 25, 2007).

41. Weart.

42. Matthew C. Nisbet, "The Polls-Trends: Twenty Years of Public Opinion About Global Warming," *Public Opinion Quarterly* 71(3): 444–470.

43. Eric Weiner, "American Conscience Waking Up to Climate Change," *National Public Radio*, December 6, 2007, http://www.np r.org/templates/story/story.php?storyId=11 787222 (accessed December 6, 2007).

44. Nisbet.

45. Weart.

46. Maxwell T. Boykoff and Jules M. Boykoff, "Climate Change and Journalistic Norms: A Case-Study of US Mass Media Coverage," *Geoforum* 38: 1190–1204.

47. Mitch Leslie, "Sifting for Truth About Global Warming. *Science* 306 (5707): 2167–2167.

48. Ruth A. Reck, "Global Climate Change: A Challenge for Civilization," paper delivered at the 2008 North American Energy Summit, University of Texas at San Antonio.

49. Aaron McCright and Riley E. Dunlap, "Defeating Kyoto: The Conservative Movement's Impact on U.S. Climate Change Policy," *Social Problems* 50(3): 348–373.

50. William J. Broad, "From a Rapt Audience, a Call to Cool the Hype," New York Times, March 13, 2007, http://nytimes.com/20 07/03/13/science/13gore.html (accessed April 2, 2007).

51. Weiner.

52. Nisbet.

53. PollingReport.com, Associated Press-Stanford University poll conducted by Ipsos Public Affairs, September 21–23, 2007, http:// www.pollingreport.com/enviro.htm (accessed December 4, 2007).

54. Nisbet.

55. John D. Sterman and Linda Booth Sweeney, "Understanding Public Complacency about Climate Change: Adults' Mental Models of Climate Change Violate Conservation of Matter," *Climate Change* 80: 213–238.

56. Barak H. Obama, *Inaugural Address*, http://www.whitehouse.gov/blog/inaugural-ad dress/ (accessed January 21, 2009).

Chapter 5

1. Walter Gibbs, "Gore and U.N. Panel Win Peace Prize for Climate Work," *New York Times*, October 13, 2007, http://www.nytim es.com/2007/10/13/world/13nobel.html (accessed October 12, 2007).

2. Marco Grasso, "A Normative Ethical Framework in Climate Change," *Climate Change* 81: 223–246.

3. U.N. News Service, "Tackling Climate Change a Moral Obligation, General Assembly President Says," *U.N. News Service*, September 24, 2007, http://www.un.org/apps/news/printn ews.asp?nid=23930 (accessed October 30, 2007).

4. Barak H. Obama, *Inaugural Address*, January 20, 2009, http://www.whitehouse.gov/ blog/inaugural-address/ (accessed January 21, 2009).

5. Grasso.

6. Simon Caney, "Environmental Degradation, Reparations, and the Moral Significance of History," *Journal of Social Philosophy* 37(3): 464–483.

7. Christina Voigt, "From Climate Change to Sustainability: An Essay on Sustainable Development, Legal and Ethical Choices," *Worldviews* 9(1): 112–137.

8. Michael Grubb, "Seeking Fair Weather: Ethics and the International Debate on Climate Change," *International Affairs* 71(3): 463–496.

9. Vaclav Havel, "Our Moral Footprint," *New York Times*, September 27, 2007, http://ww w.nytimes.com/2007/09/27/opinion/27havel. html (accessed March 27, 2009).

10. Ibid.

11. Gibbs.

12. Fen Osler Hampson and Judith Reppy, "Environmental Change and Social Justice," *Environment* 39(3): 13–35.

13. Vaughn.

14. Hampson and Reppy.

15. Mary Evelyn Tucker and John A. Grim, "Introduction: The Emerging Alliance of World Religion and Ecology," *Daedalus* 130(4): 1–22.

16. Central Intelligence Agency, *The World Factbook*, https://www.cia.gov/library/publicat ions/the-world-factbook/print/us.html (accessed December 29, 2008).

17. Pew Forum on Religion and Public Life, *Religious Affiliation*, 2007, http://religions.pewf orum.org/reports (accessed December 29, 2008).

18. Central Intelligence Agency, *The World Factbook*.

19. Grist Environmental News and Commentary, *Fifteen Green Religious Leaders*, 2007, http://www.grist.org/news/maindish/2007/07/24/religious/ (accessed September 4, 2007).

20. Donald K. Swearer, "Principles and Poetry, Places and Stories: The Resources of Buddhist Ecology," *Daedalus* 130(4): 225–241.

21. Grist Environmental News and Commentary.

22. Central Intelligence Agency. *The World Factbook* .

23. S. Nomanul Haq, "Islam and Ecology: Toward Retrieval and Reconstruction," *Daedalus* 130(4): 141–177.

24. Grist Environmental News and Commentary.

25. Central Intelligence Agency, *The World Factbook*.

26. Patricia Kopstein and Jim Salinger, "The Ecocentric Challenge: Climate Change and the Jewish Tradition," *Ecotheology* 6.1, 6.2: 60–74.

27. Grist Environmental News and Commentary.

28. Melissa Stults, *Religious Groups Becoming a Factor in Climate Policy Debate*, Global Roundtable on Climate Change, The Earth Institute at Columbia University, 2007 http://www.climate.org/topics/localaction/religion-climate-change.shtml (accessed February 28, 2007).

29. Grist Environmental News and Commentary.

30. Central Intelligence Agency, *The World Factbook*.

31. Grist Environmental News and Commentary.

32. Grist Environmental News and Commentary.

33. Stults.

34. U.S. Conference of Catholic Bishops, 1991, *Renewing the Earth,* http://conservation.catholic.org/u_s_bishops.htm (accessed October 30, 2007).

35. Stults.

36. U.S. Conference of Catholic Bishops, 2001, *Faithful Stewards of God's Creation: A Catholic Resource for Environmental Justice and Climate Change*, Climate Change Justice and Health Initiative. http://www.usccb.org/sdwp/ejp/climate/indes.shtml (accessed October 30, 2007).

37. James Macintyre, "Pope to Make Climate Action a Moral Obligation," *The Independent*, October 30, 2007, http://news.independent.co.uk/europe/article2987811.ece (accessed October 30, 2007).

38. Pope Benedict XVI, *Papal Message to Environmental Conference*, 2007, http://zenit.org/article-20435?1=english (accessed October 30, 2007).

39. John L. Carr, *Written Testimony: Religious and Moral Dimensions of Global Climate Change*, Testimony before the Committee on Environment and Public Works, United States Senate, June 7, 2007.

40. Ibid.

41. U.S. Conference of Catholic Bishops, 2007, *What Catholics are Doing*, http://www.usccb.org/sdwp/ejp/climate/wed.shtml (accessed October 20, 2007).

42. Pew Forum on Religion and Public Life.

43. Stults.

44. Stults.

45. Earthday Network, *Global Warming in the Pulpit*, 2007, http://www.earthday.net/programs/religious/default.aspx (accessed April 30, 2007).

46. Pew Forum on Religion and Public Life.

47. Southern Baptist Convention, *About Us — Meet Southern Baptists*, 2009, http://www.sbc.net/aboutus/default.asp (accessed January 1, 2009).

48. George Marsden, "Fundamentalism as an American Phenomenon, A Comparison with English Evangelicalism," *Church History*, June 1977: 215–232.

49. Evangelical Environmental Network and Creation Care Magazine, *On the Care of Creation: An Evangelical Declaration of the Care of Creation*, 1994, http://www.creationcare.org/resources/declaration/php (accessed October 23, 2007).

50. Ibid.

51. Stults.

52. Laurie Goodstein, "Living Day to Day by a Gospel of Green," *New York Times*, March 8, 2007, http://www.nytimes.com/2007/03/08/garden08ball.html (accessed March 8, 2007).

53. David Roberts, "God and the Environment," *Grist Environmental News and Commentary*, October 5, 2006, http://www.grist.org/news/maindish/2006/10/05/gate/ (accessed March 23, 2007).

54. Evangelical Climate Initiative, *Climate Change: An Evangelical Call to Action*, http://www.christiansandclimate.org/statement (accessed October 23, 2007).

55. Paula Clifford, *All Creation Groaning: A Theological Approach to Climate Change and Development* (London: Christian Aid, 2007).

56. Goodstein.

57. Brian McCammack, "Hot Damned America: Evangelicalism and the Climate Change Policy Debate," *American Quarterly*, September 2007, 645–668.

58. "An Urgent Call to Action: Scientists and Evangelicals Unite to Protect Creation," Washington, D.C.: *National Press Club*, January 17, 2007.

59. Heather Gonzales, "Evangelical, Sci-

entific Leaders Launch Effort to Protect Creation," *National Association of Evangelicals*, 2007, http://www.nae.net/index.cfm?FUSEAC TION=editor.page&pageID=413&idCatego ry=1 (accessed October 23, 2007).

60. Goodstein.

61. Brian Kaylor, "Signers of Environmental Statement Funded by ExxonMobil," ethicsd aily.com, August 10, 2006, http://www.ethicsd aily.com/print_popup.dfm?AID=7741 (accessed March 5, 2007).

62. Interfaith Stewardship Alliance, *An Open Letter to the Signers of "Climate Change: An Evangelical Call to Action*," 2006, http:// www.cornwallalliance.org/docs/an-open-lett er-to-the-signers-of-climate-change-an-evang elical-call-to-action-and-others-concerned-ab out-global-warming.pdf.

63. Adelle M. Banks, "Dobson, Others Seek Ouster of NAE Voce President," *Religion News Service*, March 2, 2007, http://www.christiantyt oday.com/ct/article_print.html?id=41357 (accessed March 5, 2007).

64. Jerry Falwell, "Falwell Confidential: America Still Trusts in God," *Jerry Falwell Ministries*, 2007, http://www.falwell.com/global_w arming.php (accessed March 5, 2007).

65. Lynne Lorenzen, Lynne, "Religion and Science: What is at Stake?" *Dialog: A Journal of Theology* 46(3): 294–300.

66. Bill Berkowitz, "Pastor John Hagee Spearheads Christians United for Isreal," *Media Transparency*, 2006, http://www.mediatransp arency.org/storyprinterfriendly.php?stroyID=1 16 (accessed March 5, 2007).

67. Glenn Scherer, "The Godly Must be Crazy," *Grist Environmental News and Commentary*, October 27, 2004, http://www.grist.or g/news/maindish/2004/10/27/scherer-christia n/ (accessed October 23, 2007).

68. Neela Banerjee, "Southern Baptists Back a Shift on Climate Change," *New York Times*, March 10, 2008, http://www.nytimes. com/2008/03/10/us/10baptists.html (accessed March 10, 2008).

69. Southern Baptist Environment and Climate Initiative, *A Southern Baptist Declaration on the Environment and Climate Change*, http:// www.baptistcreationcare.org/node/1 (accessed January 2, 2009).

Chapter 6

1. "IPCC 2000," *Good Practice Guidance and Uncertainty Management in National Greenhouse Gas Inventories*, National Greenhouse Gas Inventories Program, Intergovernmental Panel on Climate Change, Montreal, May 2000. http://www.ipcc-nggip.iges.or.j

p/public/gp/english/ (accessed January 6, 2009).

2. U.S. EPA, *Inventory of U.S. Greenhouse Gas Emissions and Sinks: 1990–2006*, http:// www.epa.gov/climatechange/emissions/usinv entoryreport.html/ (accessed January 6, 2009).

3. "IPCC 2006: The Science of Climate Change," in *Climate Change 1995*, Intergovernmental Panel on Climate Change, J.T. Houghton, L.G. Meira Filho, B.A. Callander, N. Harris, A. Kattenberg, and K. Maskell, eds. (Cambridge: Cambridge University Press, 1996).

4. U.S. EPA, *Inventory of U.S. Greenhouse Gas Emissions and Sinks: 1990–2006*, http://ww w.epa.gov/climatechange/emissions/usinventor yreport.html/ (accessed January 6, 2009).

5. Ibid.

6. Ibid.

7. Center for Sustainable Systems, *Greenhouse Gases Factsheets*, University of Michigan, 2007, http://css.snre.umich.edu/facts (accessed January 8, 2009).

8. U.S. EPA, *Inventory of U.S. Greenhouse Gas Emissions and Sinks: 1990–2006*, http://ww w.epa.gov/climatechange/emissions/usinventor yreport.html/ (accessed January 6, 2009).

9. Arjun Makhijani, *Carbon-Free and Nuclear-Free: A Roadmap for U.S. Energy Policy*. Takoma Park, MD: IEER Press and Muskegon, MI: RDR Books, 2007.

10. U.S. EPA, *Inventory of U.S. Greenhouse Gas Emissions and Sinks: 1990–2006*, http://ww w.epa.gov/climatechange/emissions/usinventor yreport.html/ (accessed January 6, 2009).

11. Ibid.

12. Center for Sustainable Systems.

13. U.S. EPA, *Inventory of U.S. Greenhouse Gas Emissions and Sinks: 1990–2006*, http:// www.epa.gov/climatechange/emissions/usinv entoryreport.html/ (accessed January 6, 2009).

14. Ibid.

15. Ibid.

16. "IPCC 2000," *Good Practice Guidance and Uncertainty Management in National Greenhouse Gas Inventories*.

17. U.S. EPA, *State Planning and Measurement*, http://www.epa.gov/climatechange/wyc d/stateandlocalgov/state_planning.html#three (accessed January 8, 2009).

18. California Climate Action Registry, *Overview*, http://www.climateregistry.org/abo ut.html (accessed April 4, 2008).

19. Gary Polakovic, "Firms Rush to Register Greenhouse Gases Early," *Los Angeles Times*, January 26, 2007.

20. The Climate Registry, *Comparison of Reporting Requirements for the Climate Registry, The California Climate Action Registry, and the California Air Resource Board's Mandatory Re-*

porting Program, 2007, http://www.climateregis try.org/resources/docs/misc/ca-voluntary-ma ndatory-reporting-matrix.pdf (accessed January 8, 2009).

21. Erik Haites and Farhana Yamin, "Overview of the Kyoto Mechanisms," *International Review for Environmental Strategies* 5(1): 199–216.

22. John Bellamy Foster, "Ecology Against Capitalism," *Monthly Review* 53(5): 1–15, http://www.monthlyreview.org/1001jbf.htm (accessed April 16, 2007).

23. Andy Peters, "Change in the Air," *Daily Report*, September 17, 2007, http://www.dailyr eportonline.com/Editorial/News/singleEdit.asp ?individual_SQL=9/17/2007@16611_Public_ .htm (accessed January 9, 2009).

24. U.S. Climate Action Partnership, "About," 2007, http://www.us-cap.org/about/ index.asp (accessed January 9, 2009).

25. U.S. Climate Action Partnership, "A Call to Action," 2007, http://www.us-cap.org/ USCAPCallForAction.pdf (accessed January 9, 2009).

26. TerraPass, *Carbon Offsets from Terra-Pass*, 2008, http://www.terrapass.com/buy-car bon-offsets/ (accessed January 9, 2009).

27. Frauke Roeser and Tim Jackson, "Early Experiences with Emissions Trading in the UK," *GMI 39* Autumn 2002: 43–54.

28. Chicago Climate Exchange, *Chicago Climate Exchange Announces Formation of the New York Climate Exchange and the Northeast Climate Exchange*, 2006, http://www.chicagocl imatex.com/news/press/release_20060314_ny cx.pdf (accessed January 9, 2009).

29. Timothy Gardner, "Chicago Climate Exchange to Expand in U.S. Northeast," *Planet Ark*, March 16, 2006, http://www.planetark. com/dailynewsstroy.cfm/newsid/35671/sto ry.htm (accessed January 9, 2009).

30. Ibid.

31. Chicago Climate Exchange.

32. World Bank, *State and Trend of the Carbon Market 2008*, http://wbcarbonfinance.org/ docs/State_of_the_Market_release_THE_FI NAL_May-7-08.pdf (accessed January 9, 2009).

33. Government Accountability Office, *International Climate Change Programs, Lessons Learned from the European Union's Emissions Trading Scheme and the Kyoto Protocol's Clean Development Mechanism*, 2008, GAO-09-151.

34. Szabo.

35. Chicago Climate Exchange.

36. Gary Mason, "What is the Cap-and-Trade System and Will it Save the World?" *The Globe and Mail*, January 12, 2008, p. S1.

37. Lawrence H. Goulder, "California's Bold New Climate Policy," *Economist's Voice*,

September 2007, www.bepress.com/ev (accessed September 30, 2007).

38. William D. Nordhaus, *Life After Kyoto: Alternative Approaches to Global Warming Policies*, National Bureau of Economic Researcher, Working Paper 11889, December 2005.

39. Sarah Van Pelt, Yael Gichon, and Jodie Carroll, "Boulder Voters Pass First Energy Tax in Nation," *City of Boulder*, November 8, 2006, http://ci.boulder.co.us/index.php?option=co m_content&task=view&id=6136&Itemid=169 (accessed January 15, 2009).

40. "CA-Global Warming Fees," *Los Angeles Times*, May 22, 2008, http://articles.lati mes.com/2008/may/22/local/me-carbontax22 (accessed January 15, 2009).

41. Andrew Clark, "Exxon Chief Backs Carbon Tax," *The Guardian*, January 9, 2009, http://www.guardian.co.uk/business/2009/jan/ 10/exxon-mobil-carbon-tax (accessed January 15, 2009).

42. R.A. Hinricks and M. Kleinbach, *Energy: Its Use and the Environment* (Forth Worth: Harcourt, 2002).

43. T.J. Brennan, K. Palmer, and S. Martinez, *Implementing Electricity Restructuring: Policies, Potholes, and Prospects*, Resources for the Future Discussion Paper 01–62, 2001.

44. M. Bolinger and R. Wiser, *Production Incentive Auctions to Support Large-Scale Renewables Projects in Pennsylvania and California*, 2002, Ernest Orlando Berkeley National Laboratory.

45. R. Wiser, R., *An Open-Ended Renewables RFP in Minnesota Funds Biomass and Innovative Wind Applications*, 2002, Ernest Orlando Berkeley National Laboratory.

46. M. Bolinger and R. Wiser, *The Use of Capital- and Performance-Based Buy-Down Programs for PV in California, Pennsylvania, and Massachusetts*, 2002, Ernest Orlando Berkeley National Laboratory.

47. American Wind Energy Association, *How a National Renewables Portfolio Standard Would Affect Utilities.* American Wind Energy Association, June 30, 1999.

48. Wilson H. Rickerson, Janet L. Sawin, and Robert C. Grace, "If the Shoe FITs: Using Feed-in-Tariffs to Meet U.S. Renewable Electricity Targets," *The Electricity Journal* 20(4): 73–86.

49. M. Bolinger and R. Wiser, *The Use of Capital- and Performance-Based Buy-Down Programs for PV in California, Pennsylvania, and Massachusetts*, 2002, Ernest Orlando Berkeley National Laboratory.

50. American Wind Energy Association, *How a National Renewables Portfolio Standard Would Affect Utilities.* American Wind Energy Association, June 30, 1999.

51. Rickerson, Wilson H., Janet L. Sawin, and Robert C. Grace. 2007. If the Shoe FITs: Using Feed-in-Tariffs to Meet U.S. Renewable Electricity Targets. *The Electricity Journal* 20(4): 73–86.

52. World Future Council. 2006. *Feed-In Tariffs — Boosting Energy for our Future*. Hamburg, Germany: World Future Council.

53. Rickerson, Sawin, and Grace.

Chapter 7

1. U.S. EPA, *Inventory of U.S. Greenhouse Gas Emissions and Sinks: 1990–2006*, http://www.epa.gov/climatechange/emissions/usinventoryreport.html/ (accessed January 6, 2009).

2. The Quad is the standard measurement us to depict energy use. A Quad is equal to 10^{15} BTUs. One BTU is the amount of energy it takes to raise the temperature of a pound of water from 39 to 40 degrees F.

3. Energy Information Administration, *Annual Energy Outlook 2005*, U.S. Department of Energy, DOE/EIA-0383(2005), http://www.eia.doe.gov/oiaf/aeo/ (accessed October 3, 2005).

4. Energy Information Administration, *Renewable Energy Trends with Preliminary Data for 2003*, U.S. Department of Energy, 2004.

5. Energy Information Administration, *Policies to Promote Non-hydro Renewable Energy in the United States and Selected Countries*, U.S. Department of Energy, 2005, http://www.eia.doe.gov/fuelrenewable.html (accessed October 3, 2005).

6. Energy Information Administration, *U.S. Energy Consumption by Energy Source*. U.S. Department of Energy, 2008, http://www.eia.doe.gov/cneaf/alternate/page/renew_energy_consump/table1.html (accessed January 31, 2009).

7. U.S. Department of Energy, *Solar Energy Industry Forecast: Perspectives on U.S. Solar Market Trajectory*, 2008, http://www.energy.gov/solar/solar_america/solar@ee.doe.gov (accessed February 2, 2009).

8. Roger A. Hinrichs and Merlin Kleinbach, *Energy: Its Use and the Environment*. 3d ed. Fort Worth: Harcourt College, 2002.

9. Makhijani.

10. Energy Information Administration, *U.S. Energy Consumption by Energy Source*.

11. Hinrichs and Kleinbach.

12. Makhijani.

13. Ibid.

14. Dianne Rahm, "The Renewables Portfolio Standard in Texas," in Rahm, ed., 48–63 (Jefferson, NC: McFarland, 2006).

15. Christina Santora, "Sustainable Energy in the Oceans: Offshore Wind in the U.S.," in Rahm, ed., 179–201 (Jefferson, NC: McFarland, 2006).

16. Makhijani.

17. U.S. Department of Energy, *Concentrating Solar Power*, 2009, http://www1.eere.energy.gov/solar/csp.html (accessed February 2, 2009).

18. U.S. Department of Energy, *Solar Heating*, 2009, http://www1.eere.energy.gov/solar/solar_heating.html (accessed February 2, 2009).

19. Hinrichs and Kleinbach.

20. U.S. Department of Energy, *Concentrating Solar Collectors Basics*, 2009, http://www1.eere.energy.gov/solar/csp_basics.html (accesses February 2, 2009).

21. Ibid.

22. U.S. Department of Energy, *Solar Heating*.

23. Energy Information Administration, *U.S. Energy Consumption by Energy Source*.

24. Makhijani.

25. Solar Buzz, *Solar Energy Costs/Prices*, 2009, http://www.solarbuzz.com/statsCosts.htm (accessed February 4, 2009).

26. Felix Matthes and Lewis J. Perelman, Short-Term Solutions to the Climate and Energy Challenge. *AICGS Policy Report*. American Institute for Contemporary German Studies, The John Hopkins University, 2008.

27. State Energy Conservation Office, *Biomass: Nature's Most Flexible Energy Resource*, State Energy Conservation Office, SECO Fact Sheet No. 15, n.d.

28. Virtus Energy Research Associates, *Texas Renewable Energy Resource Assessment: Survey, Overview, and Recommendations*, Virtus Energy Research Associates, 1995.

29. Energy Information Administration. 2008. *U. S. Energy Consumption by Energy Source*.

30. Makhijani.

31. Ken Thomas, "EPA Maps Out Renewable Fuel Standards," *Houston Chronicle*, April 10, 2007, http://www.chron.com/disp/story/mpl/business/energy/4704267.html (accessed April 12, 2007).

32. BBC News, "UN Warns on Impacts of Biofuels," http://news.bbc.co.uk/go/pr/fr/-/2/hi/science/nature/6636467.stm (accessed May 11, 2007).

33. Andrew Martin, "Farmers to Plant Largest Amount of Corn Since '44," *New York Times*, March 31, 2007, http://www.nytimes.com/2007/03/31/business/31corn.web.html (accessed March 31, 2007).

34. Laura Meckler, "Fill up With Ethanol? One Obstacle is Big Oil," *Wall Street Journal*, April 2, 2007, p. A1.

35. Janet Wilson, "Warning is Sounded on Ethanol Use," *Latimes.com*, April 18, 2007,

http://www.latimes.com/news/local/la-me-eth anol118apr18,0,7852828.story (accessed April 18, 2007).

36. U.S. Government Accountability Office, *Biofuels: DOE Lacks a Strategic Approach to Coordinate Increasing Production with Infrastructure Development and Vehicle Needs*, 2007, GAO-07–713.

37. Clifford Krauss, "Venture Capitalists Want to Put Some Algae in Your Tank," *New York Times*, March 7, 2007, http://www.nytimes.com/2007/03/07/business/07algae.html (accessed March 8, 2007).

38. Makhijani.

39. Matthes and Perelman.

40. Makhijani.

41. Renewable Northwest Project, *Wave and Tidal Energy Technology*, 2007, http://www.rnp.org/RenewTech/tech_wave.html (accessed February 8, 2009).

42. Virtus Energy Research Associates, *Texas Renewable Energy Resource Assessment: Survey, Overview, and Recommendations.*

43. National Renewable Energy Laboratory, *Geothermal Energy Basics*, 2008, http://www.nrel.gov/learning/re_geothermal.html (accessed February 8, 2009).

44. Energy Information Administration, *U.S. Energy Consumption by Energy Source.*

45. Berkeley Seismological Laboratory, *What's Going on in the Geysers?* 2009, http://seismo.berkeley.edu/faq/gey_0.html (accessed March 4,2009).

46. Hinrichs and Kleinbach.

47. Makhijani.

48. Ibid.

49. Matthes and Perelman.

50. John Deutch and Ernest Moniz, "A Future for Fossil Fuel," *Wall Street Journal*, March 15, 2007, p. A17.

51. Massachusetts Institute of Technology, *The Future of Coal: Options for a Carbon Constrained World*, MIT Study on the Future of Coal, 2007.

52. Hinrichs and Kleinbach.

53. Makhijani.

54. Jeff Goodell, *Big Coal: The Dirty Secret Behind America's Energy Future* (Boston and New York: Houghton Mifflin, 2006).

55. U.S. Department of Energy, *FutureGen: Integrated Hydrogen, Electric Power Production and Carbon Sequestration Research Initiative*, Office of Fossil Fuel. U.S. Department of Energy, 2004.

56. U.S. Department of Energy, *FutureGen — A Sequestration and Hydrogen Research Initiative*, Office of Fossil Energy, U.S. Department of Energy, project update August 2006.

57. U.S. Department of Energy, "DOE Announces Restructured FutureGen Approach to Demonstrate Carbon Capture and Storage Technology at Multiple Clean Coal Plants," *Fossil Energy Techline*, 2008, http://www.fossil.energy.gov/news/techlines/2008/08003-DOE_Announces_Restructured_FutureG.html (accessed February 6, 2009).

58. Matthew L. Wald, "In a Test of Capturing Carbon Dioxide, Perhaps a Way to Temper Global Warming," *New York Times*, March 15, 2007, http://www.nytimes.com/2007/03/15/business/15carbon.html (accessed March 15, 2007).

59. Goodell.

60. U.S. Department of Energy, *Hydrogen*, 2009, http://www.energy.gov/energysources/hydrogen.htm (accessed February 4, 2009).

61. Makhijani.

62. U.S. Department of Energy, *Hydrogen, Fuel Cells, and Infrastructure Technologies Program*, Energy Efficiency and Renewable Energy Program, U.S. Department of Energy, 2009, http://www1.eere.energy.gov/hydrogenandfuelcells (accessed February 8, 2009).

63. Energy Information Administration, *U.S. Energy Consumption by Energy Source*, U.S. Department of Energy, 2008, http://www.eia.doe.gov/cneaf/alternate/page/renew_energy_consump/table1.html (accessed January 31, 2009).

64. W. Conard Holton, "Power Surge: Renewed Interest in Nuclear Energy," *Environmental Health Perspectives* 113(11): 743–749.

65. Hinrichs and Kleinbach.

66. Ibid.

67. Holton.

68. Ibid.

69. Patrick Moore, "Going Nuclear," *Washington Post.com*, April 16, 2006, http://www.washingtonpost.com/wp-dyn/content/article/2006/04/14/AR2006041401209.html (accessed February 8, 2009).

70. Adam Vaughan, "Sweden Scraps Ban on Nuclear Power with Plan to Replace 10 Reactors, *Guardian.co.uk*, February 5, 2009, http://www.guardian.co.uk/environment/2009/feb/05/nuclear-sweden/print (accessed February 6, 2009).

71. Elizabeth Souder, "NRG Energy to Build 2 Texas Nuclear Plants," *EnergyRefuge.com*, 2006, http://www.energyrefuge.com/archives/nuclear_power_plants.htm (accessed February 8, 2009).

72. Jamia Cascio, "Plan B," *Gristmill*, 2009, http://gristmill.grist.org/print/2009/2/8/22587/75724?show+comments=no (accessed February 10, 2009).

73. Cornelia Dean, "Experts Discuss Engineering Feats, Like Space Mirrors, to Slow Climate Change," *New York Times*, November 10, 2007, http://www.nytimes.com/2007/11/10/science/earth/10geo.html (accessed November 10, 2007).

Chapter 8

1. Matthes and Perelman.
2. Hinrichs and Kleinbach.
3. Makhijani.
4. Matthes and Perelman.
5. Makhijani.
6. U.S. Green Building Council, *LEED*, 2008, http://www.usgbc.org/DisplayPage.aspx?CategoryID=19 (accessed February 14, 2009).
7. U.S. Department of Energy, *Homes*, 2007, http://www.energy.gov/energyefficiency/homes.htm (accessed February 12, 2009).
8. Makhijani.
9. Matthes and Perelman.
10. Ibid.
11. Lawrence Berkeley National Laboratory, *Standby Power*, Energy Analysis Department, 2009, http://standby.lbl.gov/ (accessed February 14, 2009).
12. Sierra Club, *Energy Efficiency Saves Money, But How Much?* 2008, http://www.sierraclub.org/quiz/energyefficiency/answer.asp (accessed February 12, 2009).
13. U.S. Department of Energy, *About Energy Star*, 2008, http://www.energystar.gov/index.cfm?c=about.ab_index (accessed February 12, 2009).
14. Makhijani.
15. Matthew L. Wald, "A U.S. Alliance to Update the Light Bulb. *New York Times*, March 14, 2007, http://www.nytimes.com/2007/03/14/business/14light.html (accessed March 15, 2007).
16. Sarah Jane Tribble, "Tech Giants Join to Cut Industry's Power Needs," *Mercury News*, February 27, 2007, http://www.mercurynews.com/mld/mercurynews/business/technology/16792775.htm (accessed February 28, 2007).
17. Government Accountability Office, *Energy Efficiency: Long-Standing Problems with DOE's Program for Setting Efficiency Standards Continue to Result in Forgone Energy Savings*, 2007, GAO-07-42.
18. John M. Broder, "Obama Orders New Rules to Raise Energy Efficiency," *New York Times*, February 6, 2009, http://www.nytimes.com/2009/02/06/us/politics/06energy.html (accessed February 12, 2009).
19. U.S. Department of Energy, *Transportation Energy Data Book*, 27th edition, 2008, http://cta.ornl.gov/data/index.shtml (accessed February 11, 2009).
20. Dianne Rahm and Jerrell D. Coggburn, "Environmentally Preferable Procurement: Greening U.S. State Government Fleets," *Public Works Management & Policy* 12(2): 400–415.
21. Plug-In Partners, *Plug-In Partner*, Plug-In Partners National Campaign, 2005, http://www.eesi.org/programs/CleanBus/PHEVS/plugin.index.htm. (accessed February 25, 2006).
22. T. Langer and D. Williams, *Greener Fleets: Fuel Economy Progress and Prospects*, American Council for an Energy-Efficient Economy, Report Number T024, 2002.
23. Henry Pulizzi, "Bush, Big Three Bypass Talk of Fuel-Economy Increases," *Wall Street Journal*, March 27, 2007, A2.
24. John M. Broder and Micheline Maynard, "Lawmakers Set Deal on Raising Fuel Efficiency," *New York Times*, December 1, 2007, http://www.nytimes.com/2007/12/01/washington/01energy.html (asccessed December 3, 2007).
25. Matthes and Perelman.
26. Ibid.
27. Nick Hodge, "Smart Grid: Smart Investing in the Smart Grid," *Wealth Daily*, June 11, 2008, http://www.wealthdaily.com/articles/smart-grid-investing/1355 (accessed February 12, 2009).
28. U.S. Department of Energy, *The Smart Grid: An Introduction*, 2008 http://www.oe.energy.gov/1165.htm (accessed February 10, 2009).
29. U.S. Department of Energy, *Federal Smart Grid Task Force*, 2008, http://www.oe.energy.gov/smartgrid_taskforce.htm (accessed February 15, 2009).
30. U.S. Department of Energy, *U.S. Climate Change Technology Program Strategic Plan*, 2006, http://www.climatetechnology.gov/stratplan/final/index.htm (accessed February 15, 2009).
31. U.S. Department of Energy, *The Smart Grid: An Introduction.*.
32. Ibid.
33. Hodge.
34. Matthes and Perelman.
35. Martin LaMonica, "Google Crashes the Smart-Grid Party. *Green Tech*, February 10, 2009, http://news.cnet.com/8301-11128_3-10160234-54.html (accessed February 15, 2009).
36. U.S. Department of Energy, *The Smart Grid: An Introduction*.
37. Ibid.
38. U.S. EPA, *Frequently Asked Questions About Landfill Gas and How it Affects Public Health, Safety, and the Environment*, 2008, http://www.epa.gov/landfill/faq-3.htm#intro (accessed February 15, 2009).
39. John Laumer, *Landfill Gas to Energy: A Growing Alternative Energy Resource*, 2008, http://www.treehugger.com/files/2008/05/landfill-gas-energy-biogas.php (accessed February 15, 2009).
40. Power Scorecard, *Electricity from Landfill Gas*, 2000, http://www.powerscorecard.org/tech_detail.cfm?resource_id=5 (accessed February 15, 2009).

41. Energy Information Administration, *Energy Efficiency*, 2008, http://www.eia.doe.g ov/kids/energyfacts/saving/ (accessed February 14, 2009).

42. Vaughn.

43. R. Neil Sampson, "Integrating Land Use, Land Use Change, and Forestry into a Mandatory National Greenhouse Gas Reduction Program," in Riggs, ed., pp.63–72 (Queenstown, MD: The Aspen Institute, 2004).

44. David Adam, "Fifth of World Carbon Emissions Soaked Up by Extra Forest Growth, Scientists Find," *Guardian.co.uk*, February 18, 2009, http://www.guardian.co.uk/envirionm ent/2009/feb/18/trees-tropics-climate-change (accessed February 23, 2009).

45. Larry West, "Top Ten Things You Can Do to Reduce Global Warming," *About.com*, 2009, http://environment.about.com/od/global warming/tp/globalwarmtips.htm (accessed February 15, 2009).

46. Matthes and Perelman.

47. The Nature Conservancy, *Climate Change: Voluntary Carbon Offset Program*, 2009, http://environment.about.com/od/global warming/tp/globalwarmtips.htm (accessed February 15, 2009).

48. The Climate Trust, "Fight Climate Change," *Carboncounter.org*, 2006, http://www. carboncounter.org/ (accessed February 15, 2009).

49. Carbonfund.org, *Reduce What You Can. Offset What You Can't*, 2009, http://www. carbonfund.org/?gclid=CLWDs4DG35gCFQs-MGgod3D0_bQ (accessed February 15, 2009).

50. Kate Galbraith, "Saving Energy with a Four-Day Work Week," *New York Times*, February 3, 2009, http://www.nytimes.com/2009/ 02/03/saving-energy-by-shutting-down-gove rnment (accessed February 4, 2009).

51. Matthes and Perelman.

Selected Bibliography

Arrow, Kenneth J. "Global Climate Change: A Challenge to Policy." *Economists' Voice*, 2007. Berkeley Electronic Press. Available at www.bepress.com/ev.

Barclay, Eliza. "Is Climate Change Affecting Dengue in the Americas?" *The Lancet* 371: 973–974.

Beggs, Paul John. "Impacts of Climate Change on Aeroallergens: Past and Future." *Clinical and Experimental Allergy* 34:1507–1513.

_____, and Hilary Jane Bambrick. "Is the Global Rise of Asthma an Early Impact of Anthropogenic Climate Change?" *Environmental Health Perspectives* 113(8): 915–919.

Bogdonoff, Sondra, and Jonathan Rubin. "The Regional Greenhouse Gas Initiative: Taking Action in Maine." *Environment* 49(2): 9–16.

Bolinger, M., and R. Wiser. *Production Incentive Auctions to Support Large-Scale Renewables Projects in Pennsylvania and California.* Ernest Orlando Berkeley National Laboratory, 2002.

_____, and _____. *The Use of Capital- and Performance-Based Buy-Down Programs for PV in California, Pennsylvania, and Massachusetts.* Ernest Orlando Berkeley National Laboratory, 2002.

Bouwer, Laurens M., Ryan P. Crompton, Ebergard Faust, and Peter Hoppe. "Confronting Disaster Losses." *Science* 318: 753.

Boykoff, Maxwell T., and Jules M. Boykoff. "Climate Change and Journalistic Norms: A Case-Study of US Mass Media Coverage." *Geoforum* 38: 1190–1204.

Byrne, John, Kristen Hughes, Wilson Rickerson, and Lado Kurdgelashvili. "American Policy Conflict in the Greenhouse: Divergent Trends in Federal, Regional, State, and Local Green Energy and Climate Change Policy." *Energy Policy* 35: 4555–4573.

Caney, Simon. "Environmental Degradation, Reparations, and the Moral Significance of History." *Journal of Social Philosophy* 37(3): 464–483.

Carr, John L. *Written Testimony: Religious and Moral Dimensions of Global Climate Change.* Testimony before the Committee on Environment and Public Works, United States Senate, June 7, 2007.

Carter, Jimmy. *Our Endangered Values: America's Moral Crisis.* New York: Simon & Schuster, 2005.

Clifford, Paula. *All Creation Groaning: A Theological Approach to Climate Change and Development.* London: Christian Aid, 2007.

The Climate Registry. *Comparison of Reporting Requirements for the Climate Registry, The California Climate Action Registry, and the California Air Resource Board's Mandatory Reporting Program.* 2008. Available at http://www.climateregistry.org/resources/docs/misc/ca-voluntary-mandatory-reporting-matrix.pdf.

Colker, Ryan M. "States Take Initiative." *ASHRAE Journal*, August 2007: 64.

Corvalan, Carlos. "Climate Change and Human Health." *Bulletin of the World Health Organization* 85(11): 830–832.

Davis, David Howard. "European Global Warming Policy." In *Handbook of Globalization and the Environment*, Khi V. Thai, Dianne Rahm, and Jerrell D. Coggburn, eds., 43–60. Boca Raton, London, and New York: CRC Press.

Declaration of the United Nations Conference on the Human Environment. 1972. Available at http://www.unep.org/Documents.Multilingual/Default.asp?DocumentID=97&ArticleID=1503.

Dlugolecki, Andrew. "Climate Change and the Insurance Sector." *The Geneva Papers* 33: 71–90.

Engel, Kirsten H. "Mitigating Global Climate Change in The United States: A Regional Approach." N.Y.U. *Environmental Law Journal* 14: 54–85.

European Environmental Agency. *Greenhouse Gas Emission Trends and Projections in Europe 2007.* 2007. Available at http://reports.eea.europa.eu/eea_report_2007_5/en.

Evangelical Climate Initiative. *Climate Change: An Evangelical Call to Action.* 2006. Available at http://www.christiansandclimate.org/statement.

Evangelical Environmental Network and Creation Care Magazine. *On the Care of Creation: An Evangelical Declaration of the Care of Creation.* 1994. Available at http://www.creationcare.org/resources/declaration/php.

ExxonMobil. *Taking on the World's Toughest Energy Challenges.* ExxonMobil Summary Annual Report. 2007. Available at http://www.exxonmobil.com/corporate/files/news_pub_sar_2007.pdf

Foster, John Bellamy. "Ecology Against Capitalism." *Monthly Review* 53(5): 1–15.

Gerwin, Virginia. "Climate Lobby Group Closes Down." *Nature* 414 (7): 567.

Goodell, Jeff. *Big Coal: The Dirty Secret Behind America's Energy Future.* Boston and New York: Houghton Mifflin, 2006.

Goulder, Lawrence H. "California's Bold New Climate Policy." *Economist's Voice*, September 2007. Available at www.bepress.com/ev.

Grasso, Marco. "A Normative Ethical Framework in Climate Change." *Climate Change* 81: 223–246.

Gross, Yvonne. "Kyoto, Congress, or Bust: The Constitutional Invalidity of State CO_2 Cap-and-Trade Programs." *Thomas Jefferson Law Review* 28: 205–236.

Grubb, Michael. "Seeking Fair Weather: Ethics and the International Debate on Climate Change." *International Affairs* 71(3): 463–496.

Haites, Erik, and Farhana Yamin. "Overview of the Kyoto Mechanisms." *International Review for Environmental Strategies* 5(1): 199–216.

Hampson, Fen Osler, and Judith Reppy. "Environmental Change and Social Justice." *Environment* 39(3): 13–35.

Haq, S. Nomanul. "Islam and Ecology: Toward Retrieval and Reconstruction." *Daedalus* 130(4): 141–177.

Hays, Samuel P. *A History of Environmental Politics Since 1945.* Pittsburg: University of Pittsburg Press, 2004.

Hinrichs, Roger A., and Merlin Kleinbach. *Energy: Its Use and the Environment.* 3d ed. Fort Worth: Harcourt College, 2002.

Hinzman, Larry, Neil Bettez, W. Robert Bolton, F. Stuart Chapin, Mark Dyurgerov, Chris Fastie, Brad Griffith, Robert Hollister, Allen Hope, Henry Huntington, Anne Jensen, Gensuo Jia, Torre Jorgenson, Douglas Kane, David Klein, Gary Kofinas, Amanda Lynch, Andrea Lloyd, A. David McGuire, Frederick Nelson, Walther Oechel, Thomas Osterkamp, Charles Racine, Vladimir Romanovsky, Robert Stone, Douglas Stow, Matthew Sturm, Craig Tweedie, George Vourlitis, Marilyn Walker, Donald Walker, Patrick Webber, Jeffrey Welker, Kevin Winker, and Kenji Yoshikawa. "Evidence and Implications of Recent Climate Change in Northern Alaska and Other Arctic Regions." *Climatic Change* 72: 251–298.

Holtkamp, James A. "Dealing With Climate Change In The United States: The Non-Federal Response." *Journal of Land, Resources, & Environmental Law* 27: 79–86.

Holton, W. Conard. "Power Surge: Renewed Interest in Nuclear Energy." *Environmental Health Perspectives* 113(11): 743–749.

Interfaith Stewardship Alliance. *An Open Letter to the Signers of "Climate Change: An Evangelical Call to Action."* 2006. Available at http://www.cornwallalliance.org/docs/an-open-letter-to-the-signers-of-climate-change-an-evangelical-call-to-action-and-others-concerned-about-global-warming.pdf.

"IPCC: 1996." *Climate Change 1995: The Science of Climate Change.* Intergovernmental Panel on Climate Change. J.T. Houghton, L.G. Meira Filho, B.A. Callander, N. Harris, A. Kattenberg, and K. Maskell, eds. Cambridge: Cambridge University Press, 1995.

"IPCC: 2000." *Good Practice Guidance and Uncertainty Management in National Greenhouse Gas Inventories.* Intergovernmental Panel on Climate Change, National Greenhouse Gas Inventories Programme, Montreal, May 2000. Available at http://www.ipcc-nggip.iges.or.jp/public/gp/english/.

"IPCC: 2005." *Guidance Notes for Lead Authors of the IPCC Fourth Assessment Report on Addressing Uncertainties.* Intergovernmental Panel on Climate Change, July 2005.

"IPCC: 2006." *2006 IPCC Guidelines for National Greenhouse Gas Inventories.* Intergovernmental Panel on Climate Change. National Greenhouse Gas Inventories Programme. Available at http://www.ipcc-nggip.iges.or.jp/public/2006gl/index.html.

"IPCC 2007: Summary for Policymakers." In *Climate Change 2007: Impacts, Adaptation and Vulnerability.* Contribution of Working Group II to the Fourth Assessment Report of the Intergovernmental Panel on Climate

Change. M.L. Parry, O.F. Canziani, J.P. Palutikof, P.J. van der Linden, and C.E. Hanson, eds. Cambridge: Cambridge University Press, 2007.

"IPCC 2007: Summary for Policymakers." In *Climate Change 2007: Mitigation.* Contribution of Working Group III to the Fourth Assessment Report of the Intergovernmental Panel on Climate Change. B. Metz, O.R. Davidson, P.R. Bosch, R. Dave, L.A. Meyer, eds. Cambridge: Cambridge University Press, 2007.

"IPCC 2007: Summary for Policymakers." In *Climate Change 2007: The Physical Science Basis.* Contribution of Working Group I to the Fourth Assessment Report of the Intergovernmental Panel on Climate Change. S. Solomon, D. Qin, M. Manning, Z. Chen, M. Marquis, K.B. Averyt, M. Tignor and H.L. Miller, eds. Cambridge: Cambridge University Press, 2007.

Kerr, Richard A. "Global Warming is Changing the World." *Science* 316: 188–190.

_____. "A Worrying Trend of Less Ice, Higher Seas." *Science* 311: 1698–1701.

Klug, Andrew. *Global Warming: A National Security Issue?* Naval War College, Newport, 2006.

Kopstein, Patricia, and Jim Salinger. "The Ecocentric Challenge: Climate Change and the Jewish Tradition." *Ecotheology* 6.1,6.2: 60–74.

Kuntsi-Reunanen, E. and J. Luukkanen. "Greenhouse Gas Emission Reductions in the Post-Kyoto Period: Emission Intensity Changes Required under the 'Contraction and Convergence' Approach." *National Resources Forum* 30: 272–279.

The Kyoto Protocol to the United Nations Framework Convention on Climate Change. 1997. Available at http://unfccc.int/kyoto_proto col/items/2830.php.

Lambright, W. Henry. "Government and Science: A Troubled, Critical Relationship and What Can Be Done About It." *Public Administration Review* January/February 2008, 5–18.

Langer, T., and D. Williams. *Greener Fleets: Fuel Economy Progress and Prospects.* American Council for an Energy-Efficient Economy, Report Number T024, 2002.

Lash, Jonathan, and Fred Wellington. "Competitive Advantage on a Warming Planet." *Harvard Business Review* 85.3: 94–102.

Laumer, John. *Landfill Gas to Energy: A Growing Alternative Energy Resource.* 2008. Available at http://www.treehugger.com/files/ 2008/05/landfill-gas-energy-biogas.php.

Lawrence Berkeley National Laboratory. *Standby Power.* Energy Analysis Department, 2009. Available at http://standby.lb l.gov/.

Leslie, Mitch. "Sifting for Truth About Global Warming." *Science* 306(5705): 2167–2167.

Le Treut, H., R. Somerville, U. Cubasch, Y. Ding, C. Mauritzen, A. Mokssit, T. Peterson and M. Prather. "2007: Historical Overview of Climate Change." In *Climate Change 2007: The Physical Science Basis.* Contribution of Working Group I to the Fourth Assessment Report of the Intergovernmental Panel on Climate Change. S. Solomon, D. Qin, M. Manning, Z. Chen, M. Marquis, K.B. Averyt, M. Tignor and H.L. Miller, eds. Cambridge: Cambridge University Press, 2007.

Lorenzen, Lynne. "Religion and Science: What is at Stake?" *Dialog: A Journal of Theology* 46(3): 294–300.

Luntz, Frank. "The Environment: A Cleaner Safer, Healthier America." *The Luntz Research Companies—Strait Talk*, 2003.

Makhijani, Arjun. *Carbon-Free and Nuclear-Free: A Roadmap for U.S. Energy Policy.* Takoma Park, MD: IEER Press and Muskegon, MI: RDR Books, 2007.

Marsden, George. "Fundamentalism as an American Phenomenon: A Comparison with English Evangelicalism." *Church History*, June 1977: 215–232.

Massachusetts Institute of Technology. *The Future of Coal: Options for a Carbon Constrained World.* MIT Study on the Future of Coal, 2007.

Matthes, Felix, and Lewis J. Perelman. "Short-Term Solutions to the Climate and Energy Challenge." *AICGS Policy Report.* American Institute for Contemporary German Studies, The John Hopkins University, 2008.

McCammack, Brian. "Hot Damned America: Evangelicalism and the Climate Change Policy Debate." *American Quarterly*, September 2007, 645–668.

McCright, Aaron M., and Riley E. Dunlap. "Challenging Global Warming as a Social Problem: An Analysis of the Conservative Movement's Counter-Claims." *Social Problems* 47(4): 499–522.

_____, and _____. "Defeating Kyoto: The Conservative Movement's Impact on U.S. Climate Change Policy." *Social Problems* 50(3): 348–373.

Military Advisory Board. *National Security and the Threat of Climate Change.* 2007. SecurityAndClimate.cna.org.

National Renewable Energy Laboratory. *Geothermal Energy Basics.* 2008. Available at http://www.nrel.gov/learning/re_geotherm al.html.

The Nature Conservancy. *Climate Change: Voluntary Carbon Offset Program.* 2009. Available at http://environment.about.com/od/globalwarming/tp/globalwarmtips.htm.

Nelson, Lisa. "The Role of the United Nations: From Stockholm to Johannesburg." In *Handbook of Globalization and the Environment*, Khi V. Thai, Dianne Rahm, and Jerrell D. Coggburn, eds., 155–176. Boca Raton, London, and New York: CRC Press.

Nisbet, Matthew C. "The Polls-Trends: Twenty Years of Public Opinion About Global Warming." *Public Opinion Quarterly* 71(3): 444–470.

Nordhaus, William D. *Life After Kyoto: Alternative Approaches to Global Warming Policies*. National Bureau of Economic Researcher, Working Paper 11889, December 2005.

Pachauri, Rajendra K. *16 Years of Scientific Assessment in Support of the Climate Convention*. Intergovernmental Panel on Climate Change, 2004. Available at http://www.ipcc.ch/pdf/10th-anniversary/anniversary-brochure.pdf.

Peterson, Thomas D., and Adam Z. Rose. "Reducing Conflicts Between Climate Policy And Energy Policy In The US: The Important Role Of The States." *Energy Policy* 34: 619–631.

Pielke, Roger, Jr., Tom Wigley and Christopher Green. "Dangerous Assumptions." *Nature* 452: 531–532.

Plug-In Partners. *Plug–In Partner*. Plug-In Partners National Campaign, 2005. Available at http://www.eesi.org/programs/CleanBus/PHEVS/plugin.index.htm.

Pope Benedict XVI. *Papal Message to Environmental Conference*. 2007. Available at http://zenit.org/article-20435?1=english.

Rabe, Barry G. *Statehouse and Greenhouse: The Emerging Politics of American Climate Change Policy*. Washington, D.C.: Brookings Institution Press, 2004.

Rahm, Dianne. "The Renewables Portfolio Standard in Texas." In *Sustainable Energy and the States: Essays on Politics, Markets, and Leadership*, Dianne Rahm, ed., 48–63. Jefferson, NC: McFarland, 2006.

_____, and Jerrell D. Coggburn. "Environmentally Preferable Procurement: Greening U.S. State Government Fleets." *Public Works Management & Policy* 12(2): 400–415.

Regional Greenhouse Gas Initiative. *Post-Model Rule Action Plan*. Regional Greenhouse Gas Initiative, 2006. Available at http://www.rggi.org/modelrule.htm.

Renewable Northwest Project. *Wave and Tidal Energy Technology*. 2007. Available at http://www.rnp.org/RenewTech/tech_wave.html.

Rickerson, Wilson H., Janet L. Sawin, and Robert C. Grace. "If the Shoe FITs: Using Feed-in- Tariffs to Meet U.S. Renewable Electricity Targets." *The Electricity Journal* 20(4): 73–86.

Rio Declaration on Environment and Development. 1992. Available at http://www.unep.org/Documents.Multilingual/Default.asp?DocumentID=78&ArticleID=1163.

Robinson, Emily. "Exxon Exposed." *Catalyst* 6(1): 2–4.

Roeser, Frauke and Tim Jackson. "Early Experiences with Emissions Trading in the UK." *GMI 39* Autumn, 2002: 43–54.

Sampson, R. Neil. "Integrating Land Use, Land Use Change, and Forestry into a Mandatory National Greenhouse Gas Reduction Program." In *A Climate Policy Framework: Balancing Policy and Politics*, John A. Riggs, ed., 63–72. Queenstown, MD: The Aspen Institute, 2004.

Santora, Christina. "Sustainable Energy in the Oceans: Offshore Wind in the U.S." In *Sustainable Energy and the States: Essays on Politics, Markets, and Leadership*, Dianne Rahm, ed., 179–201. Jefferson, NC: McFarland, 2006.

Selin, Henrik, and Stacy D. Vandeveer. "Canadian-U.S. Environmental Cooperation: Climate Change Networks and Regional Action." *American Review of Canadian Studies* 35 (2): 353–378.

Shi, Yafeng, Yongping Shen, Ersi Kang, Dongliang Li, Yongjian Ding, Gouwei Zhang, and Ruji Hu. "Recent and Future Climate Change in Northwest China." *Climatic Change* 80: 379–393.

Shulman, Seth et al. *Smoke, Mirrors & Hot Air: How ExxonMobil Uses Big Tobacco's Tactics to Manufacture Uncertainty on Climate Science*. Cambridge, MA: Union of Concerned Scientists, 2007.

Southern Baptist Environment and Climate Initiative. *A Southern Baptist Declaration on the Environment and Climate Change*. Available at http://www.baptistcreationcare.org/node/1.

Sterman, John D., and Linda Booth Sweeney. "Understanding Public Complacency about Climate Cahnge: Adults' Mental Models of Climate Change Violate Conservation of Matter." *Climate Change* 80: 213–238.

Stern, Nicholas. *The Stern Review on the Economics of Climate Change*. HM Treasury Cabinet Office, 2006. Available at http://www.hm-treasury.gov.uk/media/999/76/closed_short_executive_summary.pdf.

Swearer, Donald K. "Principles and Poetry, Places and Stories: The Resources of Buddhist Ecology." *Daedalus* 130(4): 225–241.

Tucker, Mary Evelyn, and John A. Grim. Introduction: The Emerging Alliance of

World Religion and Ecology. *Daedalus* 130(4): 1–22.

Union of Concerned Scientists. *AB 32: Global Warming Solutions Act.* 2006. Available at http://www.law.stanford.edu/program/cent ers/enrlp/pdf/AB-32-fact-sheet.pdf.

United Nations Division for Sustainable Development. 2004. *Agenda 21.* UN Department of Economic and Social Affairs, Division for Sustainable Development. Available at http://www.un.org/esa/sustd ev/documents/agenda21/index.htm.

United Nations Framework Convention on Climate Change. 1992. Available at http://un fccc.int/resource/docs/convkp/conveng.p df.

United States. Central Intelligence Agency. *The World Factbook.* Washington, D.C.: Central Intelligence Agency, 2007. Available at https://www.cia.gov/library/publications /the-world-factbook/print/us.html.

_____. Climate Action Partnership. *About USCAP.* 2007. Available at http://www.u s-cap.org/about/index.asp.

_____. Climate Action Partnership. 2007. A Call to Action. Available at http://www.us-cap.org/USCAPCallForAction.pdf.

_____. Conference of Catholic Bishops. *Faithful Stewards of God's Creation: A Catholic Resource for Environmental Justice and Climate Change.* Climate Change Justice and Health Initiative, 2001. Available at http://www.usccb.org/sdwp/ejp/climate/indes.shtml.

_____. *Renewing the Earth.* 1991. Available at http://conservation.catholic.org/u_s_bish ops.htm.

_____. Conference of Mayors. *U.S. Conference of Mayors Climate Protection Agreement.* 2005. Available at http://usmayors.org/cl imateprotection/agreement.htm.

_____. Green Building Council. 2008. *LEED.* Available at http://www.usgbc.org/Display Page.aspx?CategoryID=19.

_____. Department of Energy. *About Energy Star.* 2008. Available at http://www.ener gystar.gov/index.cfm?c=about.ab_index.

_____. _____. *Concentrating Solar Collectors Basics.* 2009. Available at http://www1. eere.energy.gov/solar/csp_basics.html.

_____. _____. *Concentrating Solar Power.* 2009. Available at http://www1.eere.energy.gov/ solar/csp.html.

_____. _____. *Federal Smart Grid Task Force.* 2008. Available at http://www.oe.energy. gov/smartgrid_taskforce.htm.

_____. _____. *FutureGen — A Sequestration and Hydrogen Research Initiative.* Project Update August 2006. Office of Fossil Energy, U.S. Department of Energy, 2006.

_____. _____. *FutureGen: Integrated Hydrogen, Electric Power Production and Carbon Sequestration Research Initiative.* Office of Fossil Fuel. U.S. Department of Energy, 2004.

_____. _____. *Homes.* 2007. Available at http://www.energy.gov/energyefficiency/homes. htm.

_____. _____. *Hydrogen.* 2009. Available at http://www.energy.gov/energysources/hyd rogen.htm.

_____. _____. *Hydrogen, Fuel Cells, and Infrastructure Technologies Program.* Energy Efficiency and Renewable Energy Program. U.S. Department of Energy, 2009. Available at http://www1.eere.energy.gov/hydroge nandfuelcells.

_____. _____. *The Smart Grid: An Introduction.* 2008. Available at http://www.oe.energy. gov/1165.htm.

_____. _____. *Solar Energy Industry Forecast: Perspectives on U.S. Solar Market Trajectory.* 2008. Available at http://www.eere.energy. gov/solar/solar_america/solar@ee.doe.gov.

_____. _____. *Solar Heating.* 2009. Available at http://www1.eere.energy.gov/solar/solar_ heating.html.

_____. _____. *Transportation Energy Data Book.* 27th ed. 2008. Available at http://cta. ornl.gov/data/index.shtml.

_____. _____. *U.S. Climate Change Technology Program Strategic Plan.* 2006. Available at http://www.climatetechnology.gov/strat plan/final/index.htm.

_____. Energy Information Administration. *Annual Energy Outlook 2005.* U.S. Department of Energy, DOE/EIA-0383, 2005.

_____. _____. *Policies to Promote Non-hydro Renewable Energy in the United States and Selected Countries.* U.S. Department of Energy, 2005. Available at http://www.eia.doe. gov/fuelrenewable.html.

_____. _____. *U. S. Energy Consumption by Energy Source.* U.S. Department of Energy, 2008. Available at http://www.eia.doe.gov/ cneaf/alternate/page/renew_energy_consu mp/table1.html.

_____. Environmental Protection Agency. *Frequently Asked Questions About Landfill Gas and How it Affects Public Health, Safety, and the Environment.* 2008. Available at http:// www.epa.gov/landfill/faq-3.htm#intro.

_____. _____. *Greenhouse Gas Emissions.* 2008. Available at http://www.epa.gov/climatec hange/emissions/.

_____. _____. *Inventory of U.S. Greenhouse Gas Emissions and Sinks: 1990–2006.* USEPA #430-R-08-005. 2008. Available at http:// www.epa.gov/climatechange/emissions/us inventoryreport.html/.

_____. _____. *State Planning and Measurement.* 2008. Available at http://www.epa.gov/climatechange/wycd/stateandlocalgov/state_planning.html#three.

_____. Government Accountability Office. *Biofuels: DOE Lacks a Strategic Approach to Coordinate Increasing Production with Infrastructure Development and Vehicle Needs.* GAO-07-713, 2007.

_____. _____. *Energy Efficiency: Long-Standing Problems with DOE's Program for Setting Efficiency Standards Continue to Result in Forgone Energy Savings.* GAO-07-42, 2007.

_____. _____. *International Climate Change Programs: Lessons Learned from the European Union's Emissions Trading Scheme and the Kyoto Protocol's Clean Development Mechanism.* GAO-09-151, 2008.

_____. _____. *Climate Change: Financial Risks to Federal and Private Insurers in Coming Decades Are Potentially Significant.* Report to the Committee on Homeland Security and Governmental Affairs, U.S. Senate. GAO-07-285, 2007.

Vaughn, Jacqueline. *Environmental Politics: Domestic and Global Dimensions.* Belmont, CA: Thomson Wadsworth, 2007.

Virtus Energy Research Associates. *Texas Renewable Energy Resource Assessment: Survey, Overview, and Recommendations.* Virtus Energy Research Associates, 1995.

Voigt, Christina. "From Climate Change to Sustainability: An Essay on Sustainable Development, Legal and Ethical Choices." *Worldviews* 9(1): 112–137.

Walker, Joe. *Draft Global Climate Science Communications Action Plan.* American Petroleum Institute memo to Global Climate Science Team, 1998. Available at http://www.euronet.nl/users/e_wesker/ew@shell/API-prop.html.

Weart, Spencer. *The Discovery of Global Warming.* Cambridge: Harvard University Press, 2003. Also available in updated version at http://www.aip.org/hsitory/climate.

Western Governors' Association. *2005–06 Strategic Agenda.* 2005. Available at http://www.westgov.org/wga_strtegic_agenda.htm.

Wilson, Jennifer Fisher. "Facing an Uncertain Climate." *Annals of Internal Medicine* 146 (2): 153–155.

Wiser, R. *An Open-Ended Renewables RFP in Minnesota Funds Biomass and Innovative Wind Applications.* Ernest Orlando Berkeley National Laboratory, 2002.

Woerdman, Edwin. "Hot Air Trading Under the Kyoto Protocol: An Environmental Problem or Not?" *European Environmental Law Review* March 2005: 71–77.

World Bank. *State and Trend of the Carbon Market 2008.* 2008. Available at http://wbcarbonfinance.org/docs/State_of_the_Market_release_THE_FINAL_May-7-08.pdf.

World Future Council. *Feed-In Tariffs — Boosting Energy for our Future.* Hamburg, Germany: World Future Council. 2006.

Index

213